ΜΙΚΡΟΝ ΕΥΧΟΛΟΓΙΟΝ

AN ORTHODOX PRAYER BOOK

ΜΙΚΡΟΝ
ΕΥΧΟΛΟΓΙΟΝ

☦

Holy Cross Orthodox Press
Brookline, Massachusetts

Edited by Fr. N. M. Vaporis

AN ORTHODOX PRAYER BOOK

Translated by
Fr. John von Holzhausen
and
Fr. Michael Gelsinger

Holy Cross Orthodox Press
Brookline, Massachusetts

Library of Congress Cataloging in Publication Data

Orthodox Eastern Church. Liturgy and ritual.
An Orthodox prayer book.

English and Greek.
I. Vaporis, Nomikos Michael. II. Title.
BX360.A5V36   *264'.01'9*   *77-77642*

ISBN 0-916586-09-X

Library of Congress Catalog Card No. 77-077642

Composition by the Holy Cross Orthodox Press
Printed in the United States of America

For

Thomas C. Lelon

William B. Conomos

George S. Venturatos

and in memory of

Dr. John G. Aspiote

PREFACE

The Holy Cross Orthodox Press is happy to respond to a need felt by many Greek Orthodox Christians—both clergy and lay—for a bilingual Prayer Book (*Euchologion*).

This is only the first of a projected series of liturgical books which we hope will prove useful to Greek Orthodox Christians in their life of prayer.

Except for some initial introductory prayers and some occasional prayers at the end, a parallel Greek and English text is provided. Moreover, the translation of the hymns has been rendered in such a way that they can be sung in English with the traditional Byzantine melodies known to most Orthodox Christians.

The translation from the Greek (slightly modified to take into account more current liturgical language) belongs to the late Father John von Holzhausen, a graduate of Harvard University and an authority in Byzantine Greek, and to the Reverend Professor Father Michael Gelsinger, Ph.D., formerly chairman of the Department of Classics at the University of Buffalo.

We are grateful to Mr. Mitchell N. Bezreh of Arlington, Massachusetts for making this translation available to the HCO Press. Thanks are due to Mrs. Sophia Caparisos, Mr. Constantine Vaporis, and Mr. Terry Tsoutsouras for their assistance in seeing the book through the press. Father Constantine Monios of Baltimore, Maryland and Mr. Deno Kristakis of Pittsburg, Pennsylvania are owed a debt of

gratitude for securing important financial assistance for the publication.

The HCO Press owes more than it can repay to the Very Reverend Archimandrite Maximos Aghiorgoussis, Professor of Dogmatic Theology at Holy Cross Greek Orthodox School of Theology, for reviewing the entire text and making numerous helpful suggestions.

Many thanks are also due to His Eminence Archbishop Iakovos for his interest and permission to publish the Prayer Book.

FR. N. M. VAPORIS
Hellenic College-Holy Cross
Greek Orthodox School of
Theology

CONTENTS

CONTENTS

CONTENTS

INTRODUCTORY PRAYERS

Priest

Blessed is God always, both now and ever, and to the ages of ages. Amen.

Great Prayer of Blessing

Blessed is the Kingdom of the Father, and of the Son, and of the Holy Spirit, both now and ever, and to the ages of ages. Amen.

* * * * *

Glory to You, O our God: Glory to You.

O Heavenly King, Comforter, Spirit of Truth, Who are in all places and fill all things, Treasury of Blessings, Bountiful Giver of Life: come, and abide in us; cleanse us of every stain of sin, and of Your goodness, O Lord, save our souls.

The Trinitarian Prayers

Holy God, Holy Mighty, Holy Immortal: have mercy on us.
Holy God, Holy Mighty, Holy Immortal: have mercy on us.
Holy God, Holy Mighty, Holy Immortal: have mercy on us.

Glory to the Father and to the Son and to the Holy Spirit, both now and ever, and to the ages of ages. Amen.

All-Holy Trinity: have mercy on us; Lord, be gracious unto our sins; Master, pardon our offenses; Holy One, visit and heal our infirmities, for Your Name's sake.

Glory to the Father and to the Son and to the Holy Spirit, both now and ever, and to the ages of ages. Amen.

Lord have mercy; Lord have mercy; Lord have mercy.

Our Father, Who are in Heaven,
Hallowed be Your Name; Your Kingdom come.
Your Will be done on earth as it is in Heaven.
Give us this day our daily bread;
And forgive us our trespasses,
As we forgive those who trespass against us.
And lead us not into temptation,
But deliver us from evil.

Priest

For Yours is the Kingdom and the Power and the Glory, of the Father, and of the Son, and of the Holy Spirit, both now and ever, and to the ages of ages. Amen.

Troparia to the Blessed Theotokos Mary

Hail! Theotokos Virgin, Mary, Full-of-Grace, the Lord is with you. Blessed are you among women, and blessed is the fruit of your womb; for from you was born the Savior of our souls.

* * * * *

To your protection do we fly, O Mary Theotokos; despise, then, not our cry. From every peril shelter us, for you alone are immaculate—the Mother of God.

* * * * *

O Theotokos Virgin, Mother of Christ our God: to Him bring our prayers, that He, for your sweet sake, will save our souls.

* * * * *

It is meet and right to call you blessed, O Lady Theotokos, Lady ever-blessed and most perfect in innocence, the Mother of our God.

Lady more honorable than the Cherubim, and, in glory past all comparing transcending the Seraphim, who without spot did give birth to God the Word: in truth the Theotokos, you, do we magnify.

* * * * *

Save, O Lord, Your people and bless Your inheritance, giving to us victory over all who assail us, and protecting Your faithful by Your Cross.

* * * * *

Lord, now let Your servant depart in peace, according to Your word; for my eyes have seen Your salvation, which You have prepared before the face of all people: a Light to lighten the Gentiles, and the Glory of Your people Israel.

* * * * *

O come (+), let us worship and fall down
before God our King.

O come (+), let us worship and fall down before Christ,
our King and our God.

O come (+), let us worship and fall down before
Christ Himself, our King and our God.

* * * * *

Alleluia, alleluia, alleluia: Glory to You, O our God. (3)

The Anastasin Christou

Having beheld the Resurrection of Christ, let us worship the Holy Lord Jesus, Who alone is without sin. Before Your Cross we bow down in worship, O Christ; and Your Holy Resurrection we praise and glorify. For You are our God:

we know none other besides You. Yours is the Name on which we call. O come all you Faithful, let us worship the Holy Resurrection of Christ; for lo! through the Cross came joy into the whole world, always blessing the Lord, we praise His Resurrection, for in that He endured the Cross for us, by death has He destroyed Death.

Prayer before the Icon of Christ

Before Your icon we bow down, O gracious Lord; and our stumblings do You forgive, O Christ our God; for it well pleased You in the flesh to ascend the Cross, to deliver us from slavery to our Foe. Wherefore, we gratefully cry unto You: "All things with gladness have you filled, O our Savior," for You did come to save the world.

Prayers before the Icon of the All-Holy Theotokos

As a Fountain welling forth mercy account us worthy of compassion, O Theotokos: look upon a people fallen into sin; manifest your might as you have ever done, for as we set our hope in you, we hail you with the self-same cry as was once intoned by Gabriel, Captain of the Bodiless Host.

* * * * *

Open for us the door of your tender compassion, O blessed Theotokos; and as we ever set our hope in you, let us never be confounded; through you may we be delivered from all adversity: you who are the salvation of all good Christian folk.

The Great Synapte (Ektenia of Peace)

In peace let us pray to the Lord.

Choir: Lord have mercy. (*And after each petition*)

For the peace from above; for the salvation of our souls; let us pray to the Lord.

For the peace of the whole world; for the stability of the earth; for peaceful seasons; let us pray to the Lord.

For this holy House, and for them that with faith, reverence, and the fear of God enter therein; let us pray to the Lord.

For our Most Reverend Archbishop (*Name*), for the venerable Priesthood, the Diaconate in Christ; for all the Clergy and for all the people; let us pray to the Lord.

For the President of the United States; for all the other Civil Authorities enabled by the American people; let us pray to the Lord.

For this City (and community); for every city and community, and for all the Faithful that dwell therein; let us pray to the Lord.

For seasonable weather, for abundance of the fruits of the earth; for peaceful seasons; let us pray to the Lord.

For all them that travel by land or sea, or in the air; for the sick, and the afflicted; for captives, and for their salvation; let us pray to the Lord.

That we may be delivered from all tribulation, wrath, danger, and necessity; let us pray to the Lord.

Help us; save us, have mercy on us; and keep us, O God, by Your Grace.

Commendation:

Calling to remembrance our all-holy, pure, exceedingly blessed and glorious Lady Theotokos and Ever-Virgin Mary, with all the Saints: let us commend ourselves and one another and all our life to Christ our God.

Choir: To You, O Lord.

Priest (intoning aloud)

For to You are due all glory, honor, and worship: to the Father and to the Son and to the Holy Spirit, both now and ever, and to the ages of ages.

Choir: Amen.

The Little Ektenia

Again and again in peace, let us pray to the Lord.

Choir: Lord have mercy. (*And after each petition*)

Help us; save us; have mercy on us; and keep us, O God, by Your Grace.

Commendation:

Calling to remembrance our all-holy, pure, exceedingly blessed and glorious Lady Theotokos and Ever-Virgin Mary, with all the Saints: let us commend ourselves and one another and all our life to Christ our God.

Choir: To You, O Lord.

Priest (intoning the Ekphonesis aloud)

For You are a good and loving God, and to You do we send up all glory: to the Father and to the Son and to the Holy Spirit, both now and ever, and to the ages of ages.

Choir: Amen.

The Triskyriac Ektenia

Let us say with all our soul, and with all our mind, let us say:

Choir: Lord have mercy. (*And after each petition*)

O Lord Almighty, God of our Fathers: we pray You, listen and have mercy.

Have mercy on us, O God, according to Your great Mercy; we pray You, listen and have mercy.

Choir: Lord have mercy. (3) (*And after each petition*)

Again we pray for our Most Reverend Archbishop (*Name*), for Priests, Deacons, and all other Clergy; for Monks and Nuns; and for all our brothers and sisters in Christ.

Again we pray for the President of the United States, and all the other Civil Authorities enabled by the American People.

Again we pray for the blessed and memorable Founders of this Holy Temple; and for all our fathers and brethren, all our kindred and friends, the Orthodox that have gone to their rest and that here and in all the world are asleep in the Lord.

Again we pray for them that bear fruit and do good works in this holy and venerable Temple by laboring and singing therein; and for the people here present who await the rich and great mercy that comes from You.

Priest (intoning the Ekphonesis aloud)

For You are a merciful and loving God, and to You do we send up glory: to the Father and to the Son and to the Holy Spirit, both now and ever, and to the ages of ages.

Choir: Amen.

The Ektenia of the Prothesis (with the Ektenia of Askings)

Let us complete our prayer to the Lord.

Choir: Lord have mercy. (*And after each petition*)

Help us; save us; have mercy on us; and keep us, O God, by Your Grace.

Ektenia of Askings

That the whole day may be made perfect, holy, peaceful, and sinless; let us ask of the Lord.

Choir: Grant this prayer, O Lord. *Paraschou Kyrie.*
(*And also after each petition*)

An angel of peace, a faithful guide, a guardian of our souls and bodies, let us ask of the Lord.

Pardon and remission of our sins and offenses; let us ask of the Lord.

All things that are good and profitable for our souls, and peace for the whole world; let us ask of the Lord.

That we may complete the remaining time of our life in peace and repentance; let us ask of the Lord.

A Christian ending to our life; painless, without shame, peaceful; and a good defense before the dread Judgment Seat of Christ; let us ask of the Lord.

Commendation:

Calling to remembrance our all-holy, pure, exceedingly blessed and glorious Lady Theotokos and Ever-Virgin Mary, with all the Saints: let us commend ourselves and one another and all our life to Christ our God.

Choir: To You, O Lord.

Priest (intoning the Ekphonesis aloud)

Through the compassion of Your Only-Begotten Son, with Whom You are blessed, together with Your All-Holy, Good and Life-creating Spirit, both now and ever, and to the ages of ages.

Choir: Amen.

THE GREAT DOXOLOGY

Glory to You, Who have shown us light; glory to God in the highest, and on earth peace to men of good will.

We praise You, we bless You, we worship You, we glorify You, we give thanks to You for Your great glory.

O Lord, Heavenly King; God, the Father Almighty: Lord, the Only-Begotten Son, Jesus Christ: and Holy Spirit.

O Lord God, Lamb of God, Son of the Father that takes away the sins of the world: have mercy on us, You, Who take away the sins of the world.

Receive our prayer, You that sit on the right hand of the Father, have mercy on us.

For You alone are Holy, You alone are the Lord, O Jesus Christ, to the Glory of the Father: Amen.

Every day I will bless You, and I will praise Your Name forever—yea, for ever and ever.

Account us worthy, O Lord, in this day to be kept secure from sin.

Blessed are You, O Lord, the God of our Fathers; and praised and glorified is Your Name unto the ages: Amen.

Let Your Mercy, O Lord, be upon us, according it as we have hoped in You.

Blessed are You, O Lord; teach me Your statutes (+).
Blessed are You, O Lord; teach me Your statutes (+).
Blessed are You, O Lord; teach me Your statutes (+).

O Lord, You have been our refuge in generation and generation; I said, "O Lord, have mercy on me; heal my soul, for I have sinned against You."

O Lord, I have fled unto You, teach me to do Your will, for You are my God.

For with You is the Fountain of Life; in Your Light shall we see light.

O continue Your Mercy unto them that know You.

Psalm 50

Have mercy on me, O God, according to Your great mercy, and according to the multitude of Your compassions blot out my transgressions. Wash me thoroughly of my wickedness, and cleanse me from my sin. For I know my iniquity, and my sin is ever before me. Against You only have I sinned, and done this evil in Your sight, that You might be justified in Your words, and victor when You are Judge. For behold I was shaped in iniquity, and in sin did my mother conceive me. For behold You love truth; the unclear and secret lore of Your wisdom have you made clear to me. You shall sprinkle me with hyssop, and I shall be clean; You shall wash me, and I shall be whiter than snow. For You shall make me hear of joy and gladness; the bones which were humbled shall rejoice. Turn away Your face from my sins, and blot out all my iniquities. Create in me, O God, a clean heart, and renew a right spirit within me. Cast me not away from Your presence, and take not Your Holy Spirit from me. Restore to me the joy of Your salvation, and with a guiding Spirit establish me. I will teach transgressors Your ways, and the ungodly shall turn back to You. Deliver me from blood-guiltiness, O God, You that are the God of my salvation: O Lord, You shall open up my lips, and my mouth shall show forth Your praise. For if You had desired sacrifice, I would have given it; with holocausts shall You not be pleased; a sacrifice for God is a broken spirit, a heart that is broken and humbled God will not despise. Do good, O Lord, in Your pleasure to Zion: rebuild the walls of Jerusalem; then shall You be pleased with a Sacrifice of Righteousness, with Oblations and Holocausts; then shall they lay young bullocks upon Your altar.

* * * * *

Grant, O Lord, to keep this day without sin. Blessed are You, O God, O God of our Fathers, and praised and glorified is Your Name unto the ages: Amen.

O Lord, may Your Mercy be upon us, as we have put our trust in You. Blessed are You, O Lord; teach me Your statutes (+). Blessed are You, O Lord; give me understanding by Your statutes (+). Blessed are You, O Lord; enlighten me in Your statutes (+). O Lord, Your Mercy endures forever, despise not then the works of Your own hands.

For to You is due praise, to You is due song, to You is due glory: to the Father and to the Son and to the Holy Spirit, both now and ever, and to the ages of ages. Amen.

* * * * *

It is a good thing to give thanks to the Lord, and to sing to Your Name, O Most High, to proclaim Your Mercy in the morning, and Your Truth every night.

*****

Christ is risen from the dead, by death trampling upon Death, and upon those in the tombs bestowing life.

*****

Lord Jesus Christ, Son of God, have mercy on me a sinner.

*****

Through the prayers of our Holy Fathers, Lord Jesus Christ have mercy upon us and save us.

$\widetilde{\text{IC}}$ $\overset{\prime\prime}{\omega}$ $\widetilde{\text{XC}}$

$\overset{c}{\text{O}}$ N

Χείρ. Δ. Δεβελιάδη.

«ΑΠΕΣΤΕΙΛΕΝ ΑΥΤΟΝ ΕΥΛΟΓΟΥΝΤΑ ΗΜΑΣ».

(Πράξ. γ΄ 26)

ΑΚΟΛΟΥΘΙΑ
ΤΟΥ ΜΙΚΡΟΥ ΑΓΙΑΣΜΟΥ

—◦—

Τελουμένου Ἁγιασμοῦ εὐτρεπίζεται μικρὰ τράπεζα καὶ τίθεται ἐπ᾿ αὐτῆς τὸ ἱερὸν Εὐαγγέλιον,
ξύλινος ἀργυρόδετος Σταυρός, θυμιατήριον (κα-
τζίον), δοχεῖον μεθ᾿ ὕδατος καθαροῦ, δύο κηροπήγια,
ἐν οἷς ἀνάπτονται κηρία καθαρά, μικρὰ δέσμη βα-
σιλικοῦ ξηροῦ καὶ λευκὸν καθαρὸν μάκτρον. Συν-
ηγμένων δὲ πάντων ἄρχεται ἡ Ἀκολουθία, τοῦ ἱερέως, ὡς καὶ ἐν πάσῃ ἱεροπραξίᾳ, φέροντος ἐπιτραχήλιον, τοῦ δὲ διακόνου στιχάριον σὺν ὀραρίῳ.

Ὁ Ἱερεὺς

Εὐλογητὸς ὁ Θεὸς ἡμῶν, πάντοτε· νῦν καὶ ἀεὶ
καὶ εἰς τοὺς αἰῶνας τῶν αἰώνων.

Ὁ Διάκονος· Ἀμήν.

13

THE ORDER FOR THE
LESSER SANCTIFICATION OF WATER

Items needed for the celebration of the Lesser Sancti-fication of Water are a small table, upon which the Priest places the Gospel; a wooden, silver-bound Cross; a censer; a bowl of water; two candlesticks with their candles; a few branches of basil and a clean white towel. The Priest wears his cassock and stole.

Priest

Blessed is our God always, both now and ever, and to the ages of ages.

Amen.

Ψαλμὸς ρμβ' (142)

Κύριε, εἰσάκουσον τῆς προσευχῆς μου,‾ ἐνώτισαι τὴν δέησίν μου ἐν τῇ ἀληθείᾳ σου, εἰσάκουσόν μου ἐν τῇ δικαιοσύνῃ σου· καὶ μὴ εἰσέλθῃς εἰς κρίσιν μετὰ τοῦ δούλου σου, ὅτι οὐ δικαιωθήσεται ἐνώπιόν σου πᾶς ζῶν. Ὅτι κατεδίωξεν ὁ ἐχθρὸς τὴν ψυχήν μου, ἐταπείνωσεν εἰς γῆν τὴν ζωήν μου, ἐκάθισέ με ἐν σκοτεινοῖς ὡς νεκροὺς αἰῶνος· καὶ ἠκηδίασεν ἐπ' ἐμὲ τὸ πνεῦμά μου; ἐν ἐμοὶ ἐταράχθη ἡ καρδία μου. Ἐμνήσθην ἡμερῶν ἀρχαίων, ἐμελέτησα ἐν πᾶσι τοῖς ἔργοις σου, ἐν ποιήμασι τῶν χειρῶν σου ἐμελέτων. Διεπέτασα πρὸς σὲ τὰς χεῖράς μου, ἡ ψυχή μου ὡς γῆ ἄνυδρός σοι. Ταχὺ εἰσάκουσόν μου, Κύριε, ἐξέλιπε τὸ πνεῦμά μου· μὴ ἀποστρέψῃς τὸ πρόσωπόν σου ἀπ' ἐμοῦ, καὶ ὁμοιωθήσομαι τοῖς καταβαίνουσιν εἰς λάκκον. Ἀκουστὸν ποίησόν μοι τὸ πρωΐ τὸ ἔλεός σου, ὅτι ἐπὶ σοὶ ἤλπισα· γνώρισόν μοι, Κύριε, ὁδόν, ἐν ᾗ πορεύσομαι, ὅτι πρὸς σὲ ἦρα τὴν ψυχήν μου· ἐξελοῦ με ἐκ τῶν ἐχθρῶν μου, Κύριε· πρὸς σὲ κατέφυγον. Δίδαξόν με τοῦ ποιεῖν τὸ θέλημά σου, ὅτι σὺ εἶ ὁ Θεός μου· τὸ πνεῦμά σου τὸ ἀγαθὸν ὁδηγήσει με ἐν γῇ εὐθείᾳ. Ἕνεκεν τοῦ ὀνόματός σου, Κύριε, ζήσεις με· ἐν τῇ δικαιοσύνῃ σου ἐξάξεις ἐκ θλίψεως τὴν ψυχήν μου· καὶ ἐν τῷ ἐλέει σου ἐξολοθρεύσεις τοὺς ἐχθρούς μου· καὶ ἀπολεῖς πάντας τοὺς θλίβοντας τὴν ψυχήν μου, ὅτι ἐγὼ δοῦλός σού εἰμι.

Εἶτα ψάλλομεν

Ἦχος δ'.

Θεὸς Κύριος καὶ ἐπέφανεν ἡμῖν· εὐλογημένος ὁ ἐρχόμενος ἐν ὀνόματι Κυρίου.

Psalm 142

O Lord, hear my prayer; give ear unto my supplication in Your truth; hear me in Your righteousness and enter not into judgment with Your servant, for before You shall not any man be justified. For the enemy has persecuted my soul: he has humbled my life to the earth. He has made me dwell in darkness like dead men of old; and anguished within me is my spirit, and within me my heart is troubled. I remembered the days of old, and I meditated on all Your works, I mused on the creations of Your hands. I stretched forth my hands to You; my soul like a waterless land thirsts for You. Quickly hear me, O Lord; my spirit has fainted away, turn not Your face from me lest I be like them that go down into the pit. Cause me to know, O Lord, the way wherein I should walk, for to You have I lifted up my soul. Rescue me from my enemies, O Lord; to You for refuge have I fled; teach me to do Your Will, for You are my God; Your good Spirit shall guide me in the land of uprightness. For Your Name's sake, O Lord, shall You quicken me. In Your righteousness shall You lead forth my soul out of tribulation, and in Your mercy shall you destroy my enemies; and You shall cut off all them that afflict my soul, for I am Your servant.

We then sing:

Tone 4

God is the Lord, and He has become manifest unto us; blessed is He who comes in the Name of the Lord.

Στίχ. α΄. Ἐξομολογεῖσθε τῷ Κυρίῳ, καὶ ἐπικαλεῖσθε τὸ ὄνομα τοῦ Ἅγιον αὐτοῦ.

Θεὸς Κύριος καὶ ἐπέφανεν ἡμῖν...

Στίχ. β΄. Πάντα τὰ ἔθνη ἐκύκλωσάν με, καὶ τῷ ὀνόματι Κυρίου ἡμυνάμην αὐτούς.

Θεὸς Κύριος καὶ ἐπέφανεν ἡμῖν...

Στίχ. γ΄. Παρὰ Κυρίου ἐγένετο αὕτη, καὶ ἔστι θαυμαστὴ ἐν ὀφθαλμοῖς ἡμῶν.

Θεὸς Κύριος καὶ ἐπέφανεν ἡμῖν...

Εἶτα τὰ παρόντα Τροπάρια.

Ἦχος δ΄. Ὁ ὑψωθεὶς ἐν τῷ Σταυρῷ.

Τῇ Θεοτόκῳ ἐκτενῶς νῦν προσδράμωμεν, ἁμαρτωλοὶ καὶ ταπεινοί, καὶ προσπέσωμεν ἐν μετανοίᾳ, κράζοντες ἐκ βάθους ψυχῆς· Δέσποινα, βοήθησον ἐφ᾽ ἡμῖν σπλαγχνισθεῖσα· σπεῦσον, ἀπολλύμεθα ὑπὸ πλήθους πταισμάτων· μὴ ἀποστρέψῃς σοὺς δούλους κενούς· σὲ γὰρ καὶ μόνην ἐλπίδα κεκτήμεθα.

Δόξα.

Καὶ νῦν.

Οὐ σιωπήσωμέν ποτε, Θεοτόκε, τὰς δυναστείας σου λαλεῖν οἱ ἀνάξιοι· εἰ μὴ γὰρ σὺ προΐστασο πρεσβεύουσα, τίς ἡμᾶς ἐρρύσατο ἐκ τοσούτων κινδύνων; Τίς δὲ διεφύλαξεν ἕως νῦν ἐλευθέρους; Οὐκ ἀποστῶμεν, Δέσποινα, ἐκ σοῦ· σοὺς γὰρ δούλους σῴζεις ἀεὶ ἐκ παντοίων δεινῶν.

Give thanks to the Lord and call upon His Name.

God is the Lord, and He has become manifest unto us; blessed is He who comes in the Name of the Lord.

All the nations encompassed me, and in the name of the Lord I crushed them.

God is the Lord . . .

This was done by the Lord, and it is wonderful in our eyes.

God is the Lord . . .

Troparia

Tone 4

To you, O Theotokos, we sinners now flee. In repentance we bow down before you, saying: "O Sovereign Lady, help us: have compassion on us, make haste to help, for we perish in the multitude of our sins. Turn us not empty away, for we have you as our only hope.

Glory . . . both now and ever . . .

Never, O Theotokos, will we, unworthy, cease to proclaim your powers: for if you did not hasten to our aid, making intercession, who would have delivered us from our manifold adversities? Who would have preserved us free to this day? We will not forsake you, O Lady, for you save your servants from all malicious foes.

Καὶ τὸν

Ψαλμὸν ν' (50) (χῦμα).

Ἐλέησόν με ὁ Θεός, κατὰ τὸ μέγα ἔλεός σου, καὶ κατὰ τὸ πλῆθος τῶν οἰκτιρμῶν σου ἐξάλειψον τὸ ἀνόμημά μου. Ἐπὶ πλεῖον πλῦνόν με ἀπὸ τῆς ἀνομίας μου, καὶ ἀπὸ τῆς ἁμαρτίας μου καθάρισόν με. Ὅτι τὴν ἀνομίαν μου ἐγὼ γινώσκω, καὶ ἡ ἁμαρτία μου ἐνώπιόν μού ἐστι διὰ παντός. Σοὶ μόνῳ ἥμαρτον, καὶ τὸ πονηρὸν ἐνώπιόν σου ἐποίησα· ὅπως ἂν δικαιωθῇς ἐν τοῖς λόγοις σου, καὶ νικήσῃς ἐν τῷ κρίνεσθαί σε. Ἰδοὺ γὰρ ἐν ἀνομίαις συνελήφθην, καὶ ἐν ἁμαρτίαις ἐκίσσησέ με ἡ μήτηρ μου. Ἰδοὺ γὰρ ἀλήθειαν ἠγάπησας· τὰ ἄδηλα καὶ τὰ κρύφια τῆς σοφίας σου ἐδήλωσάς μοι. Ῥαντιεῖς με ὑσσώπῳ, καὶ καθαρισθήσομαι· πλυνεῖς με, καὶ ὑπὲρ χιόνα λευκανθήσομαι. Ἀκουτιεῖς μοι ἀγαλλίασιν καὶ εὐφροσύνην· ἀγαλλιάσονται ὀστέα τεταπεινωμένα. Ἀπόστρεψον τὸ πρόσωπόν σου ἀπὸ τῶν ἁμαρτιῶν μου, καὶ πάσας τὰς ἀνομίας μου ἐξάλειψον. Καρδίαν καθαρὰν κτίσον ἐν ἐμοί, ὁ Θεός, καὶ πνεῦμα εὐθὲς ἐγκαίνισον ἐν τοῖς ἐγκάτοις μου. Μὴ ἀπορρίψῃς με ἀπὸ τοῦ προσώπου σου, καὶ τὸ Πνεῦμά σου τὸ ἅγιον μὴ ἀντανέλῃς ἀπ᾽ ἐμοῦ. Ἀπόδος μοι τὴν ἀγαλλίασιν τοῦ σωτηρίου σου, καὶ πνεύματι ἡγεμονικῷ στήριξόν με. Διδάξω ἀνόμους τὰς ὁδούς σου, καὶ ἀσεβεῖς ἐπὶ σὲ ἐπιστρέψουσι. Ῥῦσαί με ἐξ αἱμάτων, ὁ Θεός, ὁ Θεὸς τῆς σωτηρίας μου· ἀγαλλιάσεται ἡ γλῶσσά μου τὴν δικαιοσύνην σου. Κύριε, τὰ χείλη μου ἀνοίξεις, καὶ τὸ στόμα μου ἀναγγελεῖ τὴν αἴνεσίν σου. Ὅτι, εἰ ἠθέλησας θυσίαν, ἔδωκα ἄν· ὁλοκαυτώματα οὐκ εὐδοκήσεις. Θυσία τῷ Θεῷ πνεῦμα συντετριμμένον· καρδίαν συντετριμμένην καὶ τεταπεινωμένην ὁ Θεὸς οὐκ ἐξουδενώσει. Ἀγάθυνον, Κύριε, ἐν τῇ εὐδοκίᾳ σου τὴν

Psalm 50

Have mercy on me, O God, according to Your great mercy: and according to the multitude of Your compassions blot out my transgressions. Wash me thoroughly of my wickedness, and cleanse me from my sin. For I know my iniquity, and my sin is ever before me. Against You only have I sinned, and done this evil in Your sight, that You might be justified in Your words, and victor when You are Judge. For behold I was shaped in iniquity, and in sin did my mother conceive me. For behold You love truth; the unclear and secret lore of Your wisdom have You made clear to me. You shall sprinkle me with hyssop, and I shall be clean; You shall wash me, and I shall be whiter than snow. For You shall make me hear of joy and gladness: the bones which were humbled shall rejoice. Turn away Your face from my sins, and blot out all my iniquities. Create in me, O God, a clean heart, and renew a right spirit within me. Cast me not away from Your presence, and take not Your Holy Spirit from me. Restore to me the joy of Your salvation, and with a guiding Spirit establish me. I will teach transgressors Your ways, and the ungodly shall turn back to You. Deliver me from blood-guiltiness, O God, You that are the God of my salvation: O Lord, You shall open up my lips, and my mouth shall show forth Your praise. For if You had desired sacrifice, I would have given it; with holocausts shall You not be pleased, a sacrifice for God is a broken spirit, a heart that is broken and humbled God will not despise. Do good, O Lord, in Your pleasure unto Zion:

Σιών, καὶ οἰκοδομηθήτω τὰ τείχη Ἱερουσαλήμ. Τότε εὐδοκήσεις θυσίαν δικαιοσύνης, ἀναφορὰν καὶ ὁλοκαυτώματα. Τότε ἀνοίσουσιν ἐπὶ τὸ θυσιαστήριόν σου μόσχους.

Εἶτα ψάλλομεν τὰ ἑπόμενα Τροπάρια τῆς Θεοτόκου κατ᾽ ἀλφάβητον μετὰ Στίχου· Ὑπεραγία Θεοτόκε, σκέπε, φρούρει, φύλαττε τοὺς δούλους σου.

Ἦχος πλ. β'. Ὁ Εἱρμός.

Η ‛ τὸ χαῖρε δι᾽ ἀγγέλου δεξαμένη, καὶ τεκοῦσα τὸν Κτίστην τὸν ἴδιον, Παρθένε, σῷζε τοὺς σὲ μεγαλύνοντας (δίς).

Ἀνυμνοῦμεν τὸν Υἱόν σου, Θεοτόκε, καὶ βοῶμεν, πανάχραντε Δέσποινα, παντὸς κινδύνου ῥῦσαι τοὺς οἰκέτας σου.

Βασιλέων, Προφητῶν καὶ Ἀποστόλων καὶ Μαρτύρων ὑπάρχεις τὸ καύχημα, καὶ προστασία τοῦ κόσμου, Πανάμωμε.

Γλῶσσα πᾶσα εὐφημεῖ καὶ μακαρίζει, καὶ δοξάζει τὸν ἄχραντον τόκον σου, τῶν Ὀρθοδόξων Μαρία Θεόνυμφε.

Δός, Χριστέ μου, καὶ ἐμοὶ τῷ ἀναξίῳ ὀφλημάτων τὴν ἄφεσιν δέομαι, τῆς σὲ τεκούσης πρεσβείαις, ὡς εὔσπλαγχνος.

Ἐπὶ σέ μου τὰς ἐλπίδας ἀνεθέμην, Θεοτόκε· σῶσον ταῖς πρεσβείαις σου, καὶ δώρησαί μοι πταισμάτων τὴν ἄφεσιν.

Ζώωσόν με, ἡ τεκοῦσα Ζωοδότην καὶ Σωτῆρα· σῶσον ταῖς πρεσβείαις σου, εὐλογημένη, ἐλπὶς τῶν ψυχῶν ἡμῶν.

Ἡ τὸν Κτίστην τῶν ἁπάντων ἐν γαστρί σου συλλαβοῦσα, Παρθένε πανάμωμε, ταῖς σαῖς πρεσβείαις, σῶσον τὰς ψυχὰς ἡμῶν.

17

rebuild the walls of Jerusalem; then shall You be pleased with a Sacrifice of Righteousness, with Oblations and Holocausts; then shall they lay young bullocks upon Your altar.

Then is chanted the following verse: **All-Holy Theotokos,** guard, protect and keep your servants.

Troparia, Tone 6

O Virgin who from the Angel received, hail! And gave birth to the Life-giver Himself, your Creator, save them that magnify you. (3)

We sing of your Son, O Theotokos, and cry aloud: from all adversities save your servants, O Immaculate.

The praise of Kings, Prophets, Apostles, and Martyrs are you, and Intercessor of the world, O All-Immaculate One.

Every Orthodox tongue praises, blesses, and glorifies your immaculate Birth-giving, O Mary, Bride of God.

I beseech You, O my Christ, give to me also, though unworthy, remission of offenses, I beseech You; through the intercessions of her that bore You, in that You are compassionate.

In you, O Theotokos, have I put my hope. Save me by your prayers; grant for me remission of sins.

Give me life, you that have borne the Life-giver and Savior: save me through your prayers, O blessed Hope of our souls.

O Virgin immaculate, who did conceive in your Womb the Creator of all people: through your prayers save our souls.

Θεοτόκε, ἡ τεκοῦσα διὰ λόγου, ὑπὲρ λόγον, τὸν Λόγον, Πανύμνητε, αὐτὸν δυσώπει, σῶσαι τὰς ψυχὰς ἡμῶν.

Ἵλεών μοι τὸν Κριτήν τε καὶ Υἱόν σου, ἐπταικότι ὑπὲρ πάντα ἄνθρωπον, ταῖς σαῖς πρεσβείαις ἀπέργασαι, Δέσποινα.

Κατὰ χρέος ἐκβοῶμέν σοι τό, Χαῖρε, Θεοτόκε, ἁγνὴ ἀειπάρθενε, ἐκδυσωποῦντες πρεσβείαις σου σῴζεσθαι.

Λύτρωσαί με τοῦ πυρὸς τοῦ αἰωνίου, καὶ βασάνων τῶν ἀποκειμένων μοι, Θεογεννῆτορ, ὅπως μακαρίζω σε.

Μὴ παρίδῃς τὰς δεήσεις τῶν σῶν δούλων, δυσωποῦμεν, Πανύμνητε Δέσποινα, ἵνα ῥυσθῶμεν πάσης περιστάσεως.

Νοσημάτων καὶ παντοίων ἀλγηδόνων, καὶ κινδύνων ἡμᾶς ἐλευθέρωσον, τῇ ἱερᾷ σου σκέπῃ καταφεύγοντας.

Ξένον θαῦμα τὸ ἐν σοί, Θεοκυῆτορ· δι' ἡμᾶς γὰρ καθ' ἡμᾶς γεγέννηται ὁ πάντων Κτίστης ἐκ σοῦ καὶ Θεὸς ἡμῶν.

Ὁ ναός σου, Θεοτόκε, ἀνεδείχθη ἰατρεῖον νοσημάτων ἄμισθον, καὶ θλιβομένων ψυχῶν παραμύθιον.

Παναγία Θεοτόκε, ἡ τεκοῦσα τὸν Σωτῆρα, κινδύνων διάσωσον, καὶ πάσης ἄλλης ἀνάγκης τοὺς δούλους σου.

Ῥῦσαι πάσης ἀπειλῆς ἐπερχομένης τοὺς σοὺς δούλους, Πανάχραντε Δέσποινα, καὶ πάσης βλάβης ψυχῆς τε καὶ σώματος.

Σῶσον πάντας ταῖς πρεσβείαις σου, Παρθένε, τοὺς εἰς σέ, Θεοτόκε, προστρέχοντας, καὶ ῥῦσαι πάσης ἀνάγκης καὶ θλίψεως.

All-praised Theotokos, who through the word of an Angel, in a manner beyond reason, gave birth to the Word, pray that He will save our souls.

Through your intercessions, O Lady, make your Son a merciful Judge unto me, who am a sinner above all people.

With binding duty we cry to you, Hail! O immaculate Theotokos Ever-Virgin; through your intercessions are saved those that pray to you.

Deliver me from the fire eternal, and the torments that await me, O all-praised Lady, that I may be delivered from all tribulation.

All-praised Sovereign Lady, we pray You: do not overlook the prayers of Your servants, so that we might be delivered from all tribulation.

From every sickness and infirmity, deliver us, who have recourse unto you and your holy Protection.

Marvelous wonder shown to you, O Theotokos: for our sake the Creator of All and our God was in our likeness born to you.

Your Temple, O Theotokos, was shown forth as remedy without price of ills—the consolation of our wounded souls.

O All-Holy Theotokos, who has borne the Savior, save your servants from adversity and from all other necessity.

From every ban under which they labor deliver your servants; from every ailment of body and spirit, O you most Holy.

Through your intercessions, O Virgin Theotokos, save all that have recourse unto you; deliver all from sorrow and necessity.

Τίς προστρέχων τῷ Ναῷ σου, Θεοτόκε, οὐ λαμβάνει ταχέως τὴν ἴασιν, ψυχῆς ὁμοῦ τε καὶ σώματος, Ἄχραντε;

Ὑπὸ πάντων δυσωπούμενος, Οἰκτίρμον, τῶν Ἁγίων καὶ τῶν ἄνω Τάξεων, ἱλάσθητί μοι διὰ τῆς Τεκούσης σε.

Φεῖσαι, Σῶτερ, τῶν ψυχῶν τῶν τεθνεώντων, ἐπ᾽ ἐλπίδι ζωῆς ἀδελφῶν ἡμῶν, καὶ ἄνες, ἄφες αὐτοῖς τὰ ἐγκλήματα.

Χαῖρε κόσμου ἱλαστήριον, Παρθένε, χαῖρε στάμνε καὶ λυχνία πάγχρυσε, τοῦ θείου μάννα καὶ φωτός, Θεόνυμφε.

Τριαδικὸν

Ψάλλομέν σοι τῷ Θεῷ τῷ ἐν Τριάδι, ἐκβοῶντες φωνὴν τὴν τρισάγιον, ἐκδυσωποῦντες σωτηρίας τεύξασθαι.

Θεοτοκίον

Ὦ Παρθένε, ἡ τεκοῦσα τὸν Σωτῆρα καὶ Δεσπότην τοῦ κόσμου καὶ Κύριον, αὐτὸν δυσώπει, σῶσαι τὰς ψυχὰς ἡμῶν.

Χαῖρε ὄρος, χαῖρε βάτε, χαῖρε πύλη, χαῖρε κλῖμαξ, χαῖρε θεία τράπεζα, ἡ πάντων χαῖρε βοήθεια, Δέσποινα.

Ταῖς πρεσβείαις, Ἐλεῆμον, τῆς Μητρός σου τῆς Ἀχράντου, καὶ πάντων τῶν Ἁγίων σου, τὰ σὰ ἐλέη τῷ λαῷ σου δώρησαι.

Τῇ πρεσβείᾳ τῶν ἐνδόξων Ἀρχαγγέλων καὶ Ἀγγέλων, καὶ τῶν ἄνω Τάξεων, σοὺς δούλους, Σῶτερ, καλῶς διαφύλαξον.

Τῇ πρεσβείᾳ τοῦ τιμίου καὶ ἐνδόξου Βαπτιστοῦ σου Προφήτου Προδρόμου τε, Χριστέ μου Σῶτερ, τοὺς δούλους σου φύλαξον.

Who, having recourse unto your Temple, O Theotokos, does not receive speedy healing both of soul and body, O All-immaculate?

Entreated by the Saints and heavenly Hosts, O Merciful One, through her that bore You, do You cleanse me.

Spare, O Savior, the souls of our brethren, who died in the Hope of Life; loose, and remit their sins.

Hail! O Virgin, Mercy-Seat of the world; Hail! O Receptacle of the Manna and Candelabrum all-golden of the light divine, O Bride of God unwedded.

Triadikon

We sing unto You, O God in Three Persons, crying aloud the thrice-Holy Hymn, entreating that we may receive salvation.

Theotokion

O Virgin, who has borne the Savior, the Sovereign of the world: pray unto Him that He will save our souls.

Hail! O Mount, Hail! O Bush that burned and yet was not consumed; Hail! O Gate, Hail! O Ladder and Altar Divine, Hail! Sovereign Lady, the Helper of all.

Through the prayers of Your Holy Mother, and of Your Holy Saints, O Merciful God, to Your people grant Your great mercies.

Through the prayers of the glorious Archangels, the Angels, and all the heavenly Hosts, mightily preserve Your servants, O Savior.

Through the prayers of the glorious Prophet and Forerunner John the Baptist, and of all Your Saints, mightily preserve Your servants, O my Christ and Savior.

Τῇ πρεσβείᾳ τῶν ἐνδόξων Ἀποστόλων, καὶ Μαρτύρων, καὶ πάντων τῶν Ἁγίων σου, τὰ σὰ ἐλέη τῷ λαῷ σου δώρησαι.

Τῇ πρεσβείᾳ τῶν ἐνδόξων Ἀναργύρων, Θεοτόκε, τοὺς δούλους σου φύλαττε, ὡς προστασία τοῦ κόσμου καὶ στήριγμα.

Δόξα.

Τὸν Πατέρα καὶ Υἱὸν δοξολογοῦμεν, καὶ τὸ Πνεῦμα τὸ Ἅγιον, λέγοντες· Τριὰς Ἁγία, σῶσον τὰς ψυχὰς ἡμῶν.

Καὶ νῦν. Θεοτοκίον

Ἡ ἀρρήτως ἐπ' ἐσχάτων συλλαβοῦσα, καὶ τεκοῦσα τὸν Κτίστην τὸν ἴδιον, Παρθένε, σῷζε τοὺς σὲ μεγαλύνοντας.

Τῆς εὐσπλαγχνίας τὴν πύλην ἄνοιξον ἡμῖν, εὐλογημένη Θεοτόκε· ἐλπίζοντες εἰς σέ, μὴ ἀστοχήσωμεν· ῥυσθείημεν διὰ σοῦ τῶν περιστάσεων· σὺ γὰρ εἶ ἡ σωτηρία τοῦ γένους τῶν χριστιανῶν.

Ὁ Ἱερεὺς

Τοῦ Κυρίου δεηθῶμεν.

Ὅτι Ἅγιος εἶ ὁ Θεὸς ἡμῶν, καὶ σοὶ τὴν δόξαν ἀναπέμπομεν, τῷ Πατρί, καὶ τῷ Υἱῷ καὶ τῷ Ἁγίῳ Πνεύματι, νῦν καὶ ἀεὶ καὶ εἰς τοὺς αἰῶνας τῶν αἰώνων. Ἀμήν.

Εἶτα τὰ παρόντα Τροπάρια

Ἦχος πλ. δ'.

Νῦν ἐπέστη ὁ καιρός, ὁ πάντας ἁγιάζων, καὶ ὁ δίκαιος ἡμᾶς ἀναμένει Κριτής· ἀλλ' ἐπίστρεψον, ψυχή, πρὸς μετάνοιαν, ὡς ἡ Πόρνη κράζουσα σὺν δάκρυσι· Κύριε, ἐλέησόν με.

Through the prayers of the glorious Apostles, and the victorious Martyrs, and of all Your Saints, grant Your mercies to Your servants.

Through the prayers of the glorious Unmercenaries, O Theotokos, preserve your servants, in that you are Intercessor and Confirmer of the world.

Glory . . .

The Father and the Son and the Holy Spirit we glorify saying: O Holy Trinity, save our souls.

Both now and ever . . . *Theotokion*

O Virgin who in mystery did conceive and bring forth in these latter days Your Creator: save us who magnify you.

Open for us the door of your tender compassion, O blessed Theotokos; and as we set our hope in you, let us never be confounded; through you may we be delivered from all adversity; you, who are the salvation of all good Christian folk.

Priest

Let us pray to the Lord. Lord have mercy.

For Holy are You, O God, and to You are due all glory, honor, and adoration: to the Father and to the Son and to the Holy Spirit, both now and ever and to the ages of ages. Amen.

And the following Troparia

Tone 8

Now draws nigh the time that sanctifies all men, and a just Judge awaits us; turn then, O my soul, to repentance, like the Adulteress tearfully crying: have mercy on me, O Lord.

Νάμασιν ἐπομβρήσας, Χριστέ, πηγὴν τῶν ἰάσεων, ἐν τῷ πανσέπτῳ ναῷ τῆς Παρθένου σήμερον, τῷ τῆς σῆς εὐλογίας ῥαντισμῷ, φυγαδεύεις τὰς νόσους τῶν ἀσθενούντων, ἰατρὲ τῶν ψυχῶν καὶ τῶν σωμάτων ἡμῶν.

Παρθένος ἔτεκες ἀπειρόγαμε, καὶ Παρθένος ἔμεινας, Μήτηρ ἀνύμφευτε, Θεοτόκε, Μαρία· Χριστὸν τὸν Θεὸν ἡμῶν ἱκέτευε, σωθῆναι ἡμᾶς.

Παναγία Θεοτόκε Παρθένε, τῶν χειρῶν ἡμῶν τὰ ἔργα κατεύθυνον, καὶ συγχώρησιν τῶν πταισμάτων ἡμῶν αἴτησαι, ἐν τῷ ψάλλειν ἡμᾶς τῶν Ἀγγέλων τὸν ὕμνον.

Ἅγιος ὁ Θεός, Ἅγιος ἰσχυρός, Ἅγιος ἀθάνατος, ἐλέησον ἡμᾶς (ἐκ γ').

Δόξα. Καὶ νῦν.

Ἅγιος ἀθάνατος, ἐλέησον ἡμᾶς.

Πάλιν

Ἅγιος ὁ Θεός, Ἅγιος ἰσχυρός, Ἅγιος ἀθάνατος, ἐλέησον ἡμᾶς.

Ὁ Ἱερεύς· Πρόσχωμεν.

Προκείμενον. Ἦχος δ'.

Κύριος φωτισμός μου καὶ Σωτήρ μου.

Στίχ. Κύριος ὑπερασπιστὴς τῆς ζωῆς μου.

Ὁ Ἱερεύς· Σοφία.

O Christ, the Fountain, Who did sprinkle the waters of healing in the all-holy Temple of the Virgin, You, today, through the sprinkling of blessing did expel the maladies of ailing, O You Physician of our souls and bodies.

As a Virgin you knew not man, but gave birth; and as a Mother unwedded, a Virgin did you remain; entreat then, O Mary Theotokos, Christ our God that He will save us.

O All-Holy Theotokos Virgin, guide aright the works of our hands, and entreat pardon for our transgressions, when we chant the angelic Hymn:

Holy God, Holy Mighty, Holy Immortal: have mercy on us. (3)

Glory . . . both now and ever . . .

Holy Immortal: have mercy on us.

Again

Holy God, Holy Mighty, Holy Immortal: have mercy on us.

Priest: Let us attend.

The Prokeimenon, in Tone 4

The Lord is my Light and my Savior; whom then shall I fear? The Lord is the defender of my life; of whom then shall I be afraid?

Priest: Wisdom.

Ο Διάκονος

Πρὸς Ἑβραίους Ἐπιστολῆς Παύλου τὸ Ἀνάγνωσμα.

Ὁ Ἱερεύς· Πρόσχωμεν.

Ὁ Διάκονος

ΑΠΟΣΤΟΛΟΣ

(Κεφ. Β΄, 11—18)

Ἀδελφοί, ὁ ἁγιάζων καὶ οἱ ἁγιαζόμενοι ἐξ ἑνὸς πάντες· δι' ἣν αἰτίαν οὐκ ἐπαισχύνεται ἀδελφοὺς αὐτοὺς καλεῖν, λέγων· Ἀπαγγελῶ τὸ ὄνομά σοι τοῖς ἀδελφοῖς μου, ἐν μέσῳ ἐκκλησίας ὑμνήσω σε. Καὶ πάλιν· Ἐγὼ ἔσομαι πεποιθὼς ἐπ' αὐτῷ. Καὶ πάλιν· Ἰδοὺ ἐγὼ καὶ τὰ παιδία, ἅ μοι ἔδωκεν ὁ Θεός. Ἐπεὶ οὖν τὰ παιδία κεκοινώνηκε σαρκὸς καὶ αἵματος, καὶ αὐτὸς παραπλησίως μετέσχε τῶν αὐτῶν, ἵνα διὰ τοῦ θανάτου καταργήσῃ τὸν τὸ κράτος ἔχοντα τοῦ θανάτου, τουτέστι τὸν Διάβολον, καὶ ἀπαλλάξῃ τούτους, ὅσοι φόβῳ θανάτου διὰ παντὸς τοῦ ζῆν ἔνοχοι ἦσαν δουλείας. Οὐ γὰρ δήπου Ἀγγέλων ἐπιλαμβάνεται, ἀλλὰ σπέρματος Ἀβραὰμ ἐπιλαμβάνεται. Ὅθεν ὤφειλε κατὰ πάντα τοῖς ἀδελφοῖς ὁμοιωθῆναι, ἵνα ἐλεήμων γένηται καὶ πιστὸς Ἀρχιερεὺς τὰ πρὸς τὸν Θεόν, εἰς τὸ ἱλάσκεσθαι τὰς ἁμαρτίας τοῦ λαοῦ. Ἐν ᾧ γὰρ πέπονθεν αὐτὸς πειρασθείς, δύναται τοῖς πειραζομένοις βοηθῆσαι.

Ὁ Ἱερεὺς

Εἰρήνη σοι τῷ ἀναγινώσκοντι.

Ὁ Διάκονος

Ἀλληλούϊα. Ἦχος πλ. β΄.

Ὁ Διάκονος

Σοφία. Ὀρθοί, ἀκούσωμεν τοῦ ἁγίου Εὐαγγελίου.

Ὁ Ἱερεύς· Εἰρήνη πᾶσι.

Reader

The Lesson from the Epistle of the Holy Apostle Paul to the Hebrews. (Heb. 2:11-18)

Priest: Let us attend.

Reader

Brethren, he who sanctifies and those who are sanctified have all one origin. That is why he is not ashamed to call them brethren, saying: "I will proclaim your name to my brethren, in the midst of the congregation I will praise you." And again: "I will put my trust in him." And again: "Here am I, and the children God has given me." Since therefore the children share in flesh and blood, he himself likewise partook of the same nature, that through death he might destroy him who has the power of death, that is, the devil, and deliver all those who through fear of death were subject to lifelong bondage. For surely it is not with angels that he is concerned but with the descendants of Abraham. Therefore he had to be made like his brethren in every respect, so that he might become a merciful and faithful high priest in the service of God, to make expiation for the sins of the people. For because he himself has suffered and been tempted, he is able to help those who are tempted.

Priest

Peace be to you who read.

Choir

Alleluia, alleluia, alleluia.

Priest

Wisdom! Let us attend! Let us hear the Holy Gospel.

(+) Peace be to all.

Ὁ Διάκονος·Καὶ τῷ Πνεύματί σου.

Ὁ Ἱερεὺς

Ἐκ τοῦ κατὰ Ἰωάννην ἁγίου Εὐαγγελίου
τὸ Ἀνάγνωσμα.

Ὁ Διάκονος·Πρόσχωμεν.

Ὁ Ἱερεὺς

ΕΥΑΓΓΕΛΙΟΝ

(Κεφ. ε΄, 1-4).

Τῷ καιρῷ ἐκείνῳ, ἀνέβη ὁ Ἰησοῦς εἰς Ἱεροσό-
λυμα. Ἔστι δὲ ἐν τοῖς Ἱεροσολύμοις, ἐπὶ τῇ
Προβατικῇ, κολυμβήθρα, ἡ ἐπιλεγομένη ἑβραϊστὶ
Βηθεσδά, πέντε στοὰς ἔχουσα. Ἐν ταύταις κατέ-
κειτο πλῆθος πολὺ τῶν ἀσθενούντων, τυφλῶν, χω-
λῶν, ξηρῶν, ἐκδεχομένων τὴν τοῦ ὕδατος κίνησιν.
Ἄγγελος γὰρ κατὰ καιρὸν κατέβαινεν ἐν τῇ κολυμβήθρᾳ, καὶ ἐτάραττε τὸ ὕδωρ· ὁ οὖν πρῶτος ἐμβὰς
μετὰ τὴν ταραχὴν τοῦ ὕδατος, ὑγιὴς ἐγίνετο, ᾧ δή-
ποτε κατείχετο νοσήματι.

Ὁ Διάκονος

Δόξα σοι, Κύριε, δόξα σοι.

Εἶτα, τοῦ Διακόνου λέγοντος τὰ «Εἰρηνικά», ὁ
Ἱερεὺς ἀντιφωνεῖ καθ᾽ ἑκάστην δέησιν τὸ Κύριε,
ἐλέησον καὶ ἐν τέλει τὸ Σοί, Κύριε.

Ἐν εἰρήνῃ, τοῦ Κυρίου δεηθῶμεν.

Ὑπὲρ τῆς ἄνωθεν εἰρήνης καὶ τῆς σωτηρίας τῶν
ψυχῶν ἡμῶν, τοῦ Κυρίου δεηθῶμεν.

Ὑπὲρ τῆς εἰρήνης τοῦ σύμπαντος κόσμου, εὐσταθείας τῶν ἁγίων τοῦ Θεοῦ Ἐκκλησιῶν, καὶ τῆς
τῶν πάντων ἑνώσεως, τοῦ Κυρίου δεηθῶμεν.

Choir: **And to your spirit.**

Priest

The Holy Gospel according to St. John.
(5:1-4)
Let us attend.

Choir: **Glory to You, O God; Glory to You.**

The Gospel

At that time, there was a feast of the Jews, and Jesus went up to Jerusalem. Now there is in Jerusalem by the Sheep Gate a pool, in Hebrew called Bethesda, which has five porticoes. In these lay a multitude of invalids, blind, lame, paralyzed, waiting for the moving of the water. For an angel of the Lord went down at certain seasons into the pool and troubled the water. And whoever stepped in first after the troubling of the water was healed of whatever disease he had.

Choir

Glory to You, O God; Glory to You.

The Ektenia of Blessing

Following each petition, the Choir responds with "Lord have mercy" *and, at the end, with* "To You, O Lord."

In peace let us pray to the Lord.

For the peace from above; for the salvation of our souls; let us pray to the Lord.

For the peace of the whole world; for the stability of the holy Churches of God; and for the union of all; let us pray to the Lord.

(Ὑπὲρ τοῦ ἁγίου οἴκου τούτου, καὶ τῶν μετὰ πίστεως, εὐλαβείας καὶ φόβου Θεοῦ εἰσιόντων ἐν αὐτῷ, τοῦ Κυρίου δεηθῶμεν).

Ὑπὲρ τοῦ Ἀρχιεπισκόπου ἡμῶν (τοῦ δεῖνος), παντὸς τοῦ Κλήρου καὶ τοῦ Λαοῦ, τοῦ Κυρίου δεηθῶμεν.

(Ὑπὲρ τῶν εὐσεβεστάτων καὶ θεοφυλάκτων Βασιλέων ἡμῶν (τοῦ δεῖνος καὶ τῆς δεῖνος), τ... Διαδόχου αὐτῶν (τοῦ ἢ τῆς δεῖνος), πάσης τῆς βασιλικῆς οἰκογενείας, τοῦ κατὰ ξηράν, θάλασσαν καὶ ἀέρα φιλοχρίστου Στρατοῦ, παντὸς τοῦ εὐσεβοῦς ἡμῶν Ἔθνους καὶ πάσης Ἀρχῆς καὶ Ἐξουσίας ἐν τῷ Κράτει, τοῦ Κυρίου δεηθῶμεν).

Ὑπὲρ τῆς πόλεως (ἢ νήσου) ταύτης, πάσης πόλεως, χώρας καὶ τῶν πίστει οἰκούντων ἐν αὐταῖς, τοῦ Κυρίου δεηθῶμεν.

Ὑπὲρ εὐκρασίας ἀέρων, εὐφορίας τῶν καρπῶν τῆς γῆς, καὶ καιρῶν εἰρηνικῶν, τοῦ Κυρίου δεηθῶμεν.

Ὑπὲρ πλεόντων, ὁδοιπορούντων, νοσούντων, καμνόντων, αἰχμαλώτων καὶ τῆς σωτηρίας αὐτῶν, τοῦ Κυρίου δεηθῶμεν.

Ὑπὲρ τοῦ ἁγιασθῆναι τὸ ὕδωρ τοῦτο, τῇ δυνάμει καὶ ἐνεργείᾳ καὶ ἐπιφοιτήσει τοῦ Ἁγίου Πνεύματος, τοῦ Κυρίου δεηθῶμεν.

Ὑπὲρ τοῦ καταφοιτῆσαι τῷ ὕδατι τούτῳ τὴν καθαρτικὴν τῆς ὑπερουσίου Τριάδος ἐνέργειαν, τοῦ Κυρίου δεηθῶμεν.

Ὑπὲρ τοῦ γενέσθαι τὸ ὕδωρ τοῦτο ἰαματικὸν ψυχῶν καὶ σωμάτων, καὶ πάσης ἀντικειμένης δυνάμεως ἀποτρεπτικόν, τοῦ Κυρίου δεηθῶμεν.

Ὑπὲρ τοῦ καταπεμφθῆναι αὐτῷ τὴν χάριν τῆς ἀπολυτρώσεως, τὴν εὐλογίαν τοῦ Ἰορδάνου, τοῦ Κυρίου δεηθῶμεν.

[For this holy House; and for them that with faith, reverence, and the fear of God enter therein; let us pray to the Lord.]

For our Most Reverend Archbishop (*Name*), for all the Clergy, and the people; let us pray to the Lord.

[For the President of the United States and for all civil authorities; let us pray to the Lord.]

For this city, for every city and land, for the faithful that dwell in them; let us pray to the Lord.

For seasonable weather; for abundance of the fruits of the earth, and for peaceful seasons; let us pray to the Lord.

For all them that travel by land or sea, or in the air; for the sick, and the afflicted; for captives, and for their salvation; let us pray to the Lord.

That this water might be hallowed by the might, and operation, and descent of the Holy Spirit; let us pray to the Lord.

That there may descend upon these waters the cleansing operation of the supersubstantial Trinity; let us pray to the Lord.

That this water may be to the healing of souls and bodies, and to the banishment of every hostile power; let us pray to the Lord.

That there may be sent down upon it the Grace of Redemption, the blessing of the Jordan; let us pray to the Lord.

Ὑπὲρ πάντων τῶν χρῃζόντων τῆς παρὰ τοῦ Θεοῦ βοηθείας καὶ ἀντιλήψεως, τοῦ Κυρίου δεηθῶμεν.

Ὑπὲρ τοῦ φωτισθῆναι ἡμᾶς φωτισμὸν γνώσεως, διὰ τῆς ὁμοουσίου Τριάδος, τοῦ Κυρίου δεηθῶμεν.

Ὅπως Κύριος ὁ Θεὸς ἡμῶν ἀναδείξῃ ἡμᾶς υἱοὺς καὶ κληρονόμους τῆς βασιλείας αὐτοῦ, διὰ τῆς τοῦ ὕδατος τούτου μεταλήψεώς τε καὶ ῥαντισμοῦ, τοῦ Κυρίου δεηθῶμεν.

Ὑπὲρ τοῦ ῥυσθῆναι ἡμᾶς ἀπὸ πάσης θλίψεως, ὀργῆς, κινδύνου καὶ ἀνάγκης, τοῦ Κυρίου δεηθῶμεν.

Ἀντιλαβοῦ, σῶσον, ἐλέησον, καὶ διαφύλαξον ἡμᾶς, ὁ Θεός, τῇ σῇ χάριτι.

Τῆς παναγίας, ἀχράντου, ὑπερευλογημένης, ἐνδόξου δεσποίνης ἡμῶν Θεοτόκου καὶ ἀειπαρθένου Μαρίας, μετὰ πάντων τῶν Ἁγίων μνημονεύσαντες, ἑαυτοὺς καὶ ἀλλήλους καὶ πᾶσαν τὴν ζωὴν ἡμῶν Χριστῷ τῷ Θεῷ παραθώμεθα.

Ὅτι πρέπει σοι πᾶσα δόξα, τιμὴ καὶ προσκύνησις, τῷ Πατρὶ καὶ τῷ Υἱῷ καὶ τῷ Ἁγίῳ Πνεύματι, νῦν καὶ ἀεί καὶ εἰς τοὺς αἰῶνας τῶν αἰώνων. Ἀμήν.

Ὁ Διάκονος
Τοῦ Κυρίου δεηθῶμεν.

Ὁ Ἱερεὺς λέγει τὴν Εὐχὴν ταύτην

Κύριε ὁ Θεὸς ἡμῶν, ὁ μέγας τῇ βουλῇ καὶ θαυμαστὸς τοῖς ἔργοις, ὁ πάσης ὁρατῆς τε καὶ ἀοράτου κτίσεως δημιουργός· ὁ φυλάσσων τὴν διαθήκην σου καὶ τὸ ἔλεός σου τοῖς ἀγαπῶσί σε καὶ τηροῦσι τὰ σὰ προστάγματα· ὁ πάντων τῶν ἐν ἀνάγκαις ἐλεεινὰ προσδεχόμενος δάκρυα· διὰ γὰρ τοῦτο παραγέγονας ἐν δούλου μορφῇ, οὐ φάσμασιν ἡμᾶς ἐκδειματούμενος, ἀλλ᾽ ὑγίειαν τῷ σώματι ἀληθῆ ὀρέ-

For all of them who need God to help and give protection; let us pray to the Lord.

That He will illuminate us with the Light of understanding of the Consubstantial Trinity; let us pray to the Lord.

That the Lord our God will show us forth as sons and daughters and heirs of His Kingdom through the partaking and sprinkling of these waters; let us pray to the Lord.

That He will deliver us from all tribulation, wrath, danger, and necessity; let us pray to the Lord.

Help us; save us; have mercy on us; and keep us, O God, by Your Grace.

Calling to remembrance our all-holy, pure, exceedingly blessed glorious Lady Theotokos and Ever-Virgin Mary, with all the Saints; let us commend ourselves and one another and all our life to Christ our God.

To You, O Lord.

For to You do we send up all glory, honor, and worship: to the Father and to the Son and to the Holy Spirit, both now and ever, and to the ages of ages. Amen.

Priest

Let us pray to the Lord. Lord have mercy.

O Lord our God, Who are mighty in counsel and wondrous in all Your deeds: the Creator of all things: Who keep Your Covenant and Your mercy upon all those who love You and keep Your commandments: Who receive the devout tears of all that are in distress: for this cause did You come in the similitude of a servant, scorning not our image but giving true health to the body and saying, "Lo!

γων καὶ λέγων· Ἴδε ὑγιὴς γέγονας, μηκέτι ἁμάρτανε. Ἀλλὰ καὶ ἐκ πηλοῦ ζῶντας ὀφθαλμοὺς εἰργάσω καί, νίψασθαι κελεύσας, τὸ φῶς οἰκῆσαι παρεσκεύασας λόγῳ· ὁ τὰς τῶν ἐναντίων παθῶν σπιλάδας ταράττων. καὶ τὴν τοῦ βίου τούτου ἁλμυρὰν θάλασσαν καταστείλας, καὶ τὰ ἀχθηφόρα τῶν ἡδονῶν κατευνάσας κύματα· Αὐτὸς οὖν, φιλάνθρωπε Βασιλεῦ, ὁ δοὺς ἡμῖν χιονοφεγγόφωτον φορέσαι στολὴν ἐξ ὕδατός τε καὶ πνεύματος, καὶ διὰ τῆς τοῦ ὕδατος τούτου μεταλήψεώς τε καὶ ῥαντισμοῦ τὴν σὴν εὐλογίαν ἡμῖν κατάπεμψον, τὸν ῥύπον τῶν παθῶν ἀποσμήχουσαν. Ναί, Δέσποτα, δεόμεθα· ἐπίσκεψαι ἡμῶν, Ἀγαθέ, τὴν ἀσθένειαν καὶ ἴασαι ἡμῶν τὰς νόσους ψυχῆς τε καὶ σώματος, τῷ ἐλέει σου· πρεσβείαις τῆς παναχράντου δεσποίνης ἡμῶν Θεοτόκου καὶ ἀειπαρθένου Μαρίας· δυνάμει τοῦ τιμίου καὶ ζωοποιοῦ Σταυροῦ· προστασίαις τῶν τιμίων ἐπουρανίων Δυνάμεων Ἀσωμάτων· τοῦ τιμίου ἐνδόξου προφήτου προδρόμου καὶ βαπτιστοῦ Ἰωάννου· τῶν ἁγίων ἐνδόξων καὶ πανευφήμων Ἀποστόλων· τῶν ἐν ἁγίοις Πατέρων ἡμῶν, μεγάλων Ἱεραρχῶν καὶ οἰκουμενικῶν Διδασκάλων, Βασιλείου τοῦ Μεγάλου, Γρηγορίου τοῦ Θεολόγου καὶ Ἰωάννου τοῦ Χρυσοστόμου· τῶν ἐν Ἁγίοις Πατέρων ἡμῶν Ἀθανασίου καὶ Κυρίλλου, Ἰωάννου τοῦ Ἐλεήμονος, πατριαρχῶν Ἀλεξανδρείας· Νικολάου ἐπισκόπου Μύρων τῆς Λυκίας καὶ Σπυρίδωνος ἐπισκόπου Τριμυθοῦντος, τῶν θαυματουργῶν· τῶν ἁγίων καὶ ἐνδόξων μεγαλομαρτύρων Γεωργίου τοῦ Τροπαιοφόρου, Δημητρίου τοῦ Μυροβλύτου, Θεοδώρου τοῦ Τήρωνος καὶ Θεοδώρου τοῦ Στρατηλάτου· τῶν ἁγίων ἐνδόξων ἱερομαρτύρων Χαραλάμπους καὶ Ἐλευθερίου, τῶν ἁγίων ἐνδόξων καὶ καλλινίκων Μαρτύρων· τῶν ἁγίων καὶ δικαίων θεοπατόρων Ἰωακεὶμ καὶ Ἄννης· τῶν ἁγίων ἐνδόξων καὶ θαυματουργῶν Ἀναργύρων Κο-

You are healed, sin no more." And with clay did make man's eyes whole, and having commanded him to wash, made him by Your word rejoice in the light, putting to confusion the floods of passions of enemies; and drying up the bitter sea of life of the same, subduing the waves of sensual desires heavy to be endured: do You, the same Lord and King Who loves mankind, Who has granted to us to clothe ourselves in the garment of snowy whiteness, by water and by Spirit: send down on us Your blessing, and through the partaking of this water, through sprinkling with it, wash away the defilement of passions. Yea, we beseech You visit our weaknesses, O Good One, and heal our infirmities both of spirit and of body through Your mercy; through the prayers of the all-pure, exceedingly blessed Lady Theotokos and Ever-Virgin Mary; Through the intercessions of the precious and life-creating Cross; through the protection of the glorious bodiless Powers of the Heavens; through the intercessions of the glorious Prophet and Forerunner John the Baptist; of the holy, glorious and all-praiseworthy Apostles; of the holy and theophoric Fathers; of our Fathers among the Saints, the great Hierarchs and ecumenical Teachers, Basil the Great, Gregory the Theologian, and John Chrysostom; of our Fathers the Saints, Athanasios, Kyrillos, and John the Merciful, Patriarchs of Alexandria; of Nicholas Bishop of Myra in Lycia; of Spyridon the Wonderworker of Trymitheus; of the holy, glorious Martyrs, George the Victorious, Demetrios the Exhaler of Myrrh, Theodore of Tyron and Theodore Stratilatis; and of the holy and glorious Hieromartyrs Charalambos and Eleutherios, and of all the righteous Martyrs; of the holy and righteous forefathers Joakim and Anna; of the holy wonderworking

σμᾶ καὶ Δαμιανοῦ, Κύρου καὶ Ἰωάννου, Παντελεή-
μονος καὶ Ἑρμολάου, Σαμψὼν καὶ Διομήδους, Μω-
κίου καὶ Ἀνικήτου, Θαλλελαίου καὶ Τρύφωνος·
τοῦ Ἁγίου (τῆς ἡμέρας), οὗ καὶ τὴν μνήμην ἐπι-
τελοῦμεν· καὶ πάντων σου τῶν Ἁγίων. Καὶ φύλαττε,
Κύριε, τοὺς δούλους σου τοὺς πιστοὺς Βασιλεῖς
ἡμῶν (ἐκ γ΄)· χάρισαι αὐτοῖς ψυχῆς καὶ σώματος
τὴν ὑγίειαν, καὶ τῇ δουλικῇ σου ταύτῃ τῶν χριστιανῶν πολιτείᾳ ποίησον κατὰ πάντα ἐπιεικεῖς. Μνήσθητι, Κύριε, πάσης ἐπισκοπῆς Ὀρθοδόξων, τῶν
ὀρθοτομούντων τὸν λόγον τῆς σῆς ἀληθείας καὶ
παντὸς ἱερατικοῦ καὶ μοναχικοῦ τάγματος καὶ τῆς
σωτηρίας αὐτῶν. Μνήσθητι, Κύριε, τῶν μισούντων
καὶ ἀγαπώντων ἡμᾶς, τῶν διακονούντων ἀδελφῶν
ἡμῶν, τῶν περιεστώτων καὶ τῶν δι᾽ εὐλόγους αἰτίας ἀπολειφθέντων καὶ τῶν ἐντειλαμένων ἡμῖν
τοῖς ἀναξίοις εὔχεσθαι ὑπὲρ αὐτῶν. Μνήσθητι,
Κύριε, καὶ τῶν ἐν αἰχμαλωσίᾳ καὶ θλίψεσιν ἀδελφῶν ἡμῶν, καὶ ἐλέησον αὐτοὺς καὶ ἡμᾶς κατὰ τὸ
μέγα σου ἔλεος, πάσης ἀνάγκης ῥυόμενος.

Ὅτι σὺ εἶ ἡ πηγὴ τῶν ἰαμάτων, Χριστὲ ὁ Θεὸς
ἡμῶν, καὶ σοὶ τὴν δόξαν ἀναπέμπομεν, σὺν τῷ
ἀνάρχῳ σου Πατρί, καὶ τῷ παναγίῳ καὶ ἀγαθῷ,
καὶ ζωοποιῷ σου Πνεύματι, νῦν καὶ ἀεὶ καὶ εἰς τοὺς
αἰῶνας τῶν αἰώνων. Ἀμήν.

Εἰρήνη πᾶσι.

Ὁ Διάκονος

Τὰς κεφαλὰς ἡμῶν τῷ Κυρίῳ κλίνωμεν.

Ὁ Ἱερεύς, κλινόμενος, λέγει μυστικῶς τὴν Εὐχὴν ταύτην·

Unmercenaries, Kosmas and Damian, Kyros and John, Panteleimon and Hermolaus; Samson and Diomedes, Mokios and Anekitas, Thallelaios and Tryphon; of Saint (*Name of the Saint of the Day*), whose memory we commemorate; and of all Your Saints. Preserve, O Lord, the President of the United States, and all the other Civil Authorities enabled by the American people; save, O God, all Orthodox Bishops who rightly divide the word of Your truth, granting unto them spiritual and bodily health; be merciful unto this Christian habitation which labors for You; have in remembrance, O God, every priestly and monastic order and their salvation; have in remembrance, O God, both those that hate us and those who love us, the brethren who serve with us; the people here present; and who for any cause are worthy of blessing and have gone forth, having empowered us, unworthy though we are, to pray for them; have in remembrance, O God, our brethren who are in captivity and affliction, and show mercy unto them according to Your great Mercy, delivering them from every tribulation.

For You are the Fountain of healing, O Christ our God, and to You do we send up all glory, together with Your Eternal Father and Your All-Holy, Good, and Life-creating Spirit, both now and ever, and to the ages of ages. Amen.

Peace be to all. (+)

Choir: And to your spirit.

Priest

Let us bow our heads before the Lord.

Choir: To You, O Lord.

27

Κλῖνον, Κύριε, τὸ οὖς σου καὶ ἐπάκουσον ἡμῶν, ὁ ἐν Ἰορδάνῃ βαπτισθῆναι καταδεξάμενος καὶ ἁγιάσας τὰ ὕδατα· καὶ εὐλόγησον πάντας ἡμᾶς, τοὺς διὰ τῆς κλίσεως τοῦ ἑαυτῶν αὐχένος σημαίνοντας τὸ τῆς δουλείας πρόσχημα· καὶ καταξίωσον ἡμᾶς ἐμπλησθῆναι τοῦ ἁγιασμοῦ σου, διὰ τῆς τοῦ ὕδατος τούτου μεταλήψεώς τε καὶ ῥαντισμοῦ καὶ γενέσθω ἡμῖν, Κύριε, εἰς ὑγίειαν ψυχῆς τε καὶ σώματος.

Ἐκφώνως

Σὺ γὰρ εἶ ὁ ἁγιασμὸς τῶν ψυχῶν καὶ τῶν σωμάτων ἡμῶν, καὶ σοὶ τὴν δόξαν καὶ εὐχαριστίαν καὶ προσκύνησιν ἀναπέμπομεν, σὺν τῷ ἀνάρχῳ σου Πατρί, καὶ τῷ παναγίῳ καὶ ἀγαθῷ καὶ ζωοποιῷ σου Πνεύματι, νῦν καὶ ἀεὶ καὶ εἰς τοὺς αἰῶνας τῶν αἰώνων. Ἀμήν.

Εἶτα, λαβὼν τὸν τίμιον Σταυρόν, εὐλογεῖ τὰ ὕδατα ἐκ τρίτου, κατάγων καὶ ἀνάγων αὐτὸν ὄρθιον, καὶ ψάλλων.

Ἦχος α΄.

Σῶσον, Κύριε, τὸν λαόν σου, καὶ εὐλόγησον τὴν κληρονομίαν σου, νίκας τοῖς Βασιλεῦσι κατὰ βαρβάρων δωρούμενος, καὶ τὸ σὸν φυλάττων, διὰ τοῦ Σταυροῦ σου πολίτευμα (ἐκ γ΄).

Εἶτα, ῥαντίζων σταυροειδῶς, ψάλλει τὸ παρὸν Τροπάριον.

Ἦχος β΄.

Τῶν σῶν δωρεῶν, ἀξίους ἡμᾶς ποίησον, Θεοτόκε Παρθένε, παρορῶσα τὰ πλημμελήματα ἡμῶν, καὶ παρέχουσα ἰάματα, τοῖς ἐν πίστει λαμβάνουσι τὴν εὐλογίαν σου, Ἄχραντε.

Priest (inaudibly)

Bow down Your ear and listen to us, O Lord, Who deigned to be baptized in the river Jordan, and there sanctified the water. Bless us all who by the bowing of our heads do show forth our apprehension that we are Your servants. Grant that we may be filled with Your sanctification through the partaking of this water, and let it be for us, O Lord, for the health of soul and body.

Aloud

For You are the sanctification of our souls and bodies, and to You do we send up all glory: to the Father, and to the Son, and to the Holy Spirit, both now and ever, and to the ages of ages. Amen.

Then the Priest, taking up the venerable Cross, dips it crosswise in the Water thrice, singing the Troparion:

Tone 1

Save, O Lord, Your people, and bless Your inheritance, giving us victory over all who assail us and protecting the Church of Your faithful by Your Cross. (3)

Then the Priest sprinkles the Holy Water in the form of the Cross and sings:

Tone 2

Make us worthy of your gifts, O Virgin Theotokos, overlooking our transgressions; give healing through faith to them that accept your blessing, O Immaculate One.

Εἶτα ἀσπάζεται ὁ Ἱερεὺς τὸν τίμιον Σταυρόν· ὡσαύτως καὶ πᾶς ὁ λαός. Εἶθ᾽ οὕτω ῥαντίζει πάντα τὸν λαόν, τὸν Ναὸν (ἢ τὸν Οἶκον) διὰ τοῦ ἁγιάσματος. Ὁ δὲ Διάκονος ἢ ὁ Ἱερεὺς ψάλλει τὸ παρὸν Τροπάριον, ὅπερ καὶ πολλάκις λέγεται, μέχρι τῆς ἀποῤῥαντίσεως δηλονότι.

Ἦχος δ'.

Πηγὴν ἰαμάτων ἔχοντες, ἅγιοι Ἀνάργυροι, τὰς ἰάσεις παρέχετε πᾶσι τοῖς δεομένοις, ὡς μεγίστων δωρεῶν ἀξιωθέντες, παρὰ τῆς ἀενάου πηγῆς τοῦ Σωτῆρος Χριστοῦ. Φησὶ γὰρ πρὸς ὑμᾶς ὁ Κύριος, ὡς ὁμοζήλους τῶν Ἀποστόλων· ἰδοὺ δέδωκα ὑμῖν τὴν ἐξουσίαν κατὰ πνευμάτων ἀκαθάρτων, ὥστε αὐτὰ ἐκβάλλειν, καὶ θεραπεύειν πᾶσαν νόσον καὶ πᾶσαν μαλακίαν. Διὸ τοῖς προστάγμασιν αὐτοῦ καλῶς πολιτευσάμενοι, δωρεὰν ἐλάβετε, δωρεὰν παρέχετε, ἰατρεύοντες τὰ πάθη τῶν ψυχῶν καὶ τῶν σωμάτων ἡμῶν.

Δόξα. Καὶ νῦν. Θεοτοκίον

Νεῦσον παρακλήσεσι σῶν ἱκετῶν, Πανάμωμε, παύουσα δεινῶν ἡμῶν ἐπαναστάσεις, πάσης θλίψεως ἡμᾶς ἀπαλλάττουσα· σὲ γὰρ μόνην ἀσφαλῆ καὶ βεβαίαν ἄγκυραν ἔχομεν, καὶ τὴν σὴν προστασίαν κεκτήμεθα· μὴ αἰσχυνθῶμεν, Δέσποινα, σὲ προσκαλούμενοι. Σπεῦσον εἰς ἱκεσίαν τῶν σοὶ πιστῶς βοώντων· Χαῖρε Δέσποινα, ἡ πάντων βοήθεια, χαρὰ καὶ σκέπη, καὶ σωτηρία τῶν ψυχῶν ἡμῶν.

Καὶ τὸ

Δέσποινα πρόσδεξαι, τὰς δεήσεις τῶν δούλων σου, καὶ λύτρωσαι ἡμᾶς, ἀπὸ πάσης ἀνάγκης καὶ θλίψεως.

Then the Priest kisses the Precious Cross and blesses all the people, and he sprinkles all with the Holy Water, the Altar, and all the Temple. Meanwhile the Choir sings the following Troparia:

Tone 4

O holy Unmercenaries, who had a fountain of healing, give healing to all that ask; in that you have been given gifts most excellent from the everlasting Font of the Savior. For the Lord has said to you: Lo! to you and your fellows has been given power over all unclean spirits, to drive them off with healing and free from every ill and wound; wherefore, abiding in that command, freely have you received, freely give healing of all our passions.

Glory . . . both now and ever . . .

Regard the prayer of your servants, O all-immaculate One; allay the fierce risings against us, and assuage our every woe; for in you have we a certain hope secured; so by your intercessions, O Lady, put us not to shame when we cry to you: listen when we plead: Hail! O Lady, Helper of men, the Joy and Protection of our souls.

Accept, O Lady, the prayers of your servants, delivering us from every pain and sorrow.

Ὁ Διάκονος

Ἐλέησον ἡμᾶς, ὁ Θεός, κατὰ τὸ μέγα ἔλεός σου, δεόμεθά σου ἐπάκουσον καὶ ἐλέησον.

Μεθ᾽ ἑκάστην Δέησιν· Κύριε, ἐλέησον(γ΄).

Ἔτι δεόμεθα, ὑπὲρ τοῦ Ἀρχιεπισκόπου ἡμῶν (τοῦ δεῖνος) καὶ πάσης τῆς ἐν Χριστῷ ἡμῶν ἀδελφότητος.

Ἔτι δεόμεθα, ὑπὲρ ἐλέους, ζωῆς, εἰρήνης, ὑγίειας, σωτηρίας, ἐπισκέψεως, συγχωρήσεως καὶ ἀφέσεως τῶν ἁμαρτιῶν τῶν δούλων τοῦ Θεοῦ, πάντων τῶν εὐσεβῶν καὶ ὀρθοδόξων χριστιανῶν, τῶν κατοικούντων καὶ παρεπιδημούντων ἐν τῇ πόλει (ἢ νήσῳ) ταύτῃ, τῶν ἐνοριτῶν, ἐπιτρόπων, συνδρομητῶν καὶ ἀφιερωτῶν τοῦ ἁγίου Ναοῦ τούτου(εαν ὁ Ἁγιασμὸς τελῆται ἐν τῷ Ναῷ).

Ἔτι δεόμεθα καὶ ὑπὲρ τῶν δούλων τοῦ Θεοῦ (καὶ μνημονεύει ὀνομαστὶ τῶν δι᾽ οὓς ὁ Ἁγιασμὸς τελεῖται).

Ἔτι δεόμεθα ὑπὲρ τοῦ διαφυλαχθῆναι τὴν ἁγίαν Ἐκκλησίαν καὶ τὴν πόλιν(ἢ νῆσον) ταύτην, καὶ πᾶσαν πόλιν καὶ χώραν ἀπὸ ὀργῆς, λοιμοῦ, λιμοῦ, σεισμοῦ, καταποντισμοῦ, πυρός, μαχαίρας, ἐπιδρομῆς, ἀλλοφύλων, ἐμφυλίου πολέμου, καὶ αἰφνιδίου θανάτου· ὑπὲρ τοῦ ἵλεων, εὐμενῆ καὶ εὐδιάλλακτον γενέσθαι τὸν ἀγαθὸν καὶ φιλάνθρωπον Θεὸν ἡμῶν, τοῦ ἀποστρέψαι καὶ διασκεδάσαι πᾶσαν ὀργὴν καὶ νόσον, τὴν καθ᾽ ἡμῶν κινουμένην· καὶ ῥύσασθαι ἡμᾶς ἐκ τῆς ἐπικειμένης δικαίας αὐτοῦ ἀπειλῆς, καὶ ἐλεῆσαι ἡμᾶς.

Priest

Have mercy on us, O God, according to Your great Mercy, we beseech You: listen and have mercy.

Choir: Lord have mercy. *(And after each petition)*

Again we pray for our Most Reverend Archbishop *(Name)* and for all our brethren in Christ.

Again we pray for mercy, life, peace, health, salvation, protection, pardon and remission of the sins of the servants of God, all pious and Orthodox Christians who dwell in this city, and of the servants of God, the members, trustees, contributors, and benefactors of this Holy Church.

Again we pray for the servants of God *(names of those for whom the service is being conducted).*

Furthermore, we pray that He will save this our city and this Holy Temple, and every city and countryside from pestilence, famine, earthquake, flood, fire, and the sword; from invasion of enemies, and from civil war; and that our good God, Who loves mankind, will be graciously favorable and easy to be entreated with, and will turn away all wrath stirred up against us and deliver us from all His righteous chastisement which impends against us, and have mercy on us.

Ἔτι δεόμεθα, καὶ ὑπὲρ τοῦ εἰσακοῦσαι Κύριον τὸν Θεὸν φωνῆς τῆς δεήσεως ἡμῶν τῶν ἁμαρτωλῶν, καὶ ἐλεῆσαι ἡμᾶς.

Ὁ Ἱερεὺς

Ἐπάκουσον ἡμῶν, ὁ Θεός, ὁ Σωτὴρ ἡμῶν, ἡ ἐλπὶς πάντων τῶν περάτων τῆς γῆς καὶ τῶν ἐν θαλάσσῃ μακράν· καὶ ἵλεως, ἵλεως γενοῦ ἡμῖν, Δέσποτα, ἐπὶ ταῖς ἁμαρτίαις ἡμῶν, καὶ ἐλέησον ἡμᾶς. Ἐλεήμων γὰρ καὶ φιλάνθρωπος Θεὸς ὑπάρχεις, καὶ σοὶ τὴν δόξαν ἀναπέμπομεν, τῷ Πατρὶ καὶ τῷ Υἱῷ καὶ τῷ Ἁγίῳ Πνεύματι, νῦν καὶ ἀεὶ καὶ εἰς τοὺς αἰῶνας τῶν αἰώνων. Ἀμήν.

Εἶθ' οὕτω ποιεῖ τὴν μικρὰν Ἀπόλυσιν.

Δόξα σοι ὁ Θεός, ἡ ἐλπὶς ἡμῶν, δόξα σοι. Χριστὸς ὁ ἀληθινὸς Θεὸς ἡμῶν, ταῖς πρεσβείαις τῆς παναχράντου καὶ παναμώμου ἁγίας αὐτοῦ Μητρός, τῶν ἁγίων ἐνδόξων καὶ πανευφήμων Ἀποστόλων, τῶν ἁγίων ἐνδόξων καὶ καλλινίκων Μαρτύρων, τῶν ἁγίων καὶ θαυματουργῶν Ἀναργύρων, (τοῦ Ἁγίου τοῦ Ναοῦ), τῶν ἁγίων καὶ δικαίων θεοπατόρων Ἰωακεὶμ καὶ Ἄννης, (τοῦ Ἁγίου τῆς ἡμέρας)οὗ καὶ τὴν μνήμην ἐπιτελοῦμεν καὶ πάντων τῶν Ἁγίων, ἐλεῆσαι καὶ σῶσαι ἡμᾶς, ὡς ἀγαθὸς καὶ φιλάνθρωπος καὶ ἐλεήμων Θεός.

Δι' εὐχῶν τῶν ἁγίων Πατέρων ἡμῶν, Κύριε, Ἰησοῦ Χριστὲ ὁ Θεὸς ἡμῶν, ἐλέησον καὶ σῶσον ἡμᾶς.

Ὁ Διάκονος· Ἀμήν.

Again we pray that the Lord our God listens to the voice of the supplication of us sinners, and has mercy on us.

Priest

Hear us, O God our Savior, the Hope of all the ends of the earth and of those far off at sea, or in the air: show mercy, show mercy O Master, upon our sins, and have mercy on us. For You are a merciful God and love mankind, and to You do we send up all Glory: to the Father, and to the Son, and to the Holy Spirit, both now and ever, and to the ages of ages. Amen.

Apolysis

Glory to You, O Christ our God and our Hope, glory to You. Christ our true God, through the intercessions of His all-pure Mother; of the holy, glorious, and all-praiseworthy Apostles; of the holy, glorious, and right-victorious Martyrs; of the holy and theophoric Fathers; of Saint (*Name of the Saint of the Temple*); of the holy and righteous forefathers Joakim and Anna; of Saint (*Saint of the Day*) whose memory we commemorate, and of all Your Saints, have mercy on us and save us, as our good and loving Lord.

Through the prayers of our holy Fathers, Lord Jesus Christ, our God, have mercy on us and save us.

Amen.

ΕΥΧΑΙ
ΕΙΣ ΓΥΝΑΙΚΑ ΛΕΧΩ

Εἰσέρχεται ὁ Ἱερεὺς ἐν τῷ οἴκῳ ἔνθα τὸ βρέφος ἐγεννήθη καὶ ἵσταται πρὸ τοῦ πυλῶνος φέρων τὸ ἐπιτραχήλιον. Κἀκεῖσε λέγει·

Εὐλογητὸς ὁ Θεὸς ἡμῶν, πάντοτε· νῦν καὶ ἀεὶ καὶ εἰς τοὺς αἰῶνας τῶν αἰώνων. Ἀμήν.

Ἅγιος ὁ Θεός, Ἅγιος Ἰσχυρός, Ἅγιος Ἀθάνατος, ἐλέησον ἡμᾶς (γ').

Δόξα. Καὶ νῦν.

Παναγία Τριάς, ἐλέησον ἡμᾶς, Κύριε, ἱλάσθητι ταῖς ἁμαρτίαις ἡμῶν. Δέσποτα, συγχώρησον τὰς ἀνομίας ἡμῖν. Ἅγιε, ἐπίσκεψαι καὶ ἴασαι τὰς ἀσθενείας ἡμῶν, ἕνεκεν τοῦ ὀνόματός σου.

Κύριε, ἐλέησον· Κύριε, ἐλέησον· Κύριε, ἐλέησον.

PRAYERS ON THE BIRTH OF A CHILD

Blessed is our God always, both now and ever, and to the ages of ages. Amen.

Holy God, Holy Mighty, Holy Immortal, have mercy on us. (3)

Glory to the Father and to the Son and to the Holy Spirit, now and ever, and to the ages of ages. Amen.

All-Holy Trinity, have mercy on us. Lord, be gracious unto our sins. Master, pardon our transgressions. Holy One, visit and heal our infirmities; for Your Name's sake, and have mercy on us.

Lord have mercy; Lord have mercy; Lord have mercy.

Δόξα. Καὶ νῦν.

Πάτερ ἡμῶν ὁ ἐν τοῖς οὐρανοῖς, ἁγιασθήτω τὸ ὄνομά σου. Ἐλθέτω ἡ βασιλεία σου. Γενηθήτω τὸ θέλημά σου, ὡς ἐν οὐρανῷ καὶ ἐπὶ τῆς γῆς. Τὸν ἄρτον ἡμῶν τὸν ἐπιούσιον δὸς ἡμῖν σήμερον, καὶ ἄφες ἡμῖν τὰ ὀφειλήματα ἡμῶν, ὡς καὶ ἡμεῖς ἀφίεμεν τοῖς ὀφειλέταις ἡμῶν. Καὶ μὴ εἰσενέγκῃς ἡμᾶς εἰς πειρασμόν, ἀλλὰ ῥῦσαι ἡμᾶς ἀπὸ τοῦ πονηροῦ.

Ὅτι σοῦ ἐστιν ἡ Βασιλεία καὶ ἡ δύναμις καὶ ἡ δόξα τοῦ Πατρὸς καὶ τοῦ Υἱοῦ καὶ τοῦ Ἁγίου Πνεύματος, νῦν καὶ ἀεὶ καὶ εἰς τοὺς αἰῶνας τῶν αἰώνων. Ἀμήν.

Τοῦ Κυρίου δεηθῶμεν.

Δέσποτα, Κύριε, Παντοκράτορ, ὁ ἰώμενος πᾶσαν νόσον καὶ πᾶσαν μαλακίαν, αὐτὸς καὶ τὴν παροῦσαν, τὴν σήμερον τέξασαν δούλην σου (τὴν δὲ) ἴασαι, καὶ ἀνάστησον αὐτὴν ἀπὸ τῆς κλίνης, ἧς ἐπίκειται· ὅτ., κατὰ τὸν τοῦ προφήτου Δαυῒδ λόγον, ἐν ἀνομίαις συνελήφθημεν καὶ διὰ ῥύπου πάντες ἐσμὲν ἐνώπιόν σου. Φύλαξον ταύτην καὶ τὸ παρὸν νήπιον, ὃ ἔτεκε· σκέπασον αὐτὴν ὑπὸ τὴν σκέπην τῶν πτερύγων σου ἀπὸ τῆς σήμερον μέχρι τῆς ἐσχάτης αὐτῆς τελειώσεως· πρεσβείαις τῆς παναχράντου Θεοτόκου, καὶ πάντων τῶν Ἁγίων· Ὅτι εὐλογητὸς εἶ εἰς τοὺς αἰῶνας τῶν αἰώνων. Ἀμήν.

Τοῦ Κυρίου δεηθῶμεν.

Δέσποτα Κύριε, ὁ Θεὸς ἡμῶν, ὁ τεχθεὶς ἐκ τῆς παναχράντου Δεσποίνης ἡμῶν Θεοτόκου. καὶ ἀειπαρθένου Μαρίας, καὶ ὡς νήπιον ἐν φάτνῃ ἀνακλιθείς, καὶ ὡς βρέφος ἀναδειχθείς· αὐτὸς καὶ τὴν

Glory to the Father and to the Son and to the Holy Spirit, now and ever, and to the ages of ages. Amen.

Our Father, Who are in Heaven,
Hallowed be Your Name; Your Kingdom come.
Your Will be done on earth as it is in Heaven.
Give us this day our daily bread;
And forgive us our trespasses,
As we forgive those who trespass against us.
And lead us not into temptation,
But deliver us from evil.

For Yours is the Kingdom and the Power and the Glory, of the Father, and of the Son, and of the Holy Spirit; both now and ever, and to the ages of ages. Amen.

Let us pray to the Lord. Lord have mercy.

O Sovereign Master and Lord Almighty, Who heals every sickness and every weakness: do You Yourself heal this Your servant (*Name*) who this day has borne a child, and raise her up from the bed on which she lies. For according to the words of Your Prophet David, in sin were we conceived and all are defiled before You; protect her, and this child which she has borne; shelter her under the covering of Your wings from this day to her last; through the intercessions of the all-pure Theotokos and of all the Saints, for blessed are You to ages of ages. Amen.

Let us pray to the Lord. Lord have mercy.

Sovereign Master and Lord our God, Who was born of our all-pure Lady Theotokos and Ever Virgin Mary, Who as a Babe was laid in a manger, and as a Child was held up to be seen, do You Yourself have mercy on

παροῦσαν δούλην σου (τήνδε)τὴν σήμερον τέξασαν τὸ παρὸν παιδίον, ἐλέησον, καὶ συγχώρησον τὰ ἑκούσια καὶ τὰ ἀκούσια αὐτῆς πταίσματα καὶ διαφύλαξον αὐτὴν ἀπὸ πάσης τοῦ Διαβόλου τυραννίδος. Καὶ τὸ ἐξ αὐτῆς κυηθὲν νήπιον διατήρησον ἀπὸ πάσης φαρμακείας, ἀπὸ πάσης χαλεπότητος, ἀπὸ πάσης ζάλης τοῦ ἀντικειμένου, ἀπὸ πνευμάτων πονηρῶν, ἡμερινῶν τε καὶ νυκτερινῶν. Ταύτην δὲ διατήρησον ὑπὸ τὴν κραταιὰν χεῖρά σου, καὶ δὸς αὐτῇ ταχινὴν ἐξανάστασιν, καὶ τοῦ ῥύπου κάθαρον καὶ τοὺς πόνους θεράπευσον, καὶ ῥῶσιν καὶ εὐρωστίαν ψυχῇ τε καὶ σώματι δώρησαι, καὶ δι᾽ Ἀγγέλων φαιδρῶν καὶ φωτεινῶν ταύτην περίθαλψον, καὶ περιφρούρησον ἀπὸ πάσης ἐπελεύσεως τῶν ἀοράτων πνευμάτων. Ναί, Κύριε, ἀπὸ νόσου καὶ μαλακίας, ἀπὸ ζήλου καὶ φθόνου, καὶ ὀφθαλμῶν βασκανίας, καὶ ἐλέησον αὐτὴν καὶ τὸ βρέφος, κατὰ τὸ μέγα σου ἔλεος· καὶ καθάρισον αὐτὴν ἀπὸ τοῦ σωματικοῦ ῥύπου καὶ τῶν ποικίλων αὐτῇ ἐπερχομένων σπλαγχνικῶν ἐνοχλήσεων, καὶ ἔξαξον αὐτήν, διὰ τῆς ταχινῆς σου ἐλεημοσύνης, ἐν τῷ ταπεινῷ αὐτῆς σώματι εἰς ἐπανόρθωσιν· καὶ τὸ ἐξ αὐτῆς κυηθὲν νήπιον ἀξίωσον προσκυνῆσαι τὸν ἐπίγειον ναόν, ὃν ἡτοίμασας εἰς τὸ δοξολογεῖσθαι τὸ ὄνομά σου τὸ ἅγιον. Ὅτι πρέπει σοι πᾶσα δόξα, τιμή, καὶ προσκύνησις, τῷ Πατρὶ καὶ τῷ Υἱῷ καὶ τῷ Ἁγίῳ Πνεύματι, νῦν καὶ ἀεὶ καὶ εἰς τοὺς αἰῶνας τῶν αἰώνων. Ἀμήν.

Τοῦ Κυρίου δεηθῶμεν.

Κύριε ὁ Θεὸς ἡμῶν, ὁ εὐδοκήσας κατελθεῖν ἐκ τῶν οὐρανῶν, καὶ γεννηθῆναι ἐκ τῆς ἁγίας Θεοτόκου καὶ ἀειπαρθένου Μαρίας, διὰ τὴν σωτηρίαν ἡμῶν τῶν ἁμαρτωλῶν, ὁ γινώσκων τὸ ἀσθενὲς τῆς ἀνθρωπίνης φύσεως, συγχώρησον τῇ δούλῃ

this Your servant (*Name*) who this day has borne this child, and be gracious unto her voluntary and involuntary offenses, protecting her from every diabolical cruelty; preserve the child she has borne from every bane, from every harm, from every hostile rage, from evil spirits of the day and night; keep this woman safe under Your mighty hand. Grant to her a speedy recovery. Cleanse her of every sin; bring healing from suffering, and vouchsafe unto her health, and strength of both soul and body; and with bright, shining Angels enfold and cherish her, guarding her round about against every attack of invisible spirits—yea, Lord, from sickness and infirmity, from jealousy and envy, and from the evil eye. Have mercy on her and the newborn child according to the greatness of Your mercy. Forgive her all voluntary and involuntary sin; remove from her any travail befalling her, and through Your speedy mercy lead her to recovery in her bodily affliction; and of the infant which has been born of her do You account worthy to worship in the earthly Temple which You have prepared for the glorification of Your Holy Name. For to You are due all glory, honor, and adoration, to the Father, and to the Son, and to the Holy Spirit, both now and ever, and to the ages of ages. Amen.

Let us pray to the Lord. Lord have mercy.

O Lord our God, Who was well pleased to come down from the Heavens, and to be born of the holy Theotokos and Ever Virgin Mary for the salvation of us sinners, Who knows the frailty of human nature: according to the multitude of Your compassions forgive the sins of Your servant

σου (τῇ δε), τῇ τεξάσῃ σήμερον, κατὰ τὸ πλῆθος τῶν οἰκτιρμῶν σου. Σὺ γὰρ εἶπας, Κύριε· Αὐξάνεσθε καὶ πληθύνεσθε, καὶ πληρώσατε τὴν γῆν, καὶ κατα- κυριεύσατε αὐτῆς. Διὰ τοῦτο καὶ ἡμεῖς οἱ δοῦλοί σου δεόμεθα, καὶ θαῤῥοῦντες διὰ τῆς ἀνεξικάκου σου φιλανθρωπίας, φόβῳ βοῶμεν πρὸς τὸ τῆς βα- σιλείας σου ἅγιον ὄνομα. Ἐπίβλεψον ἐξ οὐρανοῦ, καὶ ἴδε τὴν ἀσθένειαν ἡμῶν τῶν καταδίκων, καὶ συγχώρησον τῇ δούλῃ σου (τῇ δε), καὶ παντὶ τῷ οἴκῳ, ᾧ ἐγεννήθη τὸ παιδίον, καὶ τοῖς ἁψαμένοις αὐτῆς, καὶ τοῖς ἐνθάδε εὑρισκομένοις πᾶσιν, ὡς ἀγα- θὸς καὶ φιλάνθρωπος Θεὸς συγχώρησον· ὅτι μόνος ἔχεις ἐξουσίαν ἀφιέναι ἁμαρτίας. Πρεσβείαις τῆς ἁγίας Θεοτόκου καὶ πάντων σου τῶν Ἁγίων. Ἀμήν.

Καὶ ἡ Ἀπόλυσις.

Δόξα σοι ὁ Θεός, ἡ ἐλπὶς ἡμῶν, δόξα σοι. Ὁ ἐν σπηλαίῳ γεννηθείς, καὶ ἐν φάτνῃ ἀνακλι- θεὶς διὰ τὴν ἡμῶν σωτηρίαν, Χριστὸς ὁ ἀληθινὸς Θεὸς ἡμῶν, ταῖς πρεσβείαις τῆς παναχράντου καὶ παναμώμου ἁγίας αὐτοῦ Μητρός, δυνάμει τοῦ τι- μίου καὶ ζωοποιοῦ Σταυροῦ, προστασίαις τῶν τι- μίων ἐπουρανίων Δυνάμεων ἀσωμάτων, ἱκεσίαις τοῦ τιμίου ἐνδόξου προφήτου προδρόμου καὶ βα- πτιστοῦ Ἰωάννου, τῶν ἁγίων ἐνδόξων καὶ πανευ- φήμων Ἀποστόλων, τῶν ἁγίων ἐνδόξων καὶ καλ- λινίκων Μαρτύρων, τῶν ὁσίων καὶ θεοφόρων Πα- τέρων ἡμῶν, τῶν ἁγίων καὶ δικαίων θεοπατόρων Ἰω- ακεὶμ καὶ Ἄννης καὶ πάντων τῶν Ἁγίων, ἐλεήσαι καὶ σώσαι ἡμᾶς, ὡς ἀγαθὸς καὶ φιλάνθρωπος καὶ ἐλεήμων Θεός.

Δι᾽ εὐχῶν τῶν ἁγίων Πατέρων ἡμῶν, Κύριε, Ἰησοῦ Χριστὲ ὁ Θεὸς ἡμῶν, ἐλέησον καὶ σῶσον ἡμᾶς. Ἀμήν.

(*Name*), who this day has borne a child, for You have said, O Lord, "Be fruitful, and multiply, and replenish the earth, and have dominion over it." Therefore, we, Your servants, beseech You, and trusting in Your ever patient and manbefriending love, with fear invoke the holy Name of Your Kingdom; look down from Heaven and behold the feebleness of us who are condemned, and be gracious to Your Servant (*Name*) and to all the house in which the child has been born, and to them that have touched her and to all here present, granting forgiveness as our Good and Loving God; for You alone have the power to forgive sins, through the intercessions of the holy Theotokos, and of all Your Saints. Amen.

The Apolysis

Glory to You, O Christ our God and our Hope, glory to You.

Christ our true God, Who was born in a cave and laid in a manger for our salvation, through the intercessions of His pure and spotless Mother, through the power of the precious and life-giving Cross, through the protection of the venerable and bodiless heavenly powers, through the prayers of the venerable and glorious prophet Forerunner John the Baptist, of the holy, glorious, all-praiseworthy Apostles, of the holy, glorious and victorious Martyrs, of our venerable Godbearing Fathers, of the holy, righteous ancestors of the Lord, Joachim and Anna, and of all the Saints, have mercy on us and save us as our Good and Loving God.

Through the prayers of our holy Fathers, Lord Jesus Christ, our God, have mercy and save us. Amen.

Εὐχὴ
Εἰς τὸ κατασφραγίσαι παιδίον, λαμβάνον ὄνομα τῇ ὀγδόῃ ἡμέρᾳ ἀπὸ τῆς γεννήσεως αὐτοῦ.

Ἰστέον δὲ ὅτι τῇ ὀγδόῃ ἡμέρᾳ, μετὰ τὴν γέννησιν προσάγεται ἐν τῷ Ναῷ τὸ βρέφος παρὰ τῆς μαίας καὶ ἵσταται πρὸ τῶν πυλῶν τοῦ Ναοῦ. Ὁ δὲ Ἱερεὺς φέρων, ὡς εἴθισται, τὸ Ἐπιτραχήλιον, λέγει·

Εὐλογητὸς ὁ Θεὸς ἡμῶν, πάντοτε...
Τρισάγιον. **Δόξα. Καὶ νῦν. Παναγία Τριάς. Κύριε, ἐλέησον** (γ΄). **Δόξα. Καὶ νῦν. Πάτερ ἡμῶν. Ὅτι σοῦ ἐστιν.**

Εἶτα τὸ Ἀπολυτίκιον τῆς ἡμέρας ἢ τοῦ Ἁγίου τοῦ Ναοῦ· εἶτα.

Τῇ πρεσβείᾳ, Κύριε πάντων τῶν Ἁγίων καὶ τῆς Θεοτόκου, τὴν σὴν εἰρήνην δὸς ἡμῖν καὶ ἐλέησον ἡμᾶς, ὡς μόνος οἰκτίρμων.

Εἶτα σφραγίζει τὸ μέτωπον, τὸ στόμα, καὶ τὸ στῆθος τοῦ βρέφους, λέγων τὴν ἑπομένην Εὐχήν·

PRAYER AT THE SIGNING OF A CHILD
WHEN IT RECEIVES A NAME
ON THE EIGHTH DAY AFTER ITS BIRTH

On the eighth day after birth the child is brought by the nurse or the intended Sponsor at Baptism to the Western Gates of the Temple, and stands before the doors. The Priest begins:

Blessed is our God always . . . Amen. *(See pages 32-33.)*

Trisagion. Glory . . . both now . . . O All-Holy Trinity . . . Lord have mercy (3). Glory . . . both now . . . Our Father . . . For Yours is the Kingdom . . . Amen.

Then the Apolytikion of the Day and of the Temple.

Through the prayers, O Lord, of all Your Saints and of the Theotokos, grant to us Your peace and have mercy on us, for You alone are merciful.

The Priest then makes the sign of the Cross on the child's forehead, lips, and breast, saying the following prayer:

36

Τοῦ Κυρίου δεηθῶμεν.

Κύριε ὁ Θεὸς ἡμῶν, σοῦ δεόμεθα καὶ σὲ παρα-
καλοῦμεν· Σημειωθήτω τὸ φῶς τοῦ προσώπου
σου ἐπὶ τὸν δοῦλόν σου (τόνδε), καὶ σημειωθήτω ὁ
Σταυρὸς τοῦ μονογενοῦς σου Υἱοῦ ἐν τῇ καρδίᾳ καὶ
τοῖς διαλογισμοῖς αὐτοῦ, εἰς τὸ φυγεῖν τὴν ματαιό-
τητα τοῦ κόσμου, καὶ πᾶσαν τὴν πονηρὰν ἐπιβου-
λὴν τοῦ ἐχθροῦ, ἀκολουθεῖν δὲ τοῖς προστάγμασί
σου. Καὶ δός, Κύριε, ἀνεξάρνητον μεῖναι τὸ ὄνομά σου τὸ ἅγιον ἐπ᾽ αὐτόν, συναπτόμενον ἐν καιρῷ
εὐθέτῳ τῇ ἁγίᾳ σου Ἐκκλησίᾳ καὶ τελειούμενον διὰ
τῶν φρικτῶν Μυστηρίων τοῦ Χριστοῦ σου· ἵνα,
κατὰ τὰς ἐντολάς σου πολιτευσάμενος καὶ φυλάξας
τὴν σφραγῖδα ἄθραυστον, τύχῃ τῆς μακαριότητος
τῶν ἐκλεκτῶν ἐν τῇ βασιλείᾳ σου. Χάριτι καὶ φιλανθρωπίᾳ τοῦ μονογενοῦς σου Υἱοῦ, μεθ᾽ οὗ εὐλογητὸς εἶ, σὺν τῷ παναγίῳ καὶ ἀγαθῷ καὶ ζωοποιῷ
σου Πνεύματι, νῦν καὶ ἀεὶ καὶ εἰς τοὺς αἰῶνας τῶν
αἰώνων. Ἀμήν.

Εἶτα ἀνὰ χεῖρας λαβὼν τὸ παιδίον, ἵσταται ἔμπροσθεν τῶν πυλῶν τοῦ Ναοῦ ἢ τῆς εἰκόνος τῆς
Ὑπεραγίας Θεοτόκου, καὶ ποιῶν Σταυροῦ τύπον,
λέγει·

Χαῖρε, κεχαριτωμένη Θεοτόκε Παρθένε· ἐκ σοῦ
γὰρ ἀνέτειλεν ὁ Ἥλιος τῆς δικαιοσύνης, Χριστὸς ὁ Θεὸς ἡμῶν, φωτίζων τοὺς ἐν σκότει. Εὐ-
φραίνου καὶ σύ, Πρεσβῦτα δίκαιε, δεξάμενος ἐν ἀγκάλαις τὸν ἐλευθερωτὴν τῶν ψυχῶν ἡμῶν, χαρι-
ζόμενον ἡμῖν καὶ τὴν Ἀνάστασιν.

Εἶτα ποιεῖ τὴν Ἀπόλυσιν.

Let us pray to the Lord. Lord have mercy.

O Lord our God, to You do we pray, and on You do we call. Let the Light of Your countenance be signed on this Your servant, and may he (she) be signed with the Cross of Your Only-Begotten Son in his (her) heart and understanding, that he (she) may flee the vanity of this wicked world and every evil device of the Enemy, and may follow Your commandments instead; and grant, O Lord, that Your Name may remain on him (her) unrenounced, when at a fitting time he (she) shall be conjoined with Your Holy Church, and is perfected through the dread Mysteries of Your Christ. So that, having lived according to Your commandments, and having kept the Seal unbroken, he (she) may attain the blessedness of Your elect in Your Kingdom. Through the Grace and manbefriending love of Your Only-Begotten Son, with Whom You are blessed together with Your All-Holy, Good, and Life-creating Spirit, both now and ever, and to the ages of ages. Amen.

Then, taking the child in his arms, the Priest stands before the Gates of the Temple or before the Icon of the most holy Theotokos, and moving the child to describe the shape of the Cross, he says:

Hail, O Full-of-Grace, Theotokos and Virgin, for you were the morning sky from which God poured His Light at dawning, as the Day-Star of Righteousness on them that sat in darkness. And you, too, be glad, O aged righteous man, for you in your arms have cradled the Lord, Who out of bondage has brought our souls, Who with Resurrection crowns the riches of His Grace.

Then the Apolysis.

Εὐχαὶ
εἰς τὸ ἐκκλησιάσαι παιδίον, μεθ' ἡμέρας τεσσαράκοντα.

Τῇ δὲ τεσσαρακοστῇ ἡμέρᾳ, τὸ βρέφος προσάγεται πάλιν τῷ Ναῷ ἐπὶ τῷ ἐκκλησιασθῆναι, εἴτουν ἀρχὴν λαβεῖν τοῦ εἰσάγεσθαι εἰς τὴν Ἐκκλησίαν· προσάγεται δὲ παρὰ τῆς μητρός, ἤδη κεκαθαρμένης καὶ λελουμένης οὔσης, παρόντος καὶ τοῦ μέλλοντος ἀναδέχεσθαι τοῦτο κατὰ τὸ Βάπτισμα.

Ἱσταμένης δὲ τῆς μητρὸς μετὰ τοῦ βρέφους πρὸ τῶν πυλῶν τοῦ Ναοῦ, ὁ Ἱερεὺς λέγει·

Εὐλογητὸς ὁ Θεὸς ἡμῶν... Ἅγιος ὁ Θεός. (ἐκ γ΄). Δόξα. Καὶ νῦν. Παναγία Τριάς. Κύριε, ἐλέησον (γ΄). Δόξα. Καὶ νῦν. Πάτερ ἡμῶν. Ὅτι σοῦ ἐστιν ἡ βασιλεία.

Εἶτα τὸ Ἀπολυτίκιον τῆς ἡμέρας, τὸ τυχὸν ἢ τοῦ λαχόντος Ἁγίου.

Δόξα. Καὶ νῦν.

Τῇ πρεσβείᾳ, Κύριε, πάντων τῶν Ἁγίων, καὶ τῆς Θεοτόκου, τὴν σὴν εἰρήνην δὸς ἡμῖν καὶ ἐλέησον ἡμᾶς, ὡς μόνος οἰκτίρμων.

Καὶ κλινούσης τῆς μητρὸς τὴν κεφαλήν, ἅμα τῷ βρέφει, ποιεῖ ὁ Ἱερεὺς τὴν τοῦ Σταυροῦ σφραγῖδα ἐπ' αὐτῇ καὶ ἁπτόμενος τῆς κεφαλῆς αὐτῆς, λέγει τὴν ἑπομένην Εὐχήν.

PRAYERS FOR THE CHURCHING
OF A MOTHER AND CHILD AFTER FORTY DAYS

On the fortieth day the child is brought to the Temple to be churched, that is, to begin attending church. It is brought by the mother, who has already been cleansed and washed, accompanied by the intended sponsor at the Baptism. Standing together with the mother, child and sponsor before the doors of the nave of the church, the Priest says:

Blessed is our God always, . . . (*see pp. 32-33*). The Trisagion.   O All-Holy Trinity . . .   Our Father . . . For Yours is the Kingdom . . . Amen.

Then the Apolytikion of the Day or of the Saint who is commemorated is said.

Glory . . . both now . . .

Through the prayers, O Lord, of all the Saints and of the Theotokos grant to us Your peace and mercy, for You alone are merciful.

Over the bowed heads of mother and child, the Priest makes the sign of the Cross. He then lays his hand upon the mother's head and says:

Τοῦ Κυρίου δεηθῶμεν.

Κύριε, ὁ Θεὸς ὁ παντοκράτωρ, ὁ Πατὴρ τοῦ Κυρίου ἡμῶν Ἰησοῦ Χριστοῦ, ὁ πᾶσαν φύσιν λογικήν τε καὶ ἄλογον διὰ τοῦ λόγου σου δημιουργήσας· ὁ πάντα ἐξ οὐκ ὄντων εἰς τὸ εἶναι παραγαγών, σοῦ δεόμεθα καὶ σὲ παρακαλοῦμεν· ἣν τῷ σῷ θελήματι διέσωσας δούλην σου (τήνδε), καθάρισον ἀπὸ πάσης ἁμαρτίας καὶ ἀπὸ παντὸς ῥύπου, προσερχομένην τῇ ἁγίᾳ σου Ἐκκλησίᾳ, ἵνα ἀκατακρίτως ἀξιωθῇ μετασχεῖν τῶν ἁγίων σου Μυστηρίων.

Ἰστέον ὅτι, εἰ οὐχ εὑρίσκεται ἐν τοῖς ζῶσι τὸ βρέφος, ἀναγινώσκεται ἕως ὧδε ἡ Εὐχή· εἶτα λέγει ὁ Ἱερεὺς ἐκφώνως.

Ὅτι ἀγαθὸς καὶ φιλάνθρωπος Θεὸς ὑπάρχεις, καὶ σοὶ τὴν δόξαν ἀναπέμπομεν τῷ Πατρί, καὶ τῷ Υἱῷ καὶ τῷ Ἁγίῳ Πνεύματι, νῦν καὶ ἀεὶ καὶ εἰς τοὺς αἰῶνας τῶν αἰώνων. Ἀμήν.

Εἰ δὲ τὸ βρέφος ζῇ, τότε ἁπτόμενος τῆς κεφαλῆς αὐτοῦ λέγει·

Καὶ τὸ ἐξ αὐτῆς τεχθὲν παιδίον, εὐλόγησον, αὔξησον, ἁγίασον, συνέτισον, σωφρόνισον, καλοφρόνησον· ὅτι σὺ παρήγαγες αὐτό, καὶ ἔδειξας αὐτῷ τὸ φῶς τὸ αἰσθητόν, *(ταῦτα παραλείπονται ἐὰν τὸ τέκνον ᾖ βεβαπτισμένον) ἵνα καὶ τοῦ νοητοῦ καταξιωθῇ φωτὸς ἐν καιρῷ, ᾧ προώρισας, καὶ συγκαταριθμηθῇ τῇ ἁγίᾳ σου ποίμνῃ* διὰ τοῦ μονογενοῦς σου Υἱοῦ, μεθ᾽ οὗ εὐλογητὸς εἶ, σὺν τῷ παναγίῳ καὶ ἀγαθῷ, καὶ ζωοποιῷ σου Πνεύματι, νῦν καὶ ἀεὶ καὶ εἰς τοὺς αἰῶνας τῶν αἰώνων. Ἀμήν.

Let us pray to the Lord   Lord have mercy.

O Lord God Almighty, Father of our Lord Jesus Christ, Who by Your word has made every rational and irrational creature, that brought all things out of nothingness into being: we pray to You and implore You, cleanse this Your servant (*Name*), whom by Your Will You have preserved, and who now comes into Your Holy Church, from every transgression, so that she may be accounted worthy to partake of Your holy Mysteries without condemnation.

Be it known that if the mother has come alone because the child is no longer living, the Priest ends the Prayer here with the Ekphonesis.

For You are a good and loving God, and to You we send up all glory: to the Father, and to the Son, and to the Holy Spirit, both now and ever, and to the ages of ages. Amen.

But if the child is alive, he touches its head and says:

Bless also this child which has been born of her; increase it, sanctify it, give it understanding and a prudent and virtuous mind; for You alone have brought it into being, and have shown him (her) the light which bodily sense perceives, so that he (she) might be accounted worthy also of the ideal Light and be numbered with Your holy Flock; through Your Only-Begotten Son, with Whom You are blessed, together with Your All-Holy, Good and Life-creating Spirit, both now and ever, and to the ages of ages. Amen.

Εὐχη
εἰς τὴν Μητέρα τοῦ παιδίου.

Εἰρήνη πᾶσι. Τὰς κεφαλὰς ἡμῶν τῷ Κυρίῳ κλίνωμεν.

Τοῦ Κυρίου δεηθῶμεν.

Κύριε, ὁ Θεὸς ἡμῶν, ὁ διὰ τῆς ἐνανθρωπήσεως τοῦ μονογενοῦς σου Υἱοῦ παραγενόμενος ἐπὶ σωτηρίᾳ τοῦ γένους τῶν ἀνθρώπων, παραγενοῦ καὶ ἐπὶ τὴν δούλην σου (τήνδε) καὶ καταξίωσον αὐτήν, διὰ τῶν εὐχῶν τοῦ τιμίου Πρεσβυτερίου, καταφυγεῖν ἐν τῇ ἁγίᾳ σου καθολικῇ Ἐκκλησίᾳ, καὶ τυχεῖν τῆς εἰσόδου τοῦ ναοῦ τῆς δόξης σου, καὶ ἀξίωσον αὐτὴν μεταλαβεῖν τοῦ τιμίου Σώματος καὶ Αἵματος τοῦ Χριστοῦ σου. Ἀπόπλυνον αὐτῆς τὸν ῥύπον τοῦ σώματος, καὶ τὸν σπίλον τῆς ψυχῆς, ἐν τῇ συμπληρώσει τῶν τεσσαράκοντα ἡμερῶν· ὅπως, ἀξιωθεῖσα εἰσελθεῖν ἐν τῷ ἁγίῳ ναῷ σου, δοξάσῃ σὺν ἡμῖν τὸ πανάγιον ὄνομά σου τοῦ Πατρός, καὶ τοῦ Υἱοῦ, καὶ τοῦ Ἁγίου Πνεύματος, νῦν καὶ ἀεὶ καὶ εἰς τοὺς αἰῶνας τῶν αἰώνων. Ἀμήν.

Ὧδε, εἰ μὲν τὸ βρέφος ἐβαπτίσθη ἤδη ἢ καὶ ἀπέθανε, ποιεῖ ὁ Ἱερεὺς Ἀπόλυσιν, εἰ δὲ μὴ ἀναγινώσκει καὶ τὴν ἑξῆς ἕως τέλους.

Εὐχὴ ἑτέρα εἰς τὸ Παιδίον,

ἣν ὁ Ἱερεύς, σφραγίζων τοῦτο, ἐπεύχεται.

Τοῦ Κυρίου δεηθῶμεν.

Κύριε, ὁ Θεὸς ἡμῶν, ὁ ἐν τεσσαράκοντα ἡμέραις, βρέφος τῷ νομικῷ Ναῷ προσαχθεὶς ὑπὸ Μαρίας τῆς ἀπειρογάμου καὶ ἁγίας σου Μητρός, καὶ ἐν ταῖς ἀγκάλαις τοῦ δικαίου Συμεὼν βασταχθείς, Αὐτός, Δέσποτα παντοδύναμε, καὶ τὸ προσαχθὲν τοῦτο

Prayer
for the Mother of the Child

Peace be to all. And to your spirit. Let us bow our heads before the Lord. To You, O Lord.

Let us pray to the Lord. Lord have mercy.

O Lord God, Who ever draws near for the salvation of the human race, come also to this Your servant (*Name*), and through the prayers of Your venerable Priesthood account her worthy to find refuge in Your holy Catholic Church, to obtain entrance into the Temple of Your Glory, and worthy also to partake of the Precious Body and Blood of Your Christ. In the fulfillment of the forty days, wash away from her every transgression, voluntary and involuntary, so that accounted worthy to enter Your holy Temple, she may glorify with us Your All-Holy Name, of the Father, and of the Son, and of the Holy Spirit, both now and ever, and to the ages of ages. Amen.

Another Prayer for the Child

The Priest makes again the sign of the Cross upon him (her):

Let us pray to the Lord. Lord have mercy.

O Lord our God, Who on the fortieth day was brought as a child into the Temple of the Law by Mary, the Virgin Bride and Your holy Mother, and was carried in the arms of the righteous Symeon, do You also, Sovereign Master All-Powerful, bless this presented babe that it may appear before

βρέφος, ἐμφανισθῆναί σοι τῷ πάντων Ποιητῇ, εὐλόγησον, καὶ εἰς πᾶν ἔργον ἀγαθὸν καὶ σοὶ εὐάρεστον αὔξησον, ἀποσοβῶν ἀπ᾽ αὐτοῦ πᾶσαν ἐναν-
τίαν δύναμιν, διὰ τῆς σημειώσεως τοῦ τύπου τοῦ
Σταυροῦ σου· σὺ γὰρ εἶ ὁ φυλάσσων τὰ νήπια,
Κύριε· ἵνα, καταξιωθὲν τοῦ ἁγίου Βαπτίσματος
τύχῃ τῆς μερίδος τῶν ἐκλεκτῶν τῆς βασιλείας σου,
φυλαττόμενον σὺν ἡμῖν τῇ χάριτι τῆς ἁγίας, καὶ
ὁμοουσίου, καὶ ἀδιαιρέτου Τριάδος. Σοὶ γὰρ πρέπει πᾶσα δόξα καὶ εὐχαριστία καὶ προσκύνησις,
σὺν τῷ ἀνάρχῳ σου Πατρὶ καὶ τῷ παναγίῳ καὶ
ἀγαθῷ καὶ ζωοποιῷ σου Πνεύματι, νῦν καὶ ἀεὶ καὶ
εἰς τοὺς αἰῶνας τῶν αἰώνων. Ἀμήν.

Εἰρήνη πᾶσι.

Τὰς κεφαλὰς ἡμῶν τῷ Κυρίῳ κλίνωμεν.

Ο῾ Θεός, ὁ Πατήρ, ὁ παντοκράτωρ, ὁ διὰ τοῦ
μεγαλοφωνοτάτου τῶν προφητῶν Ἡσαΐου,
προκαταγγείλας ἡμῖν τὴν ἐκ Παρθένου σάρκωσιν
τοῦ μονογενοῦς σου Υἱοῦ καὶ Θεοῦ ἡμῶν, ὃς ἐπ᾽
ἐσχάτων τῶν ἡμερῶν, εὐδοκίᾳ σῇ καὶ συνεργείᾳ
τοῦ Ἁγίου Πνεύματος, διὰ τὴν τῶν βροτῶν σωτηρίαν,
ἀμέτρῳ εὐσπλαγχνίᾳ ἐξ αὐτῆς νηπιάσαι καταδεξάμενος, καὶ κατὰ τὸ εἰθισμένον ἐν Νόμῳ ἁγίῳ
σου, μετὰ τὴν ἐκπλήρωσιν τῶν ἡμερῶν τοῦ καθα-
ρισμοῦ, τῷ Ἱερῷ προσαχθῆναι ἠνέσχετο, ἀληθὴς
νομοθέτης ὑπάρχων, καὶ ἐν ἀγκάλαις τοῦ δικαίου
Συμεὼν βασταχθῆναι κατεδέξατο, οὗπερ μυστηρίου τὴν προτύπωσιν ἐν τῷ προλεχθέντι Προ-
φήτῃ, διὰ τῆς λαβίδος τοῦ ἄνθρακος, δηλωθεῖσαν
ἐπέγνωμεν, οὗ καὶ ἡμεῖς οἱ πιστοὶ τὴν μίμησιν ἐν

You, the Creator of all things. And do You increase in him (her) every good work acceptable to You, removing from him (her) every opposing might by the sign of the likeness of Your Cross; for You are He Who guards infants, O Lord. So that, accounted worthy of holy Baptism, he (she) may obtain the portion of Your Elect of the Kingdom, being protected with us by the Grace of the Holy Consubstantial and Undivided Trinity. For unto You do we send up Glory, Honor and Worship, with Your Eternal Father and Your All-Holy, Good and Life-creating Spirit, both now and ever, and to the ages of ages. Amen.

Peace be to all (+). And to your spirit.

Let us bow our heads before the Lord. To You, O Lord.

O God, the Father Almighty, Who by the loud-voice Prophet Isaiah has foretold to us the incarnation from a Virgin of Your Only-Begotten Son and our God; Who in the latter days, by Your good pleasure and by the cooperation of the Holy Spirit have willed, through measureless love, to become a child of her for the salvation of men; and, according to the custom of Your Holy Law, after the fulfillment of the days of purification, submitted to be brought into the Sanctuary, being Himself a true lawgiver, and willed to be carried in the arms of the righteous Symeon, of which mystery we have a prototype declared in the aforementioned Prophet by the taking of coals with tongs from the Altar, and of which we Faithful also have an imitation in Grace. Do You, Who are

χάριτι κατέχομεν· Αὐτὸς καὶ νῦν, ὁ φυλάσσων τὰ νήπια, Κύριε, εὐλόγησον τὸ παιδίον τοῦτο, ἅμα τοῖς γονεῦσι καὶ ἀναδόχοις αὐτοῦ· * καὶ καταξίωσον αὐτὸ ἐν καιρῷ εὐθέτῳ καὶ τῆς δι᾿ ὕδατος καὶ πνεύματος ἀναγεννήσεως· συγκαταρίθμησον αὐτὸ τῇ ἁγίᾳ σου ποίμνῃ τῶν λογικῶν προβάτων, τῶν ἐπικεκλημένων τῷ ὀνόματι τοῦ Χριστοῦ σου.

Ὅτι σὺ εἶ ὁ ἐν ὑψηλοῖς κατοικῶν καὶ τὰ ταπεινὰ ἐφορῶν, καὶ σοὶ τὴν δόξαν ἀναπέμπομεν, τῷ Πατρὶ καὶ τῷ Υἱῷ καὶ τῷ Ἁγίῳ Πνεύματι, νῦν καὶ ἀεὶ καὶ εἰς τοὺς αἰῶνας τῶν αἰώνων. Ἀμήν.

Εἶτα, λαβὼν ὁ Ἱερεὺς τὸ παιδίον, σχηματίζει δι᾿ αὐτοῦ Σταυρὸν πρὸ τῶν πυλῶν τοῦ Ναοῦ, λέγων·

Ἐκκλησιάζεται ὁ δοῦλος τοῦ Θεοῦ (ὁ δεῖνα), **εἰς τὸ ὄνομα τοῦ Πατρὸς καὶ τοῦ Υἱοῦ καὶ τοῦ Ἁγίου Πνεύματος. Ἀμήν.**

Εἶτα εἰσάγει αὐτὸ ἐν τῷ Ναῷ λέγων·

Εἰσελεύσομαι εἰς τὸν οἶκόν σου, Κύριε, προσκυνήσω πρὸς Ναὸν ἅγιόν σου.

Καὶ εἰσέρχεται ἐν τῷ μέσῳ τοῦ Ναοῦ, λέγων.

Ἐκκλησιάζεται ὁ δοῦλος τοῦ Θεοῦ...

Ἐν μέσῳ Ἐκκλησίας ὑμνήσω σε.

Εἶτα προσάγει αὐτὸ πρὸ τῶν πυλῶν τοῦ Θυσιαστηρίου λέγων·

Ἐκκλησιάζεται ὁ δοῦλος τοῦ Θεοῦ...

Καὶ εἰσάγει αὐτὸ εἰς τὸ ἅγιον Θυσιαστήριον, εἰ μὲν εἴη ἄρρεν· εἰ δὲ θῆλυ, ἕως τῶν ὡραίων πυλῶν, λέγων τὸ

He that watches over babes, Yourself, O Lord, bless (+) this child, together with its parents and sponsors, and account it worthy, at the fitting time, to be born again of water and the Spirit. Number it with Your holy Flock of rational sheep, who are called by the Name of Your Christ. For You are He that dwells on high, and gives regard to the things which are lowly, and to You do we send up glory: to the Father, and to the Son, and to the Holy Spirit, both now and ever, and to the ages of ages. Amen.

Then, taking up the child, the Priest lifts it up in the sign of the Cross before the Gates of the Temple, saying:

The servant of God (*Name*) is churched, in the Name of the Father, and of the Son, and of the Holy Spirit. Amen.

And he carries the child into the Holy Temple, saying:

I will go into Your House. I will worship toward Your Holy Temple in fear of You.

Coming to the center of the church, he says:

The servant of God (*Name*) is churched, in the Name of the Father, and of the Son, and of the Holy Spirit. Amen. In the midst of the congregation I will sing praises to You.

Then he brings the child before the Doors of the Altar, saying:

The servant of God (*Name*) is churched, in the Name of the Father, and of the Son, and of the Holy Spirit. Amen.

If the child is male the Priest carries him into the Altar; if a female, the child is carried only as far as the Holy Doors. He then says:

Νῦν ἀπολύεις τὸν δοῦλόν σου, Δέσποτα, κατὰ τὸ ῥῆμά σου ἐν εἰρήνῃ...

Καὶ ὁ Ἱερεὺς ποιεῖ, ὡς ἔθος, Ἀπόλυσιν.

Δόξα σοι, ὁ Θεός, ἡ ἐλπὶς ἡμῶν, δόξα σοι. Ὁ ἐν ἀγκάλαις τοῦ δικαίου Συμεὼν βασταχθῆναι καταδεξάμενος, διὰ τὴν ἡμῶν σωτηρίαν, Χριστὸς ὁ ἀληθινὸς Θεὸς ἡμῶν, ταῖς πρεσβείαις τῆς παναχράντου καὶ παναμώμου ἁγίας αὐτοῦ Μητρός, δυνάμει τοῦ τιμίου καὶ ζωοποιοῦ Σταυροῦ, προστασίαις τῶν ἐπουρανίων θείων Δυνάμεων ἀσωμάτων, ἱκεσίαις τοῦ τιμίου ἐνδόξου προφήτου προδρόμου καὶ βαπτιστοῦ Ἰωάννου, τῶν ἁγίων ἐνδόξων καὶ πανευφήμων Ἀποστόλων, τῶν ἁγίων ἐνδόξων καὶ καλλινίκωνΜαρτύρων, τῶν ὁσίων καὶ θεοφόρων Πατέρων ἡμῶν, τῶν ἁγίων καὶ δικαίων θεοπατόρων Ἰωακεὶμ καὶ Ἄννης, (τοῦ ἁγίου τοῦ ναοῦ) καὶ πάντων τῶν ἁγίων ἐλεήσαι καὶ σῶσαι ἡμᾶς, ὡς ἀγαθὸς καὶ φιλάνθρωπος καὶ ἐλεήμων Θεός.

Δι' εὐχῶν...

Καὶ μετὰ τὸ Ἀμὴν σφραγίζει τὸ μέτωπον αὐτοῦ καὶ τὸ στόμα καὶ τὸ στῆθος ἐπιλέγων καὶ τὸ τῆς ἁγίας Τριάδος ὄνομα.

Καὶ οὕτως ἀποδίδωσι τὸ βρέφος τῇ μητρί.

Lord, now let Your servant depart in peace, according to Your word; for my eyes have seen Your salvation, which You have prepared before the face of all people, a Light to lighten the Gentiles, and the Glory of Your people of Israel.

Apolysis

Glory to You, O our God and our hope, glory to You.

He Who submitted to be carried in the arms of the righteous Symeon, Christ our true God, through the intercessions of His pure and spotless Mother, through the power of the precious and life-giving Cross, through the protection of the venerable and bodiless heavenly Powers, through the prayers of the venerable and glorious prophet and Forerunner John the Baptist, of the holy, glorious, all-praiseworthy Apostles, of the holy, glorious and victorious Martyrs, of our venerable Godbearing Fathers, of the holy, righteous ancestors of the Lord, Joakim and Anna, (of *the Saint of the church*), and of all the Saints, have mercy on us and save us as our Good and Loving God.

Through the prayers . . .

After the Amen, the priest makes the sign of the Cross over the forehead, mouth, and chest of the child, invoking the name of the Holy Trinity. He then returns the child to the mother.

Εὐχὴ
εἰς γυναῖκα, ὅταν ἀποβάληται.

Εὐλογητὸς ὁ Θεὸς ἡμῶν... Ἅγιος ὁ Θεός. (ἐκ γ΄). Δόξα. Καὶ νῦν. Παναγία Τριάς. Κύριε, ἐλέησον (γ΄). Δόξα. Καὶ νῦν. Πάτερ ἡμῶν. Ὅτι σοῦ ἐστιν.

Τὸ Ἀπολυτίκιον τῆς ἡμέρας καὶ τὸ Κοντάκιον, εἴ ἐστι Δεσποτικὴ ἢ Θεομητορικὴ ἑορτή. Εἶτα·

Τοῦ Κυρίου δεηθῶμεν.

Δέσποτα, Κύριε, ὁ Θεὸς ἡμῶν, ὁ τεχθεὶς ἐκ τῆς ἁγίας Θεοτόκου καὶ ἀειπαρθένου Μαρίας, καὶ ἐν φάτνῃ ὡς βρέφος ἀνακλιθείς· Αὐτὸς τὴν παροῦσαν δούλην σου (τήνδε), τὴν σήμερον ἐν ἁμαρτίαις εἰς φόνον περιπεσοῦσαν, ἑκουσίως ἢ ἀκουσίως καὶ τὸ ἐν αὐτῇ συλληφθὲν ἀποβαλομένην, ἐλέησον κατὰ τὸ μέγα σου ἔλεος· καὶ συγχώρησον αὐτῇ τὰ ἑκούσια καὶ τὰ ἀκούσια πταίσματα· καὶ διαφύλαξον ἀπὸ πάσης τοῦ Διαβόλου μηχανουργίας· καὶ τὸν ῥύπον κάθαρον· τοὺς πόνους θεράπευσον· καὶ ῥῶσιν καὶ εὐρωστίαν τῷ σώματι σὺν

44

PRAYER FOR A WOMAN
WHO HAS SUFFERED A MISCARRIAGE

Blessed is our God always . . .*(see pp. 32-33)*
The Trisagion. Glory . . .both now . . . . O All-Holy
Trinity . . . Lord have mercy (3) Glory . . . both now . . . .
Our Father . . . For Yours is the Kingdom . . .

Then the Apolytikion of the Day.

Let us pray to the Lord. Lord have mercy.

O Sovereign Master, Lord our God, Who was born of
the all-pure Theotokos and Ever-Virgin Mary, and as a babe
was laid in a manger: do You Yourself, according to Your
great mercy, have regard for this Your servant *(Name)*
who this day is in sin, having fallen even into voluntary or
involuntary sin, and has miscarried that which was conceived in her. Be gracious unto her willing and unwilling
iniquities, preserving her from every diabolical wile; cleanse
her of her sin; heal her suffering, granting to her, O Loving Lord, health and strength of body and soul. Guard her

τῇ ψυχῇ αὐτῆς, φιλάνθρωπε, δώρησαι· καὶ δι᾽ Ἀγγέλου φωτεινοῦ ταύτην περιφρούρησιν ἀπὸ πάσης ἐπελεύσεως τῶν ἀοράτων δαιμόνων. Ναί, Κύριε, ἀπὸ νόσου καὶ μαλακίας, καὶ καθάρισον αὐτὴν ἀπὸ τοῦ σωματικοῦ ῥύπου καὶ τῶν ποικίλων αὐτῇ ἐπερχομένων σπλαγχνικῶν ἐνοχλήσεων· καὶ ἔξαξον αὐτήν, διὰ τῆς πολλῆς σου ἐλεημοσύνης ἐν τῷ ταπεινῷ αὐτῆς σώματι, καὶ ἀνάστησον αὐτὴν ἀπὸ τῆς κλίνης, ἧς περίκειται· ὅτι ἐν ἁμαρτίαις συνελήφθημεν καὶ ἐν ἀνομίαις ἐκυήθημεν καὶ διὰ ῥύπου πάντες ἐσμὲν ἐνώπιόν σου, Κύριε, καὶ μετὰ φόβου βοῶμεν καὶ λέγομεν· Ἐπίβλεψον ἐξ οὐρανοῦ, καὶ ἴδε τὴν ἀσθένειαν ἡμῶν τῶν καταδίκων, καὶ συγχώρησον τῇ δούλῃ σου ταύτῃ, τῇ ἐν ἁμαρτίαις φόνῳ περιπεσούσῃ, ἑκουσίως ἢ ἀκουσίως, καὶ τὸ ἐν αὐτῇ συλληφθὲν ἀποβαλομένῃ καὶ πάντας τοὺς εὑρισκομένους καὶ ἁψαμένους αὐτῆς, κατὰ τὸ μέγα σου ἔλεος, ὡς ἀγαθὸς καὶ φιλάνθρωπος Θεός, ἐλέησον καὶ συγχώρησον, ὅτι σὺ μόνος ἔχεις ἐξουσίαν ἀφιέναι ἁμαρτίας καὶ ἀνομίας· πρεσβείαις τῆς πανάγνου σου Μητρός, καὶ πάντων τῶν Ἁγίων. Ὅτι πρέπει σοι πᾶσα δόξα, τιμή, καὶ προσκύνησις, σὺν τῷ Πατρί, καὶ τῷ Ἁγίῳ Πνεύματι, νῦν καὶ ἀεὶ καὶ εἰς τοὺς αἰῶνας τῶν αἰώνων. Ἀμήν.

Καὶ γίνεται Ἀπόλυσις.

with a shining Angel from every assault of invisible demons, yea, O Lord, from all sickness and weakness; cleanse her from bodily defilement, from diverse inward torment encompassing her; and by Your abundant mercy raise her up in her humbled body from the bed upon which she lies, for we all are conceived in sins and in transgressions, and are all defiled before You, so in fear we cry before You, saying: Look down from the Heavens, O Lord; see the helplessness of us accursed and be gracious to this Your servant (*Name*), who is in sin, having fallen even to voluntary or involuntary sin, and has aborted that which was conceived in her; and according to Your great mercy, as our Good and Loving Lord, have mercy on her, and be gracious unto her in all things that have surrounded her and have come in contact with her; for You alone have power to save and forgive sins and transgressions, through the intercessions of Your all-pure Mother and all the Saints. For to You is due all Glory, Honor, and Adoration, with Your Eternal Father and Your All-Holy, Good and Life-creating Spirit, both now and ever, and to the ages of ages. Amen.

Then the Apolysis (see p. 35).

ΤΑΞΙΣ
ΓΙΝΟΜΕΝΗ ΠΡΟ ΤΟΥ ΑΓΙΟΥ ΒΑΠΤΙΣΜΑΤΟΣ

—∞—

ΕΥΧΗ
ΕΙΣ ΤΟ ΠΟΙΗΣΑΙ ΚΑΤΗΧΟΥΜΕΝΟΝ

Ὁ Ἱερεύς, φέρων Ἐπιτραχήλιον, ἐμφυσᾷ εἰς τὸ πρόσωπον τοῦ μέλλοντος φωτισθῆναι καὶ σφραγίζει μετὰ τῆς χειρὸς αὐτοῦ τὸ μέτωπον καὶ τὸ στῆθος ἐκ τρίτου λέγων·

Εἰς τὸ ὄνομα τοῦ Πατρός, καὶ τοῦ Υἱοῦ, καὶ τοῦ Ἁγίου Πνεύματος. Ἀμήν.

Καὶ ποιήσας Εὐλογητόν, ἐπιτίθησι τὴν χεῖρα ἐπὶ τὴν κεφαλὴν αὐτοῦ, λέγων τὴν παροῦσαν

Τοῦ Κυρίου δεηθῶμεν.

Ἐπὶ τῷ ὀνόματί σου, Κύριε, ὁ Θεὸς τῆς ἀληθείας, καὶ τοῦ μονογενοῦς σου Υἱοῦ, καὶ τοῦ Ἁγίου σου Πνεύματος, ἐπιτίθημι τὴν χεῖρά μου ἐπὶ τὸν δοῦλόν σου (τόνδε)τὸν καταξιωθέντα καταφυγεῖν ἐπὶ τὸ ἅγιον ὄνομά σου, καὶ ὑπὸ τὴν σκέπην τῶν πτερύγων σου διαφυλαχθῆναι. Ἀπόστησον ἀπ᾽ αὐτοῦ τὴν παλαιὰν ἐκείνην πλάνην, καὶ ἔμπλησον αὐτὸν τῆς εἰς σὲ πίστεως καὶ ἐλπίδος καὶ ἀγάπης, ἵνα γνῷ ὅτι σὺ

ORDER BEFORE HOLY BAPTISM

PRAYERS AT THE MAKING OF A CATECHUMEN

The Priest divests him (her) that comes to be illuminated of robes and shoes and faces him (her) eastward, barefoot and clad in a single garment, hands down. Then, breathing thrice on his (her) face and signing him (her) thrice on the forehead and breast, the Priest says:

In the name of the Father, and of the Son, and of the Holy Spirit. Amen.

Blessed is our God always, both now **and** ever, and to the ages of ages. Amen.

Laying his hand upon his (her) head, the Priest says:

Let us pray to the Lord. Lord have mercy.

In Your Name, O Lord God of Truth, and in the Name of Your Only-Begotten Son, and of Your Holy Spirit, I lay my hand upon this Your servant (*Name*), who has been accounted worthy to flee unto Your Holy Name and to be sheltered under the shadow of Your wings. Remove far from him (her) that ancient error, and fill him (her) with faith and hope and love that is in You, that he (she)

εἶ Θεὸς μόνος, Θεὸς ἀληθινός, καὶ ὁ μονογενής σου Υἱός, ὁ Κύριος ἡμῶν Ἰησοῦς Χριστός, καὶ τὸ Ἅγιόν σου Πνεῦμα. Δός αὐτῷ ἐν πάσαις ταῖς ἐντολαῖς σου πορευθῆναι, καὶ τὰ ἀρεστά σοι φυλάξαι· ὅτι ἐὰν ποιήσῃ αὐτὰ ἄνθρωπος ζήσεται ἐν αὐτοῖς. Γράψον αὐτὸν ἐν βίβλῳ ζωῆς σου καὶ ἕνωσον αὐτὸν τῇ ποίμνῃ τῆς κληρονομίας σου· δοξασθήτω τὸ ὄνομά σου τὸ ἅγιον ἐπ᾽ αὐτῷ καὶ τοῦ ἀγαπητοῦ σου Υἱοῦ, Κυρίου δὲ ἡμῶν Ἰησοῦ Χριστοῦ, καὶ τοῦ ζωοποιοῦ σου Πνεύματος. Ἔστωσαν οἱ ὀφθαλμοί σου ἀτενίζοντες εἰς αὐτὸν ἐν ἐλέει διαπαντός, καὶ τὰ ὦτά σου τοῦ ἀκούειν τῆς φωνῆς τῆς δεήσεως αὐτοῦ. Εὔφρανον αὐτὸν ἐν τοῖς ἔργοις τῶν χειρῶν αὐτοῦ, καὶ ἐν παντὶ τῷ γένει αὐτοῦ· ἵνα ἐξομολογήσηταί σοι, προσκυνῶν καὶ δοξάζων τὸ ὄνομά σου τὸ μέγα καὶ ὕψιστον, καὶ αἰνέσῃ σε διαπαντὸς πάσας τὰς ἡμέρας τῆς ζωῆς αὐτοῦ. Σὲ γὰρ ὑμνεῖ πᾶσα ἡ δύναμις τῶν οὐρανῶν, καὶ σοῦ ἐστιν ἡ δόξα τοῦ Πατρὸς καὶ τοῦ Υἱοῦ καὶ τοῦ Ἁγίου Πνεύματος, νῦν καὶ ἀεὶ καὶ εἰς τοὺς αἰῶνας τῶν αἰώνων. Ἀμήν.

ΑΦΟΡΚΙΣΜΟΣ Α´

Τοῦ Κυρίου δεηθῶμεν.

Ἐπιτιμᾷ σοι Κύριος, Διάβολε, ὁ παραγενόμενος εἰς τὸν κόσμον καὶ κατασκηνώσας ἐν ἀνθρώποις, ἵνα τὴν σὴν καθέλῃ τυραννίδα καὶ τοὺς ἀνθρώπους ἐξέληται· ὃς ἐπὶ ξύλου τὰς ἀντικειμένας δυνάμεις ἐθριάμβευσεν, ἡλίου σκοτισθέντος καὶ γῆς σαλευομένης, καὶ μνημάτων ἀνοιγομένων, καὶ σωμάτων Ἁγίων ἀνισταμένων· ὃς ἔλυσε θανάτῳ τὸν θάνατον, καὶ κατήργησε τὸν τὸ κράτος ἔχοντα τοῦ θανάτου, τουτέστι, σὲ τὸν Διάβολον. Ὁρκίζω σε κατὰ τοῦ Θεοῦ, τοῦ δείξαντος τὸ ξύλον τῆς ζωῆς

may know that You alone are the True God, and Your Only-Begotten Son, our Lord Jesus Christ, and Your Holy Spirit. Grant him (her) to walk in Your commandments, and to observe those things that are acceptable before You; for if a man does such he shall find life in them. Inscribe him (her) in Your Book of Life, and unite him (her) to the flock of Your inheritance. Let Your Holy Name be glorified in him (her) and that of Your well-beloved Son, our Lord Jesus Christ, and of Your Life-creating Spirit. Let Your eyes look over him (her) in mercy, and Your ears be ever attentive unto the voice of his (her) prayer. Let him (her) ever rejoice in the works of his (her) hands, and in all his (her) generation, that he (she) may give thanks to You, worshipping and glorifying Your great and Most High Name, and may ever praise You all the days of his (her) life. For all the Powers of Heaven praise You, and Yours is the Glory, of the Father, and of the Son, and of the Holy Spirit, both now and ever, and to the ages of ages. Amen.

First Exorcism

Let us pray to the Lord. Lord have mercy.

The Lord rebukes you, O devil, He that came into the world and made His dwelling among men, that He might cast down your tyranny, and deliver men; He that upon the Tree triumphed over the opposing powers, when the sun was darkened, and the earth was shaken, and the tombs were opened, and the bodies of the Saints arose; He that by death destroyed Death, and overcame him that held the might of death, that is, even you, O devil. I abjure you by the Living God, Who has shown forth the Tree of Life, and posted the Cherubim, and

καὶ τάξαντος τὰ Χερουβὶμ καὶ τὴν φλογίνην ρομφαίαν τὴν στρεφομένην φρουρεῖν αὐτό. Ἐπιτιμήθητι καὶ ἀναχώρησον· κατ' ἐκείνου γάρ σε ὁρκίζω τοῦ περιπατήσαντος, ὡς ἐπὶ ξηρᾶς, ἐπὶ νῶτα θαλάσσης, καὶ ἐπιτιμήσαντος τῇ λαίλαπι τῶν ἀνέμων· οὗ τὸ βλέμμα ξηραίνει ἀβύσσους καὶ ἡ ἀπειλὴ τήκει ὄρη. Αὐτὸς γὰρ καὶ νῦν ἐπιτάσσει σοι δι' ἡμῶν· Φοβήθητι, ἔξελθε, καὶ ὑπαναχώρησον ἀπὸ τοῦ πλάσματος τούτου, καὶ μὴ ὑποστρέψῃς, μηδὲ ὑποκρυβῇς ἐν αὐτῷ, μηδὲ συναντήσῃς αὐτῷ ἢ ἐνεργήσῃς ἢ ἐνραγῇς, μὴ ἐν νυκτί, μὴ ἐν ἡμέρᾳ ἢ ὥρᾳ ἢ ἐν μεσημβρίᾳ· ἀλλ' ἄπελθε εἰς τὸν ἴδιον τάρταρον, ἕως τῆς ἡτοιμασμένης μεγάλης ἡμέρας τῆς κρίσεως. Φοβήθητι τὸν Θεὸν τὸν καθήμενον ἐπὶ τῶν Χερουβίμ, καὶ ἐπιβλέποντα ἀβύσσους· ὃν τρέμουσιν Ἄγγελοι, Ἀρχάγγελοι, Θρόνοι, Κυριότητες, Ἀρχαί, Ἐξουσίαι, Δυνάμεις, τὰ πολυόμματα Χερουβίμ, καὶ τὰ ἑξαπτέρυγα Σεραφίμ· ὃν τρέμει ὁ οὐρανὸς καὶ ἡ γῆ, ἡ θάλασσα καὶ πάντα τὰ ἐν αὐτοῖς. Ἔξελθε καὶ ἀναχώρησον ἀπὸ τοῦ σφραγισθέντος νεολέκτου στρατιώτου Χριστοῦ τοῦ Θεοῦ ἡμῶν· κατ' ἐκείνου γάρ σε ὁρκίζω, τοῦ περιπατοῦντος ἐπὶ πτερύγων ἀνέμων, τοῦ ποιοῦντος τοὺς Ἀγγέλους αὐτοῦ πνεύματα, καὶ τοὺς λειτουργοὺς αὐτοῦ πῦρ φλέγον. Ἔξελθε καὶ ἀναχώρησον ἀπὸ τοῦ πλάσματος τούτου σὺν πάσῃ τῇ δυνάμει καὶ τοῖς ἀγγέλοις σου. Ὅτι δεδόξασται τὸ ὄνομα τοῦ Πατρὸς καὶ τοῦ Υἱοῦ καὶ τοῦ Ἁγίου Πνεύματος, νῦν καὶ ἀεὶ καὶ εἰς τοὺς αἰῶνας τῶν αἰώνων. Ἀμήν.

ΑΦΟΡΚΙΣΜΟΣ Β'

Τοῦ Κυρίου δεηθῶμεν.

Ο Θεός, ὁ ἅγιος, ὁ φοβερὸς καὶ ἔνδοξος, ὁ ἐπὶ πᾶσι τοῖς ἔργοις καὶ τῇ ἰσχύϊ αὐτοῦ ἀκατάληπτος καὶ ἀνεξιχνίαστος ὑπάρχων· αὐτὸς ὁ προο-

the flaming sword that turns about to guard this: be rebuked, and depart, for I forbid you, through Him that walks on the waves of the sea as upon the dry land, Who forbade the storm of the winds, Whose glance dries up the deep, and Whose threatenings melt the mountains; for it is He Himself that now forbids you through us. Be afraid, and depart, and absent yourself from this creature, and come not back, neither hide yourself in him (her), nor encounter him (her), nor influence him (her) either by night or by day, nor in the morning or at noon; but get you hence to your own Tartarus, until the appointed day of Judgment. Fear God, Who sits on the throne of the Cherubim, and looks upon the depths, before Whom tremble Angels, Archangels, Thrones, Principalities, Authorities, Powers, the many-eyed Cherubim, and the six-winged Seraphim; Whom Heaven and earth fear, the sea, and all that live therein. Come forth, and depart from the sealed and newly-enlisted soldier of Christ our God; for I abjure you by Him that rides upon the wings of the winds, Who makes His Angels spirits and His Ministers a flame of fire. Come forth, and from this creature which He fashioned depart with all your power and might; for glorified is the Name of the Father, and of the Son, and of the Holy Spirit, both now and ever, and to the ages of ages. Amen.

Second Exorcism

Let us pray to the Lord. Lord have mercy.

God, the Holy, the Terrible, and the Glorious, Who concerning all His works and strength is incomprehensible and unsearchable, Who Himself has ordained for you,

ρίσας σοι, Διάβολε, τῆς αἰωνίου κολάσεως τὴν τι-
μωρίαν, δι᾽ ἡμῶν τῶν ἀχρείων αὐτοῦ δούλων κε-
λεύει σοι, καὶ πάσῃ τῇ συνεργῷ σου δυνάμει, ἀπο-
στῆναι ἀπὸ τοῦ νεωστὶ σφραγισθέντος ἐπ᾽ ὀνόματι
τοῦ Κυρίου ἡμῶν Ἰησοῦ Χριστοῦ, τοῦ ἀληθινοῦ
Θεοῦ ἡμῶν. Ὁρκίζω σε οὖν, παμπόνηρον καὶ ἀκάθαρτον καὶ μιαρὸν καὶ ἐβδελυγμένον καὶ ἀλλότριον
πνεῦμα, κατὰ τῆς δυνάμεως Ἰησοῦ Χριστοῦ, τοῦ πᾶσαν ἐξουσίαν ἔχοντος ἐν οὐρανῷ καὶ ἐπὶ γῆς, τοῦ εἰπόντος τῷ κωφῷ καὶ ἀλάλῳ δαίμονι· Ἔξελθε ἀπὸ τοῦ
ἀνθρώπου καὶ μηκέτι εἰσέλθῃς εἰς αὐτόν. Ἀναχώρησον, γνώρισον τὴν σὴν ματαίαν δύναμιν, τὴν μηδὲ
χοίρων ἐξουσίαν ἔχουσαν. Ὑπομνήσθητι τοῦ ἐπιτά-
ξαντός σοι, κατὰ τὴν σὴν αἴτησιν, εἰς τὴν ἀγέλην
τῶν χοίρων εἰσελθεῖν. Φοβήθητι τὸν Θεόν, οὗ τῷ
προστάγματι ἡ γῆ καθ᾽ ὑδάτων ἐστήρικται· τὸν κτί-
σαντα τὸν οὐρανόν, καὶ στήσαντα τὰ ὄρη σταθμῷ,
καὶ τὰς νάπας ζυγῷ, καὶ θέντα ἄμμον θαλάσσῃ ὅριον,
καὶ ἐν ὕδατι σφοδρῷ τρίβον ἀσφαλῆ· τὸν ἁπτόμενον
τῶν ὀρέων καὶ καπνίζονται· τὸν ἀναβαλλόμενον
φῶς ὡς ἱμάτιον· τὸν ἐκτείνοντα τὸν οὐρανὸν ὡσεὶ
δέρριν· τὸν στεγάζοντα ἐν ὕδασι τὰ ὑπερῷα αὐτοῦ·
τὸν θεμελιοῦντα τὴν γῆν ἐπὶ τὴν ἀσφάλειαν αὐτῆς·
οὐ κλιθήσεται εἰς τὸν αἰῶνα τοῦ αἰῶνος· τὸν προσ-
καλούμενον τὸ ὕδωρ τῆς θαλάσσης καὶ ἐκχέοντα
αὐτὸ ἐπὶ πρόσωπον πάσης τῆς γῆς. Ἔξελθε, καὶ
ἀναχώρησον ἀπὸ τοῦ πρὸς τὸ ἅγιον φώτισμα εὐτρε-
πιζομένου. Ὁρκίζω σε κατὰ τοῦ σωτηριώδους πάθους τοῦ Κυρίου ἡμῶν Ἰησοῦ Χριστοῦ, καὶ τοῦ τιμίου αὐτοῦ Σώματος καὶ Αἵματος, καὶ κατὰ τῆς ἐ-
λεύσεως αὐτοῦ τῆς φοβερᾶς. Ἥξει γάρ, καὶ οὐ χρο-
νιεῖ, κρίνων πᾶσαν τὴν γῆν, καὶ σὲ καὶ τὴν συνερ-
γόν σου δύναμιν κολάσει εἰς τὴν γέενναν τοῦ
πυρός, παραδοὺς εἰς τὸ σκότος τὸ ἐξώτερον, ὅπου ὁ

O devil, the retribution of eternal torment, through us, His unworthy servants, commands you, and all your co-operating might to go forth from him (her) that is newly sealed in the Name of our Lord God and Savior Christ. Therefore, you all evil, unclean, abominable, loathsome and alien spirit; I adjure you by the power of Jesus Christ, Who has all authority in Heaven and on earth, Who says to the deaf and dumb demon, "Get out of the man, and enter no more into him." Depart! Know the vainness of your might, which had not power even over the swine! Remember Him Who bade you, at your request, to enter into the herd of swine. Fear God, at Whose command the earth was established upon the waters; Who has found-ed the Heavens, and fixed the mountains with a line, and the valleys with a measure; Who has placed the sand for a boundary to the sea, and made safe paths through the waters; Who touched the mountains and they smoked; Who clothed Himself with Light as with a garment; Who has stretched out the Heavens as with a curtain; Who covers His upper rooms with waters; Who has founded the earth on her firm foundations, so that it shall not be moved forever; Who calls up the waters of the seas, and sprinkles it on the face of the earth. Come out! Depart from him (her) who is now being made ready for Holy Illumination; I abjure you by the saving Pas-sion of our Lord Jesus Christ, by His Precious Blood and All-Pure Body, and by His terrible Coming Again— for He shall come and not tarry, to judge all the earth, and shall punish you and your cooperating might in the Gehenna of fire, consigning you to the outer darkness where the worm dies not and the fire is not quenched;

σκώληξ ὁ ἀκοίμητος, καὶ τὸ πῦρ οὐ σβέννυται. Ὅτι τὸ κράτος Χριστοῦ τοῦ Θεοῦ ἡμῶν, σὺν τῷ Πατρὶ καὶ τῷ Ἁγίῳ Πνεύματι, νῦν καὶ ἀεὶ καὶ εἰς τοὺς αἰῶνας τῶν αἰώνων. Ἀμήν.

ΑΦΟΡΚΙΣΜΟΣ Γ΄

Τοῦ Κυρίου δεηθῶμεν.

Κ ύριε Σαβαώθ, ὁ Θεὸς τοῦ Ἰσραήλ, ὁ ἰώμενος πᾶσαν νόσον καὶ πᾶσαν μαλακίαν, ἐπίβλεψον ἐπὶ τὸν δοῦλόν σου, ἐκζήτησον, ἐξερεύνησον, καὶ ἀπέλασον ἀπ' αὐτοῦ πάντα τὰ ἐνεργήματα τοῦ Διαβόλου. Ἐπιτίμησον τοῖς ἀκαθάρτοις πνεύμασι, καὶ δίωξον αὐτά, καὶ καθάρισον τὸ ἔργον τῶν χειρῶν σου, καί, τῇ ὀξείᾳ σου χρησάμενος ἐνεργείᾳ, σύντριψον τὸν Σατανᾶν ὑπὸ τοὺς πόδας αὐτοῦ ἐν τάχει, καὶ δὸς αὐτῷ νίκας κατ' αὐτοῦ καὶ τῶν ἀκαθάρτων αὐτοῦ πνευμάτων· ὅπως, τοῦ παρὰ σοῦ ἐλέους τυγχάνων, καταξιωθῇ τῶν ἀθανάτων καὶ ἐπουρανίων σου μυστηρίων, καὶ δόξαν σοι ἀναπέμψῃ, τῷ Πατρὶ καὶ τῷ Υἱῷ καὶ τῷ Ἁγίῳ Πνεύματι, νῦν καὶ ἀεὶ καὶ εἰς τοὺς αἰῶνας τῶν αἰώνων. Ἀμήν.

ΕΥΧΗ

Τοῦ Κυρίου δεηθῶμεν.

Ο Ὤν, Δέσποτα Κύριε, ὁ ποιήσας τὸν ἄνθρωπον κατ' εἰκόνα σὴν καὶ ὁμοίωσιν, καὶ δοὺς αὐτῷ ἐξουσίαν ζωῆς αἰωνίου· εἶτα ἐκπεσόντα διὰ τῆς ἁμαρτίας μὴ παριδών· ἀλλ' οἰκονομήσας διὰ τῆς ἐνανθρωπήσεως τοῦ Χριστοῦ σου τὴν σωτηρίαν τοῦ κόσμου· Αὐτὸς καὶ τὸ πλάσμα σου τοῦτο, λυτρωσάμενος ἐκ τῆς δουλείας τοῦ ἐχθροῦ, πρόσδεξαι εἰς τὴν βασιλείαν σου τὴ·· ἐπουράνιον. Διάνοιξον

for of Christ is the Might, with the Father and the Holy
Spirit, both now and ever, and to the ages of ages. Amen.

Third Exorcism

Let us pray to the Lord. Lord have mercy.

O Lord of Sabaoth, the God of Israel, Who heals every
sickness and every wound, Look down upon this Your
servant *(Name)*; search out and try him (her), driving
away from him (her) every operation of the devil. Rebuke the unclean spirits and expel them, cleansing the
work of Your hands; and, using Your trenchant energy,
beat down Satan under his (her) feet, giving him (her)
victory over him, and over his unclean spirits; so that,
obtaining the mercy that comes from You, he (she) may
be accounted worthy of Your Immortal and Heavenly
Mysteries, and may send up all glory to You, to Father,
and to Son, and to Holy Spirit, both now and ever, and
to the ages of ages. Amen.

Prayer

Let us pray to the Lord. Lord have mercy.

You, the Existing Sovereign Master and Lord, Who made
man after Your own image and likeness and gave to him
power of eternal life; and when he had fallen through
sin did not disdain him, but did provide for him through
the Incarnation of Your Christ, the salvation of the world.
Redeeming this Your creature from the yoke of the Enemy,
receive him (her) into Your heavenly Kingdom. Open

αὐτοῦ τοὺς ὀφθαλμοὺς τῆς διανοίας, εἰς τὸ αὐγάσαι ἐν αὐτῷ τὸν φωτισμὸν τοῦ Εὐαγγελίου σου. Σύζευξον τῇ ζωῇ αὐτοῦ ῎Αγγελον φωτεινόν, ῥυόμενον αὐτὸν ἀπὸ πάσης ἐπιβουλῆς τοῦ ἀντικειμένου, ἀπὸ συναντήματος πονηροῦ, ἀπὸ δαιμονίου μεσημβρινοῦ, ἀπὸ φαντασμάτων πονηρῶν.

Καὶ ἐμφυσᾷ αὐτῷ τρίτον ὁ Ἱερεύς, καὶ σφραγίζει τὸ μέτωπον αὐτοῦ καὶ τὸ στόμα, καὶ τὸ στῆθος, λέγων·

Ἐξέλασον ἀπ᾽ αὐτοῦ πᾶν πονηρὸν καὶ ἀκάθαρτον πνεῦμα, κεκρυμμένον καὶ ἐμφωλεῦον αὐτοῦ τῇ καρδίᾳ (καὶ λέγει τοῦτο ἐκ γ'). Πνεῦμα πλάνης, πνεῦμα πονηρίας, πνεῦμα εἰδωλολατρείας καὶ πάσης πλεονεξίας· πνεῦμα ψεύδους καὶ πάσης ἀκαθαρσίας, τῆς ἐνεργουμένης κατὰ τὴν διδασκαλίαν τοῦ Διαβόλου. Καὶ ποίησον αὐτὸν πρόβατον λογικὸν τῆς ἁγίας ποίμνης τοῦ Χριστοῦ σου, μέλος τίμιον τῆς Ἐκκλησίας σου, σκεῦος ἡγιασμένον, υἱὸν φωτὸς καὶ κληρονόμον τῆς βασιλείας σου· ἵνα, κατὰ τὰς ἐντολάς σου πολιτευσάμενος, καὶ φυλάξας τὴν σφραγῖδα ἄθραυστον, καὶ διατηρήσας τὸν χιτῶνα ἀμόλυντον, τύχῃ τῆς μακαριότητος τῶν Ἁγίων ἐν τῇ βασιλείᾳ σου.

Ἐκφώνως·

Χάριτι, καὶ οἰκτιρμοῖς, καὶ φιλανθρωπίᾳ τοῦ μονογενοῦς σου Υἱοῦ, μεθ᾽ οὗ εὐλογητὸς εἶ, σὺν τῷ παναγίῳ καὶ ἀγαθῷ, καὶ ζωοποιῷ σου Πνεύματι, νῦν καὶ ἀεὶ καὶ εἰς τοὺς αἰῶνας τῶν αἰώνων. Ἀμήν.

Ἀποδυομένου δὲ καὶ ὑπολυομένου τοῦ βαπτιζομένου, εἰ ἐν ἡλικίᾳ ἐστί, στρέφει αὐτὸν ὁ Ἱερεὺς ἐπὶ δυσμάς, ἄνω τὰς χεῖρας ἔχοντα, καὶ λέγει ἐκ γ'.

the eyes of his (her) understanding, so that the Illumination of Your Gospel may dawn upon him (her). Yoke unto his (her) life a shining Angel to deliver him (her) from every plot directed against him (her) by the Adversary, from encounter with evil, from the noon-day demon, and from evil dreams.

And the Priest breathes on his (her) forehead, on his (her) mouth, and on his (her) breast, saying:

Drive out from him (her) every evil and unclean spirit, hiding and lurking in his (her) heart. (*This he does and says thrice.*) The spirit of error, the spirit of evil, the spirit of idolatry and of all covetousness that works according to the teaching of the devil. Make him (her) a reason-endowed sheep of the holy Flock of Your Christ, and honorable member of Your Church, a hallowed vessel, a child of Light, and heir of Your Kingdom. So that, having ordered his (her) life according to Your commandments, and having guarded the Seal and kept it unbroken, and having preserved his (her) garment undefiled, he (she) may attain unto the blessedness of the Saints of Your Kingdom.

Through the Grace and Compassion and Manbefriending Love of Your Only-Begotten Son, with Whom You are blessed, together with Your All-Holy, Good, and Life-creating Spirit, both now and ever, and to the ages of ages. Amen.

Then the Priest turns him (her) that is to be baptized to face westward, unclothed, barefoot, hands upraised. If the person is a child, the Sponsor holding him (her) faces West. The Priest then says thrice:

Ἀποτάσσῃ τῷ Σατανᾷ; Καὶ πᾶσι τοῖς ἔργοις αὐτοῦ; Καὶ πάσῃ τῇ λατρείᾳ αὐτοῦ; Καὶ πᾶσι τοῖς ἀγγέλοις αὐτοῦ; Καὶ πάσῃ τῇ πομπῇ αὐτοῦ;

Καὶ ἀποκρίνεται πρὸς ἕκαστον ὁ Κατηχούμενος ἢ ὁ Ἀνάδοχος αὐτοῦ, εἴ ἐστιν ὁ βαπτιζόμενος βάρβαρος ἢ παιδίον καὶ λέγει.

Ἀποτάσσομαι.

Καὶ ὅταν εἴπῃ τρίς, ἐρωτᾷ πάλιν ὁ Ἱερεὺς τὸν βαπτιζόμενον.

Ἀπετάξω τῷ Σατανᾷ;

Καὶ ἀποκρίνεται ὁ Κατηχούμενος ἢ ὁ Ἀνάδοχος αὐτοῦ.

Ἀπεταξάμην.

Καὶ ὅταν εἴπῃ τρίς, λέγει ὁ Ἱερεύς.

Καὶ ἐμφύσησον, καὶ ἔμπτυσον αὐτῷ.

Καὶ τοῦτο ποιήσαντος, στρέφει αὐτὸν ὁ Ἱερεὺς κατὰ ἀνατολάς, κάτω τὰς χεῖρας ἔχοντα καὶ λέγει αὐτῷ τρίς.

Συντάσσῃ τῷ Χριστῷ;

Καὶ ἀποκρίνεται ὁ Κατηχούμενος ἢ ὁ Ἀνάδοχος, λέγων·

Συντάσσομαι. (ἐκ τρίτου)

Εἶτα πάλιν λέγει αὐτῷ ὁ Ἱερεὺς ἐκ τρίτου.

Συνετάξω τῷ Χριστῷ;

Καὶ ἀποκρίνεται.

Συνεταξάμην.

Καὶ πάλιν λέγει·

Καὶ πιστεύεις αὐτῷ;

Καὶ ἀποκρίνεται.

Πιστεύω αὐτῷ, ὡς Βασιλεῖ καὶ Θεῷ.

Do you renounce Satan, and all his works, and all his worship, and all his angels, and all his pomp?

Each time the Catechumen (or the Sponsor if the person to be baptized is a child or a foreigner) answers and says:

I do renounce him.

Again the Priest asks him (her) that is to be baptized: (3 times)

Have you renounced Satan?

And the Catechumen or the Sponsor answers (3 times):

I have renounced him.

After the third time, the Priest says:

Then blow and spit upon him.

And this being done, the Priest turns the Catechumen to the East with lowered hands, and repeats the following three times:

Do you join Christ?

The question is answered three times:

I do join Him.

Again the Priest asks three times:

Have you joined Christ?

Catechumen (or Sponsor):

I have joined Him.

Again the Priest asks:

And do you believe in Him?

Catechumen (or Sponsor):

I believe in Him as King and as God.

Καὶ λέγει τὸ Σύμβολον τῆς πίστεως·

Π ιστεύω εἰς ἕνα Θεόν, Πατέρα Παντοκράτορα, Ποιητὴν οὐρανοῦ καὶ γῆς, ὁρατῶν τε πάντων καὶ ἀοράτων.

Καὶ εἰς ἕνα Κύριον Ἰησοῦν Χριστόν, τὸν Υἱὸν τοῦ Θεοῦ, τὸν μονογενῆ, τὸν ἐκ τοῦ Πατρὸς γεννηθέντα πρὸ πάντων τῶν αἰώνων. Φῶς ἐκ Φωτός, Θεὸν ἀληθινόν, ἐκ Θεοῦ ἀληθινοῦ, γεννηθέντα, οὐ ποιηθέντα, ὁμοούσιον τῷ Πατρί, δι᾽ οὗ τὰ πάντα ἐγένετο. Τὸν δι᾽ ἡμᾶς τοὺς ἀνθρώπους καὶ διὰ τὴν ἡμετέραν σωτηρίαν κατελθόντα ἐκ τῶν οὐρανῶν καὶ σαρκωθέντα ἐκ Πνεύματος Ἁγίου καὶ Μαρίας τῆς Παρθένου καὶ ἐνανθρωπήσαντα. Σταυρωθέντα τε ὑπὲρ ἡμῶν ἐπὶ Ποντίου Πιλάτου, καὶ παθόντα καὶ ταφέντα. Καὶ ἀναστάντα τῇ τρίτῃ ἡμέρᾳ κατὰ τὰς Γραφάς. Καὶ ἀνελθόντα εἰς τοὺς οὐρανοὺς καὶ καθεζόμενον ἐκ δεξιῶν τοῦ Πατρός. Καὶ πάλιν ἐρχόμενον μετὰ δόξης, κρῖναι ζῶντας καὶ νεκρούς· οὗ τῆς βασιλείας οὐκ ἔσται τέλος. Καὶ εἰς τὸ Πνεῦμα τὸ Ἅγιον, τὸ Κύριον, τὸ Ζωοποιόν, τὸ ἐκ τοῦ Πατρὸς ἐκπορευόμενον, τὸ σὺν Πατρὶ καὶ Υἱῷ συμπροσκυνούμενον καὶ συνδοξαζόμενον, τὸ λαλῆσαν διὰ τῶν Προφητῶν. Εἰς Μίαν, Ἁγίαν, Καθολικὴν καὶ Ἀποστολικὴν Ἐκκλησίαν. Ὁμολογῶ ἓν Βάπτισμα εἰς ἄφεσιν ἁμαρτιῶν. Προσδοκῶ ἀνάστασιν νεκρῶν. Καὶ ζωὴν τοῦ μέλλοντος αἰῶνος. Ἀμήν.

Καὶ ὅταν πληρώσῃ τὸ ἅγιον Σύμβολον, λέγει πάλιν πρὸς αὐτὸν ἐκ τρίτου·

Συνετάξω τῷ Χριστῷ κ.λ.π., ἀποκρινομένου καθ᾽ ἕκαστον τοῦ Κατηχουμένου ἢ τοῦ Ἀναδόχου,

The Creed (Symbol of the Faith)

I believe in one God, Father, Almighty, Creator of heaven and earth, and of all things visible and invisible.

And in one Lord, Jesus Christ, the only begotten Son of God, begotten of the Father before all ages. Light of Light, true God of true God, begotten, not created, of one essence with the Father, through whom all things were made.

For us all and for our salvation, He came down from heaven and was incarnate by the Holy Spirit and the Virgin Mary and became man.

He was crucified for us under Pontius Pilate, and He suffered and was buried.

On the third day He rose according to the Scriptures.

He ascended into heaven and is seated at the right hand of the Father.

He will come again in glory to judge the living and the dead. His kingdom will have no end.

And in the Holy Spirit, the Lord, the Giver of Life, who proceeds from the Father, who together with the Father and the Son is worshiped and glorified, who spoke through the prophets.

In one, holy, catholic, and apostolic Church.

I acknowledge one baptism for the forgiveness of sins.

I expect the resurrection of the dead.

And the life of the age to come. Amen.

ὡς εἴρηται. Ἐρωτηθέντος δὲ τρίς, καὶ ἐκ τρίτου εἰπόντος τὸ ἅγιον Σύμβολον, ἐρωτᾷ αὐτὸν ἐκ τρίτου·

Συνετάξω τῷ Χριστῷ;

Καὶ ἀποκρίνεται·

Συνεταξάμην.

Καὶ λέγει ὁ Ἱερεύς·

Καὶ προσκύνησον αὐτῷ.

Καὶ προσκυνεῖ λέγων·

Προσκυνῶ Πατέρα, Υἱόν, καὶ Ἅγιον Πνεῦμα, Τριάδα ὁμοούσιον καὶ ἀχώριστον.

Ὁ Ἱερεύς, ἐκφώνως·

Εὐλογητὸς ὁ Θεός, ὁ πάντας ἀνθρώπους θέλων· σωθῆναι καὶ εἰς ἐπίγνωσιν ἀληθείας ἐλθεῖν, νῦν καὶ ἀεὶ καὶ εἰς τοὺς αἰῶνας τῶν αἰώνων. Ἀμήν.

Καὶ οὕτως ἐπεύχεται λέγων·

Τοῦ Κυρίου δεηθῶμεν.

Δέσποτα, Κύριε, ὁ Θεὸς ἡμῶν, προσκάλεσαι τὸν δοῦλόν σου (τόνδε) πρὸς τὸ ἅγιόν σου φώτισμα, καὶ καταξίωσον αὐτὸν τῆς μεγάλης ταύτης χάριτος τοῦ ἁγίου σου Βαπτίσματος. Ἀπόδυσον αὐτοῦ τὴν παλαιότητα, καὶ ἀνακαίνισον αὐτὸν εἰς τὴν ζωὴν τὴν αἰώνιον, καὶ πλήρωσον αὐτὸν τῆς τοῦ Ἁγίου σου Πνεύματος δυνάμεως, εἰς ἕνωσιν τοῦ Χριστοῦ σου· ἵνα μηκέτι τέκνον. σώματος ᾖ, ἀλλὰ τέκνον τῆς σῆς Βασιλείας. Εὐδοκίᾳ καὶ χάριτι τοῦ μονογενοῦς σου Υἱοῦ, μεθ' οὗ εὐλογητὸς εἶ, σὺν τῷ παναγίῳ καὶ ἀγαθῷ καὶ ζωοποιῷ σου Πνεύματι, νῦν καὶ ἀεὶ καὶ εἰς τοὺς αἰῶνας τῶν αἰώνων. Ἀμήν.

Ἀπόλυσις.

Δόξα σοι, ὁ Θεός, ἡ ἐλπίς, ἡμῶν δόξα σοι, Χριστὸς ὁ ἀληθινὸς ἡμῶν...

Δι' εὐχῶν τῶν ἁγίων Πατέρων ἡμῶν...

After the completion of the Creed, the Priest asks thrice:

Have you joined Christ?

Catechumen (or Sponsor):

I have joined Him.

Then the Priest says:

Then bow before Him and worship Him.

Catechumen (or Sponsor) bows down, saying:

I bow down before the Father, and the Son, and the Holy Spirit; Trinity One in Essence and Undivided.

Priest

Blessed is God Who desires that all people should be saved, and come to the knowledge of the Truth; both now and ever, and to the ages of ages. Amen.

Let us pray to the Lord. Lord have mercy.

Sovereign Master, Lord our God, call this Your servant (*Name*) to Your Holy Illumination, and account him (her) worthy of this great Grace and Your Holy Baptism. Put off from him (her) the old man, and renew him (her) unto everlasting life; fill him (her) with the power of Your Holy Spirit, unto union with Your Christ; that he (she) may no longer be a child of the body, but a child of Your Kingdom; through the good pleasure and Grace of Your Only-Begotten Son, with Whom You are blessed, together with Your All-Holy, Good, and Life-creating Spirit, both now and ever, and to the ages of ages. Amen.

Apolysis

Glory to You, O Christ our God and our Hope, glory to You. Christ our True God . . .

Through the prayers of our holy Fathers. . .

ΑΚΟΛΟΥΘΙΑ
ΤΟΥ ΑΓΙΟΥ ΒΑΠΤΙΣΜΑΤΟΣ

Εἰσέρχεται ὁ Ἱερεύς, καὶ ἀλλάσσει λευκὴν ἱερα-τικὴν στολήν, ἤτοι ἐπιτραχήλιον καὶ φελώνιον· καὶ ἁπτομένων πάντων τῶν κηρῶν, λαβὼν θυμια-τόν, ἀπέρχεται ἐν τῇ Κολυμβήθρᾳ καὶ θυμιᾷ κύκλῳ καὶ ἀποδοὺς τὸ θυμιατόν, προσκυνεῖ.

Ὁ Ἱερεύς, ἐκφώνως·

Εὐλογημένη ἡ βασιλεία τοῦ Πατρὸς καὶ τοῦ Υἱοῦ καὶ τοῦ Ἁγίου Πνεύματος, νῦν καὶ ἀεὶ καὶ εἰς τοὺς αἰῶνας τῶν αἰώνων. Ἀμήν.

Ὁ Διάκονος ἢ αὐτὸς ὁ Ἱερεὺς

Ἐν εἰρήνῃ τοῦ Κυρίου δεηθῶμεν.

Ὁ Χορός, μεθ᾽ ἑκάστην δέησιν· Κύριε, ἐλέησον.

Ὑπὲρ τῆς ἄνωθεν εἰρήνης, καὶ τῆς σωτηρίας τῶν ψυχῶν ἡμῶν, τοῦ Κυρίου δεηθῶμεν.

THE SERVICE OF HOLY BAPTISM

The Priest enters the Altar and arrays himself in white vestments. While the candles are being lit, he takes up the Censer, goes to the Font, and censes round about. And giving up the Censer, he makes a Reverence.

Priest

Blessed is the Kingdom of the Father, and of the Son, and of the Holy Spirit, both now and ever, and to the ages of ages. Amen.

In peace let us pray to the Lord. Lord have mercy.

After each petition: Lord have mercy.

For the peace from above; for the salvation of our souls; let us pray to the Lord.

Ὑπὲρ τῆς εἰρήνης τοῦ σύμπαντος κόσμου, εὐσταθείας τῶν ἁγίων τοῦ Θεοῦ Ἐκκλησιῶν, καὶ τῆς τῶν πάντων ἑνώσεως, τοῦ Κυρίου δεηθῶμεν.

Ὑπὲρ τοῦ ἁγίου Οἴκου τούτου, καὶ τῶν μετὰ πίστεως, εὐλαβείας καὶ φόβου Θεοῦ εἰσιόντων ἐν αὐτῷ, τοῦ Κυρίου δεηθῶμεν.

Ὑπὲρ τοῦ Ἀρχιεπισκόπου ἡμῶν (τοῦ δεῖνος), τοῦ τιμίου πρεσβυτερίου, τῆς ἐν Χριστῷ διακονίας, παντὸς τοῦ κλήρου καὶ τοῦ λαοῦ, τοῦ Κυρίου δεηθῶμεν.

Ὑπὲρ τοῦ ἁγιασθῆναι τὸ ὕδωρ τοῦτο, τῇ ἐπιφοιτήσει καὶ δυνάμει καὶ ἐνεργείᾳ τοῦ Ἁγίου Πνεύματος, τοῦ Κυρίου δεηθῶμεν.

Ὑπὲρ τοῦ καταπεμφθῆναι αὐτῷ τὴν χάριν τῆς ἀπολυτρώσεως, τὴν εὐλογίαν τοῦ Ἰορδάνου, τοῦ Κυρίου δεηθῶμεν.

Ὑπὲρ τοῦ καταφοιτῆσαι τοῖς ὕδασι τούτοις τὴν καθαρτικὴν τῆς ὑπερουσίου Τριάδος ἐνέργειαν, τοῦ Κυρίου δεηθῶμεν.

Ὑπὲρ τοῦ φωτισθῆναι ἡμᾶς φωτισμὸν γνώσεως καὶ εὐσεβείας, διὰ τῆς ἐπιφοιτήσεως τοῦ ἁγίου Πνεύματος, τοῦ Κυρίου δεηθῶμεν.

Ὑπὲρ τοῦ ἀναδειχθῆναι τὸ ὕδωρ τοῦτο ἀποτρόπαιον πάσης ἐπιβουλῆς ὁρατῶν καὶ ἀοράτων ἐχθρῶν, τοῦ Κυρίου δεηθῶμεν.

Ὑπὲρ τοῦ ἄξιον γενέσθαι τῆς ἀφθάρτου βασιλείας τὸν ἐν αὐτῷ βαπτιζόμενον, τοῦ Κυρίου δεηθῶμεν.

Ὑπὲρ τοῦ νῦν προσερχομένου τῷ ἁγίῳ Φωτίσματι καὶ τῆς σωτηρίας αὐτοῦ, τοῦ Κυρίου δεηθῶμεν.

Ὑπὲρ τοῦ ἀναδειχθῆναι αὐτὸν υἱὸν φωτὸς καὶ κληρονόμον τῶν αἰωνίων ἀγαθῶν, τοῦ Κυρίου δεηθῶμεν.

For the peace of the whole world; for the stability of the holy Churches of God, and for the union of all; let us pray to the Lord.

For this holy House, and for them that with faith, reverence, and the fear of God enter therein; let us pray to the Lord.

For our Most Reverend Archbishop (*Name*), for the venerable Priesthood, the Diaconate in Christ; for all the Clergy, and for all the people; let us pray to the Lord.

That this water may be hallowed by the might, and operation, and descent of the Holy Spirit; let us pray to the Lord.

That there may be sent down upon it the Grace of Redemption, the blessing of the Jordan; let us pray to the Lord.

That there may come down upon this water the cleansing operation of the Supersubstantial Trinity; let us pray to the Lord.

That we may be illumined with the Light of Knowledge and Piety through the descent of the Holy Spirit; let us pray to the Lord.

That this water may prove effectual for the averting of every plot of visible and invisible enemies; let us pray to the Lord.

That he (she) that is about to be baptized herein may become worthy of the incorruptible Kingdom; let us pray to the Lord.

That he (she) that now comes to holy Illumination, and for his (her) salvation; let us pray to the Lord.

That he (she) may prove to be a child of Light, and an inheritor of eternal blessings; let us pray to the Lord.

Ὑπὲρ τοῦ γενέσθαι αὐτὸν σύμφυτον καὶ κοινωνὸν τοῦ θανάτου καὶ τῆς ἀναστάσεως Χριστοῦ τοῦ Θεοῦ ἡμῶν, τοῦ Κυρίου δεηθῶμεν.

Ὑπὲρ τοῦ διαφυλαχθῆναι αὐτῷ τὴν στολὴν τοῦ Βαπτίσματος, καὶ τὸν ἀρραβῶνα τοῦ Πνεύματος, ἄσπιλον καὶ ἀμώμητον ἐν τῇ ἡμέρᾳ τῇ φοβερᾷ Χριστοῦ τοῦ Θεοῦ ἡμῶν, τοῦ Κυρίου δεηθῶμεν.

Ὑπὲρ τοῦ γενέσθαι αὐτῷ τὸ ὕδωρ τοῦτο λουτρὸν παλιγγενεσίας, εἰς ἄφεσιν ἁμαρτιῶν, καὶ ἔνδυμα ἀφθαρσίας, τοῦ Κυρίου δεηθῶμεν.

Ὑπὲρ τοῦ εἰσακοῦσαι Κύριον τὸν Θεὸν φωνῆς τῆς δεήσεως ἡμῶν, τοῦ Κυρίου δεηθῶμεν.

Ὑπὲρ τοῦ ῥυσθῆναι αὐτόν τε καὶ ἡμᾶς ἀπὸ πάσης θλίψεως, ὀργῆς, κινδύνου καὶ ἀνάγκης, τοῦ Κυρίου δεηθῶμεν.

Ἀντιλαβοῦ, σῶσον, ἐλέησον, καὶ διαφύλαξον ἡμᾶς, ὁ Θεός, τῇ σῇ χάριτι.

Τῆς Παναγίας, ἀχράντου, ὑπερευλογημένης, ἐνδόξου δεσποίνης ἡμῶν Θεοτόκου, καὶ ἀειπαρθένου Μαρίας μετὰ πάντων τῶν ἁγίων μνημονεύσαντες, ἑαυτοὺς καὶ ἀλλήλους, καὶ πᾶσαν τὴν ζωὴν ἡμῶν Χριστῷ τῷ Θεῷ παραθώμεθα.

Καὶ τοῦ Διακόνου λέγοντος ταῦτα, ὁ Ἱερεὺς λέγει καθ' ἑαυτὸν τὴν Ε ὐ χ ὴ ν ταύτην μυστικῶς.

Τοῦ Κυρίου δεηθῶμεν.

Ο῾ εὔσπλαγχνος καὶ ἐλεήμων Θεός, ὁ ἐτάζων καρδίας καὶ νεφρούς, καὶ τὰ κρύφια τῶν ἀνθρώπων ἐπιστάμενος μόνος· οὐ γάρ ἐστι πρᾶγμα ἀφανὲς ἐνώπιόν σου, ἀλλὰ πάντα γυμνὰ καὶ τετραχηλισμένα τοῖς ὀφθαλμοῖς σου· ὁ γινώσκων τὰ κατ' ἐμέ, μὴ βδελύξῃ με, μηδὲ τὸ πρόσωπόν σου ἀποστρέψῃς ἀπ' ἐμοῦ, ἀλλὰ πάριδέ μου τὰ παρα-

That he (she) may grow in, and become a partaker of the Death and Resurrection of Christ our God; let us pray to the Lord.

That he (she) may preserve the garment of Baptism, and the earnest of the Spirit undefiled and blameless in the terrible Day of Christ our God; let us pray to the Lord.

That this water may be for him (her) a laver of Regeneration unto the remission of sins, and a garment of incorruption; let us pray to the Lord.

That the Lord may listen to the voice of our prayer; let us pray to the Lord.

That He may deliver him (her) and us from tribulation, wrath, danger, and necessity; let us pray to the Lord.

Help us; save us; have mercy on us; and keep us, O God, by Your Grace.

Calling to remembrance our all-holy, pure, exceedingly blessed glorious Lady Theotokos and Ever-Virgin Mary, with all the Saints; let us commend ourselves and one another and all our life to Christ our God.

Priest (inaudibly)

Let us pray to the Lord.

O compassionate and merciful God, Who tries the heart and reigns, and Who alone knows the secrets of men, for no deed is secret in Your sight, but all things are exposed and naked in Your eyesight: do You Yourself, Who perceives that which concerns me, neither turn away Your face from me, but overlook my offenses in this hour, O You that

πτώματα ἐν τῇ ὥρᾳ ταύτῃ, ὁ παρορῶν ἀνθρώπων ἁμαρτήματα εἰς μετάνοιαν, καὶ ἀπόπλυνόν μου τὸν ῥύπον τοῦ σώματος, καὶ τὸν σπίλον τῆς ψυχῆς, καὶ ὅλον με ἁγίασον ὁλοτελῆ τῇ δυνάμει σου τῇ ἀοράτῳ καὶ πνευματικῇ δεξιᾷ· ἵνα μή, ἐλευθερίαν ἄλλοις ἐπαγγελλόμενος καὶ ταύτην παρέχων πίστει τῇ ἠρτημένῃ τῆς σῆς ἀφάτου φιλανθρωπίας, αὐτὸς ὡς δοῦλος ἁμαρτίας ἀδόκιμος γένωμαι. Μή, Δέσποτα, ὁ μόνος ἀγαθὸς καὶ φιλάνθρωπος, μὴ ἀποστραφείην τεταπεινωμένος καὶ κατῃσχυμένος· ἀλλ' ἐξαπόστειλόν μοι δύναμιν ἐξ ὕψους, καὶ ἐνίσχυσόν με πρὸς τὴν διακονίαν τοῦ προκειμένου σου Μυστηρίου, τοῦ μεγάλου καὶ ἐπουρανίου. Καὶ μόρφωσόν σου τὸν Χριστὸν ἐν τῷ μέλλοντι ἀναγεννᾶσθαι διὰ τῆς ἐμῆς ἐλεεινότητος· καὶ οἰκοδόμησον αὐτὸν ἐν τῷ θεμελίῳ τῶν Ἀποστόλων καὶ Προφητῶν σου· καὶ μὴ καθέλῃς, ἀλλὰ φύτευσον αὐτὸν φύτευμα ἀληθείας ἐν τῇ ἁγίᾳ σου Καθολικῇ καὶ Ἀποστολικῇ Ἐκκλησίᾳ, καὶ μὴ ἐκτίλῃς. Ὅπως προκόπτοντος αὐτοῦ ἐν εὐσεβείᾳ, δοξάζηται καὶ δι' αὐτοῦ τὸ πανάγιον ὄνομά σου, τοῦ Πατρός, καὶ τοῦ Υἱοῦ, καὶ τοῦ Ἁγίου Πνεύματος, νῦν καὶ ἀεὶ καὶ εἰς τοὺς αἰῶνας τῶν αἰώνων. Ἀμήν.

Δεῖ δὲ εἰδέναι, ὅτι καθ' ἑαυτὸν λέγει καὶ τὴν Ἐκφώνησιν καὶ τό, Ἀμήν.

Μετὰ δὲ τὸ συμπληρωθῆναι τὰ Εἰρηνικά, ἄνευ Ἐκφωνήσεως, λέγει ὁ Ἱερεὺς τὴν Εὐχὴν ταύτην μεγαλοφώνως καὶ μετὰ φόβου Θεοῦ καὶ ἐξ ὅλης ψυχῆς καὶ συντετριμμένης καρδίας.

Μ έγας εἶ, Κύριε, καὶ θαυμαστὰ τὰ ἔργα σου, καὶ οὐδεὶς λόγος ἐξαρκέσει πρὸς ὕμνον τῶν θαυμασίων σου . Σὺ γὰρ βουλήσει ἐξ οὐκ ὄντων εἰς τὸ εἶναι παραγαγὼν τὰ σύμπαντα, τῷ σῷ κράτει συνέχεις τὴν κτίσιν, καὶ τῇ σῇ προνοίᾳ διοικεῖς τὸν

overlook the sins of men that they repent. Wash away the defilement of my body and the stain of my soul. Sanctify me wholly by Your all-effectual, invisible might, and by Your spiritual right hand, lest, by preaching liberty to others, and offering this in the perfect faith of Your unspeakable love for humankind, I may be condemned as a servant of sin. Nay, Sovereign Master that alone are good and loving, let me not be turned away humbled and shamed, but send forth to me power from on high, and strengthen me for the ministration of this Your present, great, and most heavenly Mystery. Form the Image of Your Christ in him (her) who is about to be born again through my humility. Build him (her) on the foundation of Your Apostles and Prophets. Cast him (her) not down, but plant him (her) as a plant of truth in Your Holy, Catholic, and Apostolic Church. Pluck him (her) not out, that, by his (her) advancing in piety, by the same may be glorified Your Most Holy Name, of Father, and of Son, and of Holy Spirit, both now and ever, and to the ages of ages. Amen.

The Priest reads aloud:

The Blessing of the Baptismal Waters

Great are You, O Lord, and wondrous are Your works, and no word will suffice to hymn Your wonders. (3) For by Your Will have You out of nothingness brought all things into being and by Your power sustain all creation,

κόσμον. Σὺ ἐκ τεσσάρων στοιχείων τὴν κτίσιν συναρμόσας, τέτταρσι καιροῖς τὸν κύκλον τοῦ ἐνιαυτοῦ ἐστεφάνωσας. Σὲ τρέμουσιν αἱ νοεραὶ πᾶσαι Δυνάμεις· σὲ ὑμνεῖ ἥλιος· σὲ δοξάζει σελήνη· σοὶ ἐντυγχάνει τὰ ἄστρα· σοὶ ὑπακούει τὸ φῶς· σὲ φρίττουσιν ἄβυσσοι· σοὶ δουλεύουσιν αἱ πηγαί. Σὺ ἐξέτεινας τὸν οὐρανὸν ὡσεὶ δέρριν· σὺ ἐστερέωσας τὴν γῆν ἐπὶ τῶν ὑδάτων· σὺ περιετείχισας τὴν θάλασσαν ψάμμῳ· σὺ πρὸς ἀναπνοὰς τὸν ἀέρα ἐξέχεας. Ἀγγελικαὶ Δυνάμεις σοὶ λειτουργοῦσιν, οἱ τῶν Ἀρχαγγέλων χοροὶ σὲ προσκυνοῦσι, τὰ πολυόμματα Χερουβίμ, καὶ τὰ ἐξαπτέρυγα Σεραφίμ, κύκλῳ ἑστῶτα, καὶ περιϊπτάμενα, φόβῳ τῆς ἀπροσίτου σου δόξης κατακαλύπτεται. Σὺ γάρ, Θεὸς ὢν ἀπερίγραπτος ἄναρχός τε καὶ ἀνέκφραστος, ἦλθες ἐπὶ τῆς γῆς, μορφὴν δούλου λαβών, ἐν ὁμοιώματι ἀνθρώπων γενόμενος· οὐ γὰρ ἔφερες, Δέσποτα, διὰ σπλάγχνα ἐλέους σου, θεᾶσθαι ὑπὸ τοῦ διαβόλου τυραννούμενον τὸ γένος τῶν ἀνθρώπων, ἀλλ᾽ ἦλθες καὶ ἔσωσας ἡμᾶς. Ὁμολογοῦμεν τὴν χάριν, κηρύττομεν τὸν ἔλεον, οὐ κρύπτομεν τὴν εὐεργεσίαν. Τὰς τῆς φύσεως ἡμῶν γονὰς ἠλευθέρωσας, παρθενικὴν ἡγίασας μήτραν τῷ τόκῳ σου, πᾶσα ἡ κτίσις ὕμνησέ σε ἐπιφανέντα. Σὺ γάρ, ὁ Θεὸς ἡμῶν, ἐπὶ τῆς γῆς ὤφθης καὶ τοῖς ἀνθρώποις συνανεστράφης· Σὺ καὶ τὰ Ἰορδάνεια ῥεῖθρα ἡγίασας, οὐρανόθεν καταπέμψας αὐτοῖς τὸ Πανάγιόν σου Πνεῦμα, καὶ τὰς κεφαλὰς τῶν ἐκεῖσε ἐμφωλευόντων συνέτριψας δρακόντων. Αὐτὸς οὖν, φιλάνθρωπε Βασιλεῦ, πάρεσο καὶ νῦν διὰ τῆς ἐπιφοιτήσεως τοῦ Ἁγίου σου Πνεύματος καὶ ἁγίασον τὸ ὕδωρ τοῦτο (τρίς). Καὶ δὸς αὐτῷ τὴν χάριν τῆς ἀπολυτρώσεως, τὴν εὐλογίαν τοῦ Ἰορδάνου. Ποίησον αὐτὸ ἀφθαρσίας πηγήν, ἁγιασμοῦ δῶρον, ἁμαρτημάτων λυτήριον, νοσημά-

and by Your Providence direct the world. You from the four elements have formed creation and have crowned the cycle of the year with the four seasons; all the spiritual powers tremble before You; the sun praises You; the moon glorifies You; the stars in their courses meet with You; the Light hearkens unto You; the depths shudder at Your presence; the springs of water serve You; You have stretched out the Heavens as a curtain; You have founded the earth upon the waters; You have bounded the sea with sand; You have poured forth the air for breathing; the angelic Powers minister unto You; the Choirs of Archangels worship before You; the many-eyed Cherubim and the six-winged Seraphim, as they stand and fly around You, veil themselves with fear of Your unapproachable Glory; for You, being boundless and beginningless and unutterable, did come down on earth, taking the form of a servant, being made in the likeness of men; for You, O Master, through the tenderness of Your Mercy, could not endure the race of men tormented by the devil, but You did come and saved us. We confess Your Grace; we proclaim Your benificence; we do not hide Your Mercy; You have set at liberty the generations of our nature; You did hallow the virginal Womb by Your Birth; all creation praises You, Who did manifest Yourself, for You were seen upon the earth, and did sojourn with men. You hallowed the streams of Jordan, sending down from the Heavens Your Holy Spirit, and crushed the heads of dragons that lurked therein. DO YOU YOURSELF, O LOVING KING, BE PRESENT NOW ALSO THROUGH THE DESCENT OF YOUR HOLY SPIRIT AND HALLOW THIS WATER (3). And give to it the Grace of Redemption, the Blessing of Jordan. Make it a fountain of incorruption, a gift of sanctification, a loosing

των ἀλεξιτήριον, δαίμοσιν ὀλέθριον, ταῖς ἐναντίαις δυνάμεσιν ἀπρόσιτον, ἀγγελικῆς ἰσχύος πεπληρωμένον. Φυγέτωσαν ἀπ' αὐτοῦ οἱ ἐπιβουλεύοντες τῷ πλάσματί σου· ὅτι τὸ ὄνομά σου, Κύριε, ἐπεκαλεσάμην, τὸ θαυμαστὸν καὶ ἔνδοξον καὶ φοβερὸν τοῖς ὑπεναντίοις.

Καὶ ἐμφυσᾷ εἰς τὸ ὕδωρ τρίς· καὶ σφραγίζει τῇ δεξιᾷ τρίτον καὶ ἐπεύχεται, λέγων·

Συντριβήτωσαν ὑπὸ τὴν σημείωσιν τοῦ τύπου τοῦ τιμίου Σταυροῦ σου πᾶσαι αἱ ἐναντίαι δυνάμεις (τρίς). Ὑποχωρησάτωσαν ἡμῖν πάντα τὰ ἐναέρια καὶ ἀφανῆ εἴδωλα, καὶ μὴ ὑποκρυβήτω τῷ ὕδατι τούτῳ δαιμόνιον σκοτεινόν, μηδὲ συγκαταβήτω τῷ βαπτιζομένῳ, δεόμεθά σου, Κύριε, πνεῦμα πονηρόν, σκότωσιν λογισμῶν καὶ ταραχὴν διανοίας ἐπάγον. Ἀλλὰ σύ, Δέσποτα τῶν ἁπάντων, ἀνάδειξον τὸ ὕδωρ τοῦτο, ὕδωρ ἀπολυτρώσεως, ὕδωρ ἁγιασμοῦ, καθαρισμὸν σαρκὸς καὶ πνεύματος, ἄνεσιν δεσμῶν, ἄφεσιν παραπτωμάτων, φωτισμὸν ψυχῆς, λουτρὸν παλλιγγενεσίας, ἀνακαινισμὸν πνεύματος, υἱοθεσίας χάρισμα, ἔνδυμα ἀφθαρσίας, πηγὴν ζωῆς. Σὺ γὰρ εἶπας, Κύριε· Λούσασθε, καὶ καθαροὶ γίνεσθε, ἀφέλετε τὰς πονηρίας ἀπὸ τῶν ψυχῶν ὑμῶν. Σὺ ἐχαρίσω ἡμῖν τὴν ἄνωθεν ἀναγέννησιν, δι' ὕδατος καὶ Πνεύματος. Ἐπιφάνηθι, Κύριε, τούτῳ· καὶ δὸς μεταποιηθῆναι τὸν ἐν αὐτῷ βαπτιζόμενον, εἰς τὸ ἀποθέσθαι μὲν τὸν παλαιὸν ἄνθρωπον, τὸν φθειρόμενον κατὰ τὰς ἐπιθυμίας τῆς ἀπάτης, ἐνδύσασθαι δὲ τὸν νέον, τὸν ἀνακαινούμενον κατ' εἰκόνα τοῦ κτίσαντος αὐτόν· ἵνα, γενόμενος σύμφυτος τῷ ὁμοιώματι τοῦ θανάτου σου διὰ τοῦ Βαπτίσματος, κοινωνὸς καὶ τῆς ἀναστάσεώς σου γένηται· καὶ φυλάξας τὴν δωρεὰν τοῦ Ἁγίου σου Πνεύματος καὶ αὐξήσας τὴν παρακαταθήκην τῆς χάριτος, δέ-

of sins, a healing of sicknesses, a destruction of demons, unapproachable by hostile powers, filled with angelic might; and let them that take counsel together against Your creature flee therefrom, for I have called upon Your Name, O Lord, which is wonderful, and glorious, and terrible unto adversaries.

And he signs the water thrice, dipping his fingers in it; and breathing upon it, he says:

LET ALL ADVERSE POWERS BE CRUSHED BENEATH THE SIGNING OF YOUR MOST PRECIOUS CROSS (3). We pray You, O Lord, let every airy and invisible spectre withdraw itself from us, and let not a demon of darkness conceal himself in this water; neither let an evil spirit, bringing obscurity of purpose and rebellious thoughts, descend into it with him (her) that is about to be baptized. But do You, O Master of All, declare this water to be water of redemption, water of sanctification, a cleansing of flesh and spirit, a loosing of bonds, a forgiveness of sins, an illumination of soul, a laver of regeneration, a renewal of the spirit, a gift of sonship, a garment of incorruption, a fountain of life. For You have said, O Lord: "Wash, and be clean; put away evil from your souls." You have bestowed upon us regeneration from on high by water and the spirit. Manifest Yourself, O Lord, in this water, and grant that he (she) that is to be baptized may be transformed therein to the putting away of the old man, which is corrupt according to the deceitful lusts, and to the putting on of the new, which is renewed according to the Image of Him that created him (her). That, being planted in the likeness of Your death through Baptism, he (she) may become a sharer of Your Resurrection; and, preserving the Gift of Your Holy Spirit, and increasing the deposit of Grace, he (she) may attain unto prize of his

ξηται τὸ βραβεῖον τῆς ἄνω κλήσεως, καὶ συγκαταριθμηθῇ τοῖς πρωτοτόκοις, τοῖς ἀπογεγραμμένοις ἐν οὐρανῷ, ἐν σοὶ τῷ Θεῷ καὶ Κυρίῳ ἡμῶν Ἰησοῦ Χριστῷ. Ὅτι σοὶ πρέπει δόξα, κράτος, τιμὴ καὶ προσκύνησις, ἅμα τῷ ἀνάρχῳ σου Πατρί, καὶ τῷ παναγίῳ καὶ ἀγαθῷ καὶ ζωοποιῷ σου Πνεύματι, νῦν καὶ ἀεὶ καὶ εἰς τοὺς αἰῶνας τῶν αἰώνων.

Ὁ Χορός· Ἀμήν.

Ὁ Ἱερεύς· Εἰρήνη πᾶσι.

Ὁ Χορός· Καὶ τῷ πνεύματί σου.

Ὁ Διάκονος

Τὰς κεφαλὰς ἡμῶν τῷ Κυρίῳ κλίνωμεν.

Ὁ Χορός· Σοὶ Κύριε.

Καὶ ἐμφυσᾷ ὁ Ἱερεὺς εἰς τὸ ἀγγεῖον τοῦ ἐλαίου, βασταζόμενον ὑπὸ τοῦ Διακόνου καὶ σφραγίζει διὰ τῆς χειρὸς τρὶς τοῦτο, ἤτοι τὸ ἔλαιον.

Τοῦ Κυρίου δεηθῶμεν.

Ὁ Χορός. Κύριε, ἐλέησον

ΕΥΧΗ ΤΟΥ ΕΛΑΙΟΥ

Δέσποτα, Κύριε, ὁ Θεὸς τῶν Πατέρων ἡμῶν, ὁ τοῖς ἐν τῇ κιβωτῷ τοῦ Νῶε περιστερὰν ἀποστείλας, κάρφος ἐλαίας ἔχουσαν ἐπὶ τοῦ στόματος, καταλλαγῆς σύμβολον, σωτηρίας τε τῆς ἀπὸ τοῦ κατακλυσμοῦ, καὶ τὸ τῆς χάριτος μυστήριον δι᾽ ἐκείνων προτυπώσας· ὁ καὶ τῆς ἐλαίας τὸν καρπὸν εἰς πλήρωσιν τῶν ἁγίων σου Μυστηρίων χορηγήσας, ὁ δι᾽ αὐτοῦ καὶ τοὺς ἐν νόμῳ Πνεύματος Ἁγίου πληρώσας καὶ τοὺς ἐν χάριτι τελειῶν· Αὐτὸς εὐλόγησον καὶ

(her) high calling, and accounted among the number of the first-born, whose names are written in Heaven, in You our God and Lord Jesus Christ, to Whom be all Glory and Might, together with Your Eternal Father and with Your All-Holy, Good, and Life-creating Spirit, both now and ever, and to the ages of ages.

Choir: Amen.

Priest: Peace be to all. (+)

Choir: And to your spirit.

Priest

Let us bow our heads before the Lord.

Choir: To You, O Lord.

The Priest breathes thrice upon the Oil and signs it thrice, while it is held by the Godparent.

Priest

Let us pray to the Lord. Lord have mercy.

The Blessing of the Oil

Sovereign Lord and Master, God of our Fathers, Who did send to them in the Ark of Noah a dove bearing a twig of olive in its beak as a sign of reconciliation and salvation from the Flood, and through these things prefigured the Mystery of Grace; and thereby have filled them that were under the Law with the Holy Spirit, and perfected them that are under Grace: do You Yourself bless this Oil

τοῦτο τὸ ἔλαιον, τῇ δυνάμει καὶ ἐνεργείᾳ καὶ ἐπιφοιτήσει τοῦ Ἁγίου σου Πνεύματος, ὥστε γενέσθαι αὐτὸ χρίσμα ἀφθαρσίας, ὅπλον δικαιοσύνης, ἀνακαινισμὸς ψυχῆς καὶ σώματος, πάσης διαβολικῆς ἐνεργείας ἀποτρόπαιον, εἰς ἀπαλλαγὴν κακῶν, πᾶσι τοῖς χριομένοις αὐτὸ ἐν πίστει, ἢ καὶ μεταλαμβάνουσιν ἐξ αὐτοῦ.

Εἰς δόξαν σήν, καὶ τοῦ μονογενοῦς σου Υἱοῦ, καὶ τοῦ παναγίου καὶ ἀγαθοῦ καὶ ζωοποιοῦ σου Πνεύματος, νῦν καὶ ἀεὶ καὶ εἰς τοὺς αἰῶνας τῶν αἰώνων.

Ὁ Χορός· Ἀμήν.

Ὁ Διάκονος· Πρόσχωμεν.

Ὁ δὲ Ἱερεύς, λαβὼν τὸ ἀγγεῖον τοῦ ἐλαίου καταχέει ἐξ αὐτοῦ ἐν τῇ κολυμβήθρᾳ, ποιῶν σταυροὺς γ΄ καὶ ψάλλων ἐν ἑκάστῳ σταυρῷ τὸ Ἀλληλούϊα (γ΄).

Εἶτα ἐκφωνεῖ·
Εὐλογητὸς ὁ Θεός, ὁ φωτίζων καὶ ἁγιάζων πάντα ἄνθρωπον, ἐρχόμενον εἰς τὸν κόσμον, νῦν καὶ ἀεὶ καὶ εἰς τοὺς αἰῶνας τῶν αἰώνων.

Ὁ Χορός· Ἀμήν.

Καὶ προσφέρεται ὁ βαπτιζόμενος. Ὁ δὲ Ἱερεὺς λαμβάνει ἐκ τοῦ ἁγίου ἐλαίου διὰ τῶν τριῶν δακτύλων τῆς δεξιᾶς καὶ ποιεῖ Σταυροῦ τύπον ἐπὶ τοῦ μετώπου, καὶ τοῦ στήθους, καὶ τῶν μεταφρένων τοῦ βαπτιζομένου, λέγων.

Χρίεται ὁ δοῦλος τοῦ Θεοῦ (ὁ δεῖνα), ἔλαιον ἀγαλλιάσεως, εἰς τὸ ὄνομα τοῦ Πατρός, καὶ τοῦ Υἱοῦ, καὶ τοῦ Ἁγίου Πνεύματος. Ἀμήν.

Καὶ σφραγίζων αὐτοῦ τὰ στῆθος καὶ τὰ μετάφρενα, λέγει·

Εἰς μὲν τὸ στῆθος·
Εἰς ἴασιν ψυχῆς καὶ σώματος.

by the power (+) and operation (+) and descent of the Holy Spirit (+) that it may become an anointing of incorruption, a shield of righteousness, a renewal of soul and body, and averting of every operation of the devil, to the removal of all evils from them that are anointed with it in faith, or that are partakers of it.

To Your Glory, and to that of Your Only-Begotten Son, and of Your All-Holy, Good, and Life-creating Spirit, both now and ever, and to the ages of ages.

Choir: Amen.

Priest: Let us attend.

The Priest, singing Alleluia thrice with the people, makes three Crosses with the Oil upon the water.

Alleluia, alleluia, alleluia.

Blessed is God that enlightens and sanctifies every man that comes into the world, both now and ever, and to the ages of ages.

Choir: Amen.

The Priest pours some Oil into the hands of the Godparent. He then takes Oil and makes the Sign of the Cross on the child's forehead, breast, and between his (her) shoulders, saying:

The servant of God (*Name*) is anointed with the Oil of Gladness, in the Name of the Father, and of the Son, and of the Holy Spirit, both now and ever, and to the ages of ages. Amen.

And he signs his (her) breast and between his (her) shoulders, saying:

For healing of soul and body.

Εἰς δὲ τὰς ἀκοάς·

Εἰς ἀκοὴν πίστεως.

Εἰς τοὺς πόδας·

Τοῦ πορεύεσθαι τὰ διαβήματά σου.

Εἰς τὰς χεῖρας·

Αἱ χεῖρές σου ἐποίησάν με, καὶ ἔπλασάν με.

Καὶ ὅταν χρισθῇ ἐκ τοῦ ἐλαίου ὅλον τὸ σῶμα ὑπὸ τοῦ Ἀναδόχου, βαπτίζει αὐτὸν ὁ Ἱερεύς, ὄρθιον αὐτὸν κατέχων καὶ βλέποντα κατὰ ἀνατολὰς καὶ λέγων.

Βαπτίζεται ὁ δοῦλος τοῦ Θεοῦ (ὁ δεῖνα) εἰς τὸ ὄνομα τοῦ Πατρός, Ἀμήν· καὶ τοῦ Υἱοῦ, Ἀμήν· καὶ τοῦ Ἁγίου Πνεύματος, Ἀμήν, (ἑκάστῃ προσρήσει κατάγων αὐτὸν καὶ ἀνάγων).

Καὶ λούει αὐτοῦ ὁ Ἱερεύς, ὅλον τὸ σῶμα καλῶς.

Εἶτα λαμβάνει αὐτὸν ὁ Ἀνάδοχος ἐκ τῆς ἁγίας Κολυμβήθρας διὰ τῶν χειρῶν τοῦ Ἱερέως ὑπτίαις χερσί, σαβάνου [σινδονίου] λευκοῦ πρότερον ἐφαπλωθέντος ἐν ταῖς χερσίν.

Ὁ Χορὸς ψάλλει·

Ψαλμὸς λα΄ (31)

Μακάριοι, ὧν ἀφέθησαν αἱ ἀνομίαι, καὶ ὧν ἐπεκαλύφθησαν αἱ ἁμαρτίαι (ἐκ γ΄). Μακάριος ἀνήρ, ᾧ οὐ μὴ λογίσηται Κύριος ἁμαρτίαν, οὐδέ ἐστιν ἐν τῷ στόματι αὐτοῦ δόλος. Ὅτι ἐσίγησα, ἐπαλαιώθη τὰ ὀστᾶ μου, ἀπὸ τοῦ κράζειν με ὅλην τὴν ἡμέραν. Ὅτι ἡμέρας καὶ νυκτὸς ἐβαρύνθη ἐπ᾽ ἐμὲ ἡ χείρ σου, ἐστράφην εἰς ταλαιπωρίαν ἐν τῷ ἐμπαγῆναί μοι ἄκανθαν. Τὴν ἀνομίαν μου ἐγνώρισα καὶ τὴν ἁμαρτίαν μου οὐκ ἐκάλυψα. Εἶπα· Ἐξαγορεύσω κατ᾽ ἐμοῦ τὴν ἀνομίαν μου τῷ Κυρίῳ, καὶ σὺ ἀφῆκας τὴν ἀσέβειαν τῆς καρδίας μου. Ὑπὲρ ταύτης προσεύξεται

And on the ears, saying:

For the hearing of Faith.

And on the feet, saying:

That he (she) may walk in the paths of Your commandments.

And on the hands, saying:

Your hands have made me, and fashioned me.

The Baptizing

When he has anointed the whole body, the Priest baptizes him (her), holding him (her) erect, and looking towards the East, says:

The servant of God (*Name*) is baptized in the Name of the Father. Amen. And of the Son, Amen. And of the Holy Spirit, Amen.

At each invocation the Priest immerses him (her) and raises him (her) up again.

After the baptizing, the Priest places the child in a linen sheet held by the Godparent.

The Choir sings:

Psalm 31

Blessed are they whose iniquities are forgiven, and whose sins are covered. (3) Blessed is the man whom the Lord imputes not sin, and in whose mouth there is no guile. Because I have kept silence, my bones waxed old through my crying all the day long. For day and night Your hand was heavy on me. I was turned into lowliness while the thorn was fastened in me. My sin I have acknowledged, and my iniquity I have not hid. I said,"I will confess against myself my sin unto the Lord." And You forgave the ungodliness of my heart. For this shall everyone who is holy pray

πρὸς σὲ πᾶς ὅσιος, ἐν καιρῷ εὐθέτῳ. Πλὴν ἐν κατακλυσμῷ ὑδάτων πολλῶν, πρὸς αὐτὸν οὐκ ἐγγιοῦσι. Σύ μου εἶ καταφυγὴ ἀπὸ θλίψεως τῆς περιεχούσης με· τὸ ἀγαλλίαμά μου, λύτρωσαί με ἀπὸ τῶν κυκλωσάντων με. Συνετιῶ σε καὶ συμβιβῶ σε ἐν ὁδῷ ταύτῃ ᾗ πορεύσῃ, ἐπιστηριῶ ἐπὶ σὲ τοὺς ὀφθαλμούς μου. Μὴ γίνεσθε ὡς ἵππος καὶ ἡμίονος, οἷς οὐκ ἔστι σύνεσις· ἐν κημῷ καὶ χαλινῷ τὰς σιαγόνας αὐτῶν ἄγξαις, τῶν μὴ ἐγγιζόντων πρὸς σέ. Πολλαὶ αἱ μάστιγες τοῦ ἁμαρτωλοῦ, τὸν δὲ ἐλπίζοντα ἐπὶ Κύριον ἔλεος κυκλώσει. Εὐφράνθητε ἐπὶ Κύριον καὶ ἀγαλλιᾶσθε, δίκαιοι, καὶ καυχᾶσθε πάντες οἱ εὐθεῖς τῇ καρδίᾳ.

Καὶ μετὰ τοῦτο λέγει ὁ Ἱερεὺς τὴν Εὐχὴν ταύτην·

Τοῦ Κυρίου δεηθῶμεν.

Ὁ Χορός, **Κύριε, ἐλέησον.**

ΕΥΧΗ ΤΟΥ ΜΥΡΟΥ

Εὐλογητὸς εἶ, Κύριε, ὁ Θεὸς ὁ Παντοκράτωρ, ἡ πηγὴ τῶν ἀγαθῶν, ὁ ἥλιος τῆς δικαιοσύνης, ὁ λάμψας τοῖς ἐν σκότει φῶς σωτηρίας, διὰ τῆς ἐπιφανείας τοῦ μονογενοῦς σου Υἱοῦ καὶ Θεοῦ ἡμῶν καὶ χαρισάμενος ἡμῖν τοῖς ἀναξίοις τὴν μακαρίαν κάθαρσιν ἐν τῷ ἁγίῳ Βαπτίσματι, καὶ τὸν θεῖον ἁγιασμὸν ἐν τῷ ζωοποιῷ χρίσματι· ὁ καὶ νῦν εὐδοκήσας ἀναγεννῆσαι τὸν δοῦλόν σου τὸν νεοφώτιστον δι' ὕδατος καὶ Πνεύματος, καὶ τὴν τῶν ἑκουσίων καὶ ἀκουσίων ἁμαρτημάτων ἄφεσιν αὐτῷ δωρησάμενος· Αὐτὸς οὖν, Δέσποτα παμβασιλεῦ εὔσπλαγχνε, χάρισαι αὐτῷ καὶ τὴν σφραγῖδα τῆς δωρεᾶς τοῦ ἁγίου καὶ παντοδυνάμου, καὶ προσκυνητοῦ σου Πνεύματος,

to You in a seasonable time; moreover in a flood of many waters shall the billows not come nigh to him. For You are my refuge from the tribulation which surrounds me. O my rejoicing, deliver me from them that have encircled me. The Lord says: "I will give you understanding, and will teach you in this My way which you shall go; I will fix My eyes on you. Be not as the horse, or as the mule, which have no understanding. With bit and bridle would you bind their jaws; lest they come near to you." Many are the scourges of the sinner, but with mercy shall I encircle them that hope on the Lord. Be glad in the Lord, and rejoice, you righteous; and shout for joy, all you that are upright of heart.

The Priest says the Prayer of Confirmation.

Let us pray to the Lord.

Choir: Lord have mercy.

The Prayer of Confirmation

Blessed are You, Lord God Almighty, Fountain of Blessings, Sun of Righteousness, Who made to shine forth for those in darkness a light of salvation through the manifestation of Your Only-Begotten Son and our God, granting unto us, though we are unworthy, blessed cleansing in Holy Water, and divine sanctification in the Life-effecting Anointing; Who now also has been well-pleased to regenerate this Your servant newly illuminated through Water and Spirit, giving him (her) forgiveness of his (her) voluntary and involuntary sins: do You Yourself, Sovereign Master, Compassionate King of All, bestow upon him (her) also the Seal of Your omnipotent and adorable Holy Spirit, and the

καὶ τὴν μετάληψιν τοῦ ἁγίου Σώματος, καὶ τοῦ τιμίου Αἵματος τοῦ Χριστοῦ σου. Φύλαξον αὐτὸν ἐν
τῷ σῷ ἁγιασμῷ· βεβαίωσον ἐν τῇ Ὀρθοδόξῳ πίστει·
ῥῦσαι ἀπὸ τοῦ πονηροῦ, καὶ πάντων τῶν ἐπιτηδευ-
μάτων αὐτοῦ, καὶ τῷ σωτηρίῳ σου φόβῳ, ἐν ἁγνείᾳ
καὶ δικαιοσύνη τὴν ψυχὴν αὐτοῦ διατήρησον·
ἵνα, ἐν παντὶ ἔργῳ καὶ λόγῳ εὐαρεστῶν σοι, υἱὸς καὶ
κληρονόμος τῆς ἐπουρανίου σου γένηται βασιλείας.

Ἐκφώνως
Ὅτι σὺ εἶ ὁ Θεὸς ἡμῶν, Θεὸς τοῦ ἐλεεῖν καὶ
σῴζειν, καὶ σοὶ τὴν δόξαν ἀναπέμπομεν, τῷ Πατρί,
καὶ τῷ Υἱῷ, καὶ τῷ Ἁγίῳ Πνεύματι, νῦν καὶ ἀεὶ
καὶ εἰς τοὺς αἰῶνας τῶν αἰώνων.

Ὁ Χορός· Ἀμήν.

Καὶ μετὰ τὴν Εὐχήν, χρίει τὸν βαπτισθέντα ὁ
Ἱερεὺς τῷ ἁγίῳ Μύρῳ, ποιῶν τοῦ Σταυροῦ τύπον ἐπὶ
τοῦ μετώπου, τῶν ὀφθαλμῶν, τῶν μυκτήρων, τοῦ
στόματος, τῶν δύο ὤτων, τοῦ στήθους, τῶν χειρῶν
καὶ τῶν ποδῶν, λέγων·

Σφραγὶς δωρεᾶς Πνεύματος Ἁγίου. Ἀμήν.

Εἶτα ἐνδύων αὐτὸν τὸν χιτῶνα λέγει.

Ἐνδύεται ὁ δοῦλος τοῦ Θεοῦ (ὁ δεῖνα) χιτῶνα
δικαιοσύνης, εἰς τὸ ὄνομα τοῦ Πατρός, καὶ τοῦ
Υἱοῦ, καὶ τοῦ Ἁγίου Πνεύματος. Ἀμήν.

Καὶ ψάλλεται Τροπάριον εἰς ἦχον πλ. δ΄.

Χιτῶνά μοι παράσχου φωτεινόν, ὁ ἀναβαλλόμενος
φῶς ὡς ἱμάτιον, πολυέλεε Χριστὲ ὁ Θεὸς ἡμῶν.

Ὁ Ἱερεὺς νιψάμενος, θυμιᾷ τὴν Κολυμβήθραν,
περιερχόμενος αὐτὴν γύρωθεν μετὰ τοῦ Ἀναδόχου,
κατ᾽ ἐνώπιον ἱσταμένου καὶ βαστάζοντος τὸ νεοφώτιστον βρέφος, καὶ ψάλλων εἰς ἦχον α΄.

Communion of the Holy Body and Most Precious Blood of Your Christ; keep him (her) in Your sanctification; confirm him (her) in the Orthodox Faith; deliver him (her) from the Evil One and all his devices; preserve his (her) soul, through Your saving fear, in purity and righteousness, that in every work and word, being acceptable before You, he (she) may become a child and heir of Your heavenly Kingdom.

For You are our God, the God of Mercy and Salvation, and to You do we send up Glory, to the Father, and to the Son, and to the Holy Spirit, both now and ever, and to the ages of ages.

Choir: Amen.

And after the Prayer of Confirmation, the Priest chrismates the baptized and he makes on the person the Sign of the Cross with the Holy Chrism (Holy Myron), on the forehead, the eyes, the nostrils, the mouth, the ears, the breast, the hands, and the feet. At each anointing and sealing, he says:

SEAL OF THE GIFT OF THE HOLY SPIRIT, AMEN.

The Priest invests the baptized in a new clean robe, saying:

Clothed is the servant of God *(Name)* with the garment of righteousness, in the Name of the Father, and of the Son, and of the Holy Spirit. Amen.

The Troparion, in Tone 8

A robe of divine light bestow upon me, O You that for vesture array Yourself with Light; and bestow many mercies, O Christ our God, who are plentious in mercy.

Then the Priest makes, together with the Godparent and the child, a circumambulation around the Font, three times; and for each of the three rounds the Choir sings:

Ὅσοι εἰς Χριστὸν ἐβαπτίσθητε, Χριστὸν ἐνεδύσασθε, Ἀλληλούϊα (ἐκ τρίτου).

Δόξα. Καὶ νῦν.

Χριστὸν ἐνεδύσασθε. Ἀλληλούϊα.

Ὁ Διάκονος· Δύναμις.

Ὁ Χορὸς

Ὅσοι εἰς Χριστὸν ἐβαπτίσθητε, Χριστὸν ἐνεδύσασθε. Ἀλληλούϊα.

Ὁ Διάκονος· Πρόσχωμεν.

Ὁ Ἀναγνώστης

Προκείμενον. Ἦχος γ΄.

Κύριος φωτισμός μου καὶ σωτήρ μου.

Στίχ. Κύριος ὑπερασπιστὴς τῆς ζωῆς μου.

Ὁ Διάκονος· Σοφία.

Ὁ Ἀναγνώστης

Πρὸς Ῥωμαίους ἐπιστολῆς Παύλου τὸ Ἀνάγνωσμα.

(Κεφ. ϛ΄ 3-11)

Ὁ Διάκονος· Πρόσχωμεν.

Ὁ Ἀναγνώστης

Ἀδελφοί, ὅσοι εἰς Χριστὸν ἐβαπτίσθημεν, εἰς τὸν θάνατον αὐτοῦ ἐβαπτίσθημεν. Συνετάφημεν οὖν αὐτῷ διὰ τοῦ βαπτίσματος εἰς τὸν θάνατον, ἵνα, ὥσπερ ἠγέρθη Χριστὸς ἐκ νεκρῶν διὰ τῆς δόξης τοῦ Πατρός, οὕτω καὶ ἡμεῖς ἐν καινότητι ζωῆς περιπατήσωμεν. Εἰ γὰρ σύμφυτοι γεγόναμεν τῷ ὁμοιώματι τοῦ θανάτου αὐτοῦ, ἀλλὰ καὶ τῆς ἀναστάσεως ἐσόμεθα, τοῦτο γινώσκοντες, ὅτι ὁ παλαιὸς ἡμῶν ἄνθρωπος συνεσταυρώθη, ἵνα καταργηθῇ τὸ σῶμα τῆς ἁμαρτίας, τοῦ μηκέτι δουλεύειν ἡμᾶς, τῇ ἁμαρτίᾳ. Ὁ γὰρ ἀποθανὼν δεδικαίωται ἀπὸ τῆς ἁμαρτίας. Εἰ δὲ ἀπεθάνομεν σὺν Χριστῷ, πιστεύομεν ὅτι καὶ συζήσομεν αὐτῷ, εἰδότες ὅτι Χριστός, ἐγερ-

As many of you as have been baptized into Christ, have put on Christ. Alleluia. (3)

Glory ... Both now ...
As many ... Alleluia.

Priest: Louder.

Choir

As many of you as have been baptized into Christ, have put on Christ. Alleluia.

Priest: Let us attend.

The Prokeimenon in Tone 3

The Lord is my light and my salvation; of whom then shall I fear? The Lord is the Protector of my life; of whom then shall I be afraid?

Priest: Wisdom!

The Reader

The Reading from the Epistle of the Holy Apostle Paul to the Romans. (Rom. 6:3-11)

Priest: Let us attend.

The Reader

Brethren, do you not know that all of us who have been baptized into Christ Jesus were baptized into his death? We were buried therefore with him by baptism into death, so that as Christ was raised from the dead by the glory of the Father, we too might walk in newness of life. For if we have been united with him in a death like his, we shall certainly be united with him in a resurrection like his. We know that our old self was crucified with him so that the sinful body might be destroyed, and we might no longer be enslaved to sin. For he who has died is freed from sin. But if we have died with Christ, we believe that we shall also live with him. For we know that Christ being

θεὶς ἐκ νεκρῶν, οὐκέτι ἀποθνήσκει, θάνατος αὐτοῦ οὐκέτι κυριεύει. Ὁ γὰρ ἀπέθανε τῇ ἁμαρτίᾳ, ἀπέθανεν ἐφάπαξ, ὃ δὲ ζῇ, ζῇ τῷ Θεῷ. Οὕτω καὶ ὑμεῖς λογίζεσθε ἑαυτοὺς νεκροὺς μὲν εἶναι τῇ ἁμαρτίᾳ, ζῶντας δὲ τῷ Θεῷ ἐν Χριστῷ Ἰησοῦ τῷ Κυρίῳ ἡμῶν.

Ὁ Ἱερεύς· Εἰρήνη σοι τῷ ἀναγινώσκοντι.

Ὁ Χορὸς
Ἀλληλούϊα, ἀλληλούϊα, ἀλληλούϊα.

Ὁ Διάκονος
Σοφία· ὀρθοί· ἀκούσωμεν τοῦ ἁγίου Εὐαγγελίου.

Ὁ Ἱερεύς· Εἰρήνη πᾶσι.

Ὁ Χορός· Καὶ τῷ πνεύματί σου.

Ὁ Ἱερεὺς
Ἐκ τοῦ κατὰ Ματθαῖον ἁγίου Εὐαγγελίου
τὸ Ἀνάγνωσμα.

(Κεφ. κη´ 16-20)

Ὁ Διάκονος· Πρόσχωμεν.

Ὁ Ἱερεὺς

Τῷ καιρῷ ἐκείνῳ, οἱ ἔνδεκα Μαθηταὶ ἐπορεύθησαν εἰς τὴν Γαλιλαίαν, εἰς τὸ ὄρος, οὗ ἐτάξατο αὐτοῖς ὁ Ἰησοῦς. Καὶ ἰδόντες αὐτόν, προσεκύνησαν αὐτῷ· οἱ δὲ ἐδίστασαν. Καὶ προσελθὼν ὁ Ἰησοῦς ἐλάλησεν αὐτοῖς, λέγων· Ἐδόθη μοι πᾶσα ἐξουσία ἐν οὐρανῷ καὶ ἐπὶ γῆς. Πορευθέντες οὖν, μαθητεύσατε πάντα τὰ ἔθνη, βαπτίζοντες αὐτοὺς εἰς τὸ ὄνομα τοῦ Πατρὸς καὶ τοῦ Υἱοῦ καὶ τοῦ Ἁγίου Πνεύματος, διδάσκοντες αὐτοὺς τηρεῖν πάντα ὅσα ἐνετειλάμην ὑμῖν· καὶ ἰδού, ἐγὼ μεθ᾽ ὑμῶν εἰμι πάσας τὰς ἡμέρας, ἕως τῆς συντελείας τοῦ αἰῶνος. Ἀμήν.

Ὁ Χορός· Δόξα σοι, Κύριε, δόξα σοι.

raised from the dead will never die again; death no longer has dominion over him. The death he died he died to sin, once for all, but the life he lives he lives to God. So you also must consider yourselves dead to sin and alive to God in Christ Jesus.

Priest: Peace be to you that read. And to your spirit.

Choir

Alleluia, alleluia, alleluia.

Priest

Wisdom! Let us attend! Let us hear the Holy Gospel.

Peace be to all (+).

Choir: And with your spirit.

Priest

The Reading from the Holy Gospel

according to St. Matthew. Let us attend.

(Matt. 28:16-20)

Choir: Glory to You, O Lord; Glory to You.

Priest

At that time, the eleven disciples went to Galilee, to the mountain to which Jesus had directed them. And when they saw him, they worshipped him; but some doubted. And Jesus came and said to them, "All authority in heaven and on earth has been given to me. Go therefore and make disciples of all nations, baptizing them in the name of the Father and of the Son and of the Holy Spirit, teaching them to observe all that I have commanded to you; and lo, I am with you always, to the close of the age. Amen."

Choir: Glory to You, O Lord; Glory to You.

ΕΥΧΑΙ ΤΗΣ ΑΠΟΛΟΥΣΕΩΣ

Ὁ Ἱερεύς· **Εἰρήνη πᾶσι.**

Ὁ Χορός· **Καὶ τῷ πνεύματί σου.**

Ὁ Διάκονος

Τὰς κεφαλὰς ἡμῶν τῷ Κυρίῳ κλίνωμεν.

Ὁ Χορός· **Σοί, Κύριε.**

Ὁ Διάκονος

Τοῦ Κυρίου δεηθῶμεν.

Ὁ Χορός· **Κύριε, ἐλέησον.**

Ὁ Ἱερεὺς τὴν Ε ὐ χ ή ν·

Ὁ λύτρωσιν ἁμαρτιῶν, διὰ τοῦ ἁγίου Βαπτίσματος, τῷ δούλῳ σου δωρησάμενος, καὶ ζωὴν ἀναγεννήσεως αὐτῷ χαρισάμενος· Αὐτός, Δέσποτα Κύριε, τὸν φωτισμὸν τοῦ προσώπου σου ἐν τῇ καρδίᾳ αὐτοῦ ἐναυγάζειν διὰ παντὸς εὐδόκησον· τὸν θυρεὸν τῆς πίστεως αὐτοῦ ἀνεπιβούλευτον ἐχθροῖς διατήρησον· τὸ τῆς ἀφθαρσίας ἔνδυμα, ὃ περιεβάλετο, ἀρρύπωτον ἐν αὐτῷ καὶ ἀμόλυντον διαφύλαξον· ἄθραυστον ἐν αὐτῷ τὴν πνευματικὴν σφραγῖδα τῇ χάριτί σου διατηρῶν, καὶ ἵλεως αὐτῷ τε καὶ ἡμῖν γενόμενος, κατὰ τὸ πλῆθος τῶν οἰκτιρμῶν σου. Ὅτι ηὐλόγηται καὶ δεδόξασται τὸ πάντιμον καὶ μεγαλοπρεπὲς ὄνομά σου, τοῦ Πατρὸς καὶ τοῦ Υἱοῦ καὶ τοῦ Ἁγίου Πνεύματος, νῦν καὶ ἀεὶ καὶ εἰς τοὺς αἰῶνας τῶν αἰώνων.

Ὁ Χορός· **Ἀμήν.**

Ὁ Διάκονος

Τοῦ Κυρίου δεηθῶμεν.

Ὁ Χορός· **Κύριε, ἐλέησον.**

THE ABLUTION

Priest: **Peace be to all. (+)**

Choir: **And with your spirit.**

Priest

Let us bow our heads before the Lord.

Choir: **To You, O Lord.**

Priest

Let us pray to the Lord.

Choir: **Lord have mercy.**

Priest says the Prayer:

You that through Holy Baptism have granted forgiveness of sins to this Your servant, bestowing on him (her) a life of regeneration: do You Yourself, Sovereign Master and Lord, be pleased that the Light of Your countenance evermore shine in his (her) heart; maintain the shield of his (her) faith against the plotting of enemies; preserve in him (her) the garment of incorruption, which he (she) has put on undefiled and unstained; preserve in him (her) the Seal of Your Grace, being gracious unto us, and unto him (her) according to the multitude of Your compassions, for glorified and blessed is Your all-honorable and majestic Name: of Father, and of Son, and of Holy Spirit, both now and ever, and to the ages of ages.

Choir: **Amen.**

Priest

Let us pray to the Lord.

Choir: **Lord have mercy.**

Ὁ Ἱερεὺς τὴν Ε ὐ χ ή ν·

Δέσποτα Κύριε, ὁ Θεὸς ἡμῶν, ὁ διὰ τῆς κολυμβήθρας τὴν οὐράνιον ἔλλαμψιν τοῖς βαπτιζομένοις παρέχων· ὁ ἀναγεννήσας τὸν δοῦλόν σου τὸν νεοφώτιστον δι' ὕδατος καὶ πνεύματος, καὶ τὴν τῶν ἑκουσίων καὶ ἀκουσίων ἁμαρτημάτων ἄφεσιν αὐτῷ δωρησάμενος, ἐπίθες αὐτῷ τὴν χεῖρά σου τὴν κραταιάν, καὶ φύλαξον αὐτὸν ἐν τῇ δυνάμει τῆς σῆς ἀγαθότητος· ἄσυλον τὸν ἀρραβῶνα διαφύλαξον· καὶ ἀξίωσον αὐτὸν εἰς τὴν ζωὴν τὴν αἰώνιον, καὶ εἰς τὴν σὴν εὐαρεστίαν. Ὅτι σὺ εἶ ὁ ἁγιασμὸς ἡμῶν, καὶ σοὶ τὴν δόξαν ἀναπέμπομεν τῷ Πατρὶ καὶ τῷ Υἱῷ καὶ τῷ Ἁγίῳ Πνεύματι, νῦν καὶ ἀεὶ καὶ εἰς τοὺς αἰῶνας τῶν αἰώνων. Ἀμήν.

Ὁ αὐτός· Εἰρήνη πᾶσι.

Ὁ Χορός· Καὶ τῷ Πνεύματί σου.

Ὁ Διάκονος

Τὰς κεφαλὰς ἡμῶν τῷ Κυρίῳ κλίνωμεν.

Ὁ Χορός· Σοί, Κύριε.

Ὁ Διάκονος

Τοῦ Κυρίου δεηθῶμεν.

Ὁ Χορός· Κύριε, ἐλέησον.

Ὁ Ἱερεὺς μυστικῶς τὴν Ε ὐ χ ή ν·

Ὁ ἐνδυσάμενος σέ, τὸν Χριστὸν καὶ Θεὸν ἡμῶν, σοὶ ὑπέκλινε σὺν ἡμῖν τὴν ἑαυτοῦ κεφαλήν· ὃν διαφύλαξον ἀήττητον ἀγωνιστὴν διαμεῖναι κατὰ τῶν μάτην ἔχθραν φερομένων κατ' αὐτοῦ τε καὶ ἡμῶν· τῷ δὲ σῷ ἀφθάρτῳ στεφάνῳ μέχρι τέλους νικητὰς πάντας ἀνάδειξον.

Ἐκφώνως

Ὅτι σόν ἐστι τὸ ἐλεεῖν καὶ σῴζειν ἡμᾶς, καὶ σοὶ τὴν δόξαν ἀναπέμπομεν, σὺν τῷ ἀνάρχῳ σου Πατρὶ

Priest

Sovereign Master and Lord our God, Who through the baptismal Font bestows heavenly Illumination to them that are baptized; Who has regenerated this Your servant, bestowing upon him (her) forgiveness of his (her) voluntary and involuntary sins; do You lay upon him (her) Your mighty hand, and guard him (her) in the power of Your goodness. Preserve unspotted his (her) pledge of Faith in You. Account him (her) worthy of Life everlasting and Your good favor. For You are our sanctification, and to You do we send up all Glory; to the Father, and to the Son, and to the Holy Spirit, both now and ever, and to the ages of ages. Amen.

Peace be to all. (+)

Choir: And to your spirit.

Priest

Let us bow our heads before the Lord.

Choir: To You, O Lord.

Priest

Let us pray to the Lord.

Choir: Lord have mercy.

Priest

He (She) that has put on You, O Christ, with us bows his (her) head unto You; ever protect him (her) a warrior invincible against them who vainly raise up enmity against him (her), or, as might be, against us; and by Your Crown of Incorruption at the last declare us all to be the victorious ones.

For Yours it is to have mercy and to save, and unto You, as to Your Eternal Father and Your All-Holy, Good, and

καὶ τῷ παναγίῳ καὶ ἀγαθῷ καὶ ζωοποιῷ σου Πνεύματι, νῦν καὶ ἀεὶ καὶ εἰς τοὺς αἰῶνας τῶν αἰώνων.

Ὁ Χορός· Ἀμήν.

Ὁ Ἱερεὺς λύει τὸ ζωνάριον τοῦ παιδίου καὶ τὸ σάβανον [μυρόπανον] καί, ἑνώσας τὰς ἄκρας αὐτῶν, βρέχει μετὰ ὕδατος καθαροῦ αὐτὰς καὶ ῥαίνει τὸ παιδίον, λέγων·

Ἐδικαιώθης, ἐφωτίσθης.

Καὶ λαβὼν σπόγγον καινὸν ἢ βάμβακα μεθ' ὕδατος, ἀποσπογγίζει τὸ πρόσωπον αὐτοῦ, σὺν τῇ κεφαλῇ, καὶ τὸ στῆθος καὶ τὰ λοιπά, λέγων·

Ἐβαπτίσθης, ἐφωτίσθης, ἐμυρώθης, ἡγιάσθης, ἀπελούσθης εἰς τὸ ὄνομα τοῦ Πατρὸς καὶ τοῦ Υἱοῦ καὶ τοῦ Ἁγίου Πνεύματος. Ἀμήν.

ΕΥΧΗ ΕΙΣ ΤΡΙΧΟΚΟΥΡΙΑΝ

Ὁ Διάκονος

Τοῦ Κυρίου δεηθῶμεν.

Ὁ Χορός· Κύριε, ἐλέησον.

Ὁ Ἱερεὺς τὴν Εὐχήν·

Δέσποτα Κύριε, ὁ Θεὸς ἡμῶν, ὁ τῇ εἰκόνι σου τιμήσας τὸν ἄνθρωπον, ἐκ ψυχῆς λογικῆς καὶ υωματος εὐπρεποῦς κατασκευάσας αὐτόν, ὡς ἂν τὸ σῶμα ἐξυπηρετῆσαι τῇ λογικῇ ψυχῇ· κεφαλὴν μὲν ἐπὶ τῶν ὑψηλοτάτων θείς, καὶ ἐν αὐτῇ τὰς πλείστας τῶν αἰσθήσεων καθιδρύσας, μὴ παρεμποδιζούσας ἀλλήλαις· ταῖς δὲ θριξὶ τὴν κεφαλὴν ὀροφώσας, πρὸς τὸ μὴ βλάπτεσθαι ταῖς μεταβολαῖς τῶν ἀέρων, καὶ πάντα τὰ μέλη αὐτῷ χρησίμως ἐμφυτεύσας, ἵνα διὰ πάντων εὐχαριστῇ σοι τῷ ἀριστοτέχνῃ. Αὐτός, Δέσποτα, ὁ διὰ τοῦ σκεύους τῆς ἐκλογῆς σου Παύλου τοῦ Ἀποστόλου ἐντειλάμενος

Life-creating Spirit, do we send up all Glory, both now and ever, and to the ages of ages.

Choir: Amen.

The Priest loosens the child's girdle and garment, and, joining the ends of these, he soaks them with clean water and sprinkles the child, saying aloud:

You are justified; you are illumined.

And taking a new sponge dipped in water, the Priest wipes his (her) head, the breast, and the rest, saying:

You are baptized; you are illuminated; you are anointed with the Holy Myrrh; you are hallowed; you are washed clean, in the Name of Father, and of Son, and of Holy Spirit. Amen.

THE TONSURE

Priest

Let us pray to the Lord.

Choir: Lord have mercy.

Priest

Sovereign Master and Lord our God, Who honored man with Your own Image, providing him with reason-endowed soul and comely body, that the body might serve the reason-endowed soul; for You did set his head on high, and therein planted the greater number of the senses, which impede not one another, covering the head that it might not be injured by the changes of the weather, and did fit all the members serviceably thereunto, that by all it might render thanks unto You, the excellent Artist; do You Yourself, O Sovereign Master, Who by the Vessel of Your Election, Paul the Apostle, to do all things unto Your

ἡμῖν πάντα εἰς δόξαν σὴν ποιεῖν, τὸν προσελθόντα δοῦλόν σου (τόνδε) ἀπαρχὴν ποιήσασθαι κείρασθαι τὴν κόμην τῆς κεφαλῆς αὐτοῦ, εὐλόγησον, ἅμα τῷ αὐτοῦ ἀναδόχῳ· καὶ δὸς αὐτοῖς πάντα μελετᾶν ἐν τῷ νόμῳ σου καὶ τὰ εὐάρεστά σοι πράττειν. Ὅτι ἐλεήμων καὶ φιλάνθρωπος Θεὸς ὑπάρχεις, καὶ σοὶ τὴν δόξαν ἀναπέμπομεν, τῷ Πατρὶ καὶ τῷ Υἱῷ καὶ τῷ Ἁγίῳ Πνεύματι, νῦν καὶ ἀεὶ καὶ εἰς τοὺς αἰῶνας τῶν αἰώνων.

Ὁ Χορός· **Ἀμήν.**

Ὁ Ἱερεύς· **Εἰρήνη πᾶσι.**

Ὁ Χορός· **Καὶ τῷ πνεύματί σου.**

Ὁ Διάκονος

Τὰς κεφαλὰς ἡμῶν τῷ Κυρίῳ κλίνωμεν.

Ὁ Χορός· **Σοί, Κύριε.**

Ὁ Διάκονος

Τοῦ Κυρίου δεηθῶμεν.

Ὁ Χορός· **Κύριε ἐλέησον.**

Ὁ Ἱερεύς, κρατῶν τὴν δεξιὰν αὐτοῦ ἐπὶ τὴν κεφαλὴν τοῦ βαπτισθέντος, ἐπεύχεται·

Κύριε ὁ Θεὸς ἡμῶν, ὁ ἐκ τοῦ πληρώματος τῆς κολυμβήθρας διὰ τῆς σῆς ἀγαθότητος ἁγιάσας τοὺς εἰς σὲ πιστεύοντας, εὐλόγησον τὸ παρὸν νήπιον, καὶ ἐπὶ τὴν κεφαλὴν αὐτοῦ ἡ εὐλογία σου καταβήτω. Καὶ ὡς εὐλόγησας διὰ τοῦ προφήτου Σαμουήλ, Δαυὶδ τὸν βασιλέα. εὐλόγησον καὶ τὴν κεφάλην τοῦ δούλου σου (τοῦδε), διὰ χειρὸς ἐμοῦ τοῦ ἁμαρτωλοῦ, ἐπιφοιτῶν αὐτῷ τῷ Πνεύματί σου τῷ Ἁγίῳ, ὅπως προκόπτων ἐν ἡλικίᾳ καὶ πολιᾷ γήρως, δόξαν σοι ἀναπέμψῃ, καὶ ἴδῃ τὰ ἀγαθὰ Ἱερουσαλὴμ πάσας τὰς ἡμέρας τῆς ζωῆς αὐτοῦ.

Glory, bless (+) this Your servant (*Name*), who is come now to make offering the firstlings of hair shorn from his (her) head; and bless his (her) Sponsor (+); granting them in all things to be diligent followers of Your Law, and to do all those things that are well pleasing unto You, for a merciful and loving God are You, and to You do we send up all Glory, to the Father, and to the Son, and to the Holy Spirit, both now and ever, and to the ages of ages.

Choir: **Amen.**

Priest: **Peace be to all. (+)**

Choir: And to your spirit.

Priest

Let us bow our heads before the Lord.

Choir: To You, O Lord.

Priest

Let us pray to the Lord.

Choir: Lord have mercy.

The Priest lays his right hand upon the head of the child and prays:

O Lord our God, Who through the fulfillment of the baptismal Font have, by Your Goodness, sanctified them that believe in You: (+) do You bless this child here present, and may Your blessings come down upon his (her) head; as You did bless the head of Your servant David the King through the Prophet Samuel, (+) so also bless the head of this servant (*Name*), through the hand of me, the unworthy Priest, visiting him (her) with Your Holy Spirit, that as he (she) goes forward to the prime of his (her) years, and the grey hairs of old age, he (she) may send up Glory to You, beholding the good things of Jerusalem all the days of his (her) life.

Ἐκφώνως

Ὅτι πρέπει σοι πᾶσα δόξα, τιμὴ καὶ προσκύνησις, τῷ Πατρὶ καὶ τῷ Υἱῷ καὶ τῷ Ἁγίῳ Πνεύματι, νῦν καὶ ἀεὶ καὶ εἰς τοὺς αἰῶνας τῶν αἰώνων.

Ὁ Χορός· Ἀμήν.

Ὁ Ἱερεὺς κείρει τὴν κόμην τῆς κεφαλῆς τοῦ παιδίου σταυροειδῶς, λέγων·

Κείρεται ὁ δοῦλος τοῦ Θεοῦ (ὁ δεῖνα) τὴν κόμην τῆς κεφαλῆς αὐτοῦ, εἰς τὸ ὄνομα τοῦ Πατρός, καὶ τοῦ Υἱοῦ, καὶ τοῦ Ἁγίου Πνεύματος.

Ὁ Χορός, Ἀμήν.

Ὁ Διάκονος

Ἐλέησον ἡμᾶς ὁ Θεός, κατὰ τὸ μέγα ἔλεός σου, δεόμεθά σου, ἐπάκουσον, καὶ ἐλέησον.

Ὁ Χορὸς Κύριε, ἐλέησον.

Ὁ Διάκονος

Ἔτι δεόμεθα ὑπὲρ ἐλέους, ζωῆς, εἰρήνης, ὑγίειας καὶ σωτηρίας τῶν δούλων σου, τοῦ νεοφωτίστου (τοῦ δεῖνος), τοῦ ἀναδόχου (τοῦ δεῖνος) καὶ παντὸς τοῦ περιεστῶτος λαοῦ.

Ὁ Ἱερεὺς

Ὅτι ἐλεήμων, καὶ φιλάνθρωπος Θεὸς ὑπάρχεις καὶ σοὶ τὴν δόξαν ἀναπέμπομεν, τῷ Πατρὶ καὶ τῷ Υἱῷ καὶ τῷ Ἁγίῳ Πνεύματι, νῦν καὶ ἀεὶ καὶ εἰς τοὺς αἰῶνας τῶν αἰώνων.

Ὁ Χορός· Ἀμήν.

Εἶθ᾽ οὕτως ἡ Ἀπόλυσις, τοῦ Βαπτίσματος ὡς ἀκολούθως·

Ὁ Ἱερεὺς

Δόξα σοι, ὁ Θεός, ἡ ἐλπὶς ἡμῶν, δόξα σοι.

For to You are due all glory, honor and worship, to the Father, and to the Son, and to the Holy Spirit, both now and ever, and to the ages of ages.

Choir: Amen.

The Priest shears him (her) in the form of a Cross, snipping off four locks of hair, front, back, and over each ear, cross-fashion, saying:

The servant of God (*Name*) is shorn in the Name of the Father, and of the Son, and of the Holy Spirit.

Choir: Amen.

Priest

Have mercy on us, O God, according to Your great mercy. We beseech You, listen, and have mercy.

Choir: Lord have mercy.

Priest

Again let us pray for mercy, life, peace, health, and salvation for the servants of God, the newly illumined (*Name*), the Godparents, and all those who have come here together for this holy Sacrament.

For You are a merciful and loving God, and to You do we send up all Glory, to the Father, and to the Son, and to the Holy Spirit, both now and ever, and to the ages of ages.

Choir: Amen.

The Apolysis

Priest

Glory to You, O Christ our God and our hope; glory to You.

Ο Διάκονος

Δόξα Πατρὶ καὶ Υἱῷ καὶ Ἁγίῳ Πνεύματι. Καὶ νῦν καὶ ἀεὶ καὶ εἰς τοὺς αἰῶνας τῶν αἰώνων. Ἀμήν. Κύριε, ἐλέησον· Κύριε, ἐλέησον· Κύριε, ἐλέησον. Πάτερ ἅγιε, εὐλόγησον.

Ο Ἱερεύς

Ο ἐν Ἰορδάνῃ ὑπὸ Ἰωάννου βαπτισθῆναι καταδεξάμενος διὰ τὴν ἡμῶν σωτηρίαν, Χριστὸς ὁ ἀληθινὸς Θεὸς ἡμῶν, ταῖς πρεσβείαις τῆς παναχράντου καὶ παναμώμου ἁγίας αὐτοῦ Μητρός, τοῦ τιμίου, ἐνδόξου προφήτου, προδρόμου καὶ βαπτιστοῦ Ἰωάννου, τῶν ἁγίων ἐνδόξων καὶ πανευφήμων Ἀποστόλων, (τοῦ ἁγίου οὗ τὸ ὄνομα ἔλαβεν ὁ νεοφώτιστος), καὶ πάντων τῶν Ἁγίων, ἐλεήσαι καὶ σώσαι ἡμᾶς ὡς ἀγαθὸς καὶ φιλάνθρωπος.

Δι᾽ εὐχῶν τῶν ἁγίων...

Ο Χορός· Ἀμήν.

Priest

Glory to the Father, and to the Son, and to the Holy Spirit, both now and ever, and to the ages of ages. Amen. Lord have mercy; Lord have mercy; Lord have mercy. Master, bid the blessing.

He Who deigned to be baptized in the Jordan by John for our salvation, Christ our true God—through the intercessions of His all-pure Mother, of the holy and glorious prophet, Forerunner and Baptist John, of the holy, glorious all-praiseworthy Apostles, *(Name of Saint whose name the child has received),* and of all the Saints; have mercy and save us as our good and loving Lord.

Through the prayers of our holy Fathers...

Choir: Amen.

ΑΚΟΛΟΥΘΙΑ
ΕΠΙ ΜΝΗΣΤΡΟΙΣ

Μετὰ τὴν θείαν Λειτουργίαν, τοῦ Ἱερέως ἑστῶτος ἐν τῷ Ἱερατείῳ, παρίστανται οἱ μέλλοντες ζεύγνυσθαι πρὸ τῶν ἁγίων Θυρῶν· ὁ μὲν ἀνὴρ ἐκ δεξιῶν, ἡ δὲ γυνὴ ἐξ εὐωνύμων. Ἀπόκεινται δὲ ἐν τῷ δεξιῷ μέρει τῆς ἁγίας Τραπέζης δακτύλιοι αὐτῶν δύο, χρυσοῦς καὶ ἀργυροῦς· ὁ μὲν ἀργυροῦς ἀπονεύων πρὸς τὰ δεξιά, ὁ δὲ χρυσοῦς πρὸς τὰ ἀριστερά, σύνεγγυς ἀλλήλων. Ὁ δὲ Ἱερεύς, ἐλθὼν ἐν τῷ νάρθηκι σφραγίζει τὰς κεφαλὰς τῶν νεονύμφων ἐκ γ΄ καὶ δίδωσιν αὐτοῖς κηροὺς ἁπτομένους· καὶ εἰσάξας αὐτοὺς ἔνδον τοῦ Ναοῦ, θυμιᾷ σταυροειδῶς.

Καὶ ἐρωτᾷ αὐτοὺς ὁ Ἱερεύς, πρὸς ὁμολογίαν, ἐὰν θέλῃ ἡ νύμφη τὸν νυμφίον· ὁμοίως καὶ ὁ νυμφίος τὴν νύμφην. Εἶτα λέγει·

74

THE SERVICE OF BETROTHAL

The priest stands before the Royal Doors, looking towards the two who are to be Betrothed; and they stand outside the Royal Doors, the man to the right, and the woman on the left. On the right side of the Holy Altar are placed the two rings. The priest takes up the censer and censes the holy icons, the bridal pair, and the people.

Then the priest asks the bride is she wishes to marry the groom, and the groom if he wishes to marry the bride. The priest then says:

Ὁ Ἱερεύς, ἐκφώνως·

Εὐλογητὸς ὁ Θεὸς ἡμῶν, πάντοτε· νῦν καὶ ἀεὶ καὶ εἰς τοὺς αἰῶνας τῶν αἰώνων.

Ὁ Χορός· Ἀμήν.

Ὁ Διάκονος

Ἐν εἰρήνῃ τοῦ Κυρίου δεηθῶμεν.

Ὁ Χορός· Κύριε, ἐλέησον.

Ὁ Διάκονος

Ὑπὲρ τῆς ἄνωθεν εἰρήνης καὶ τῆς σωτηρίας τῶν ψυχῶν ἡμῶν, τοῦ Κυρίου δεηθῶμεν.

Ὑπὲρ τῆς εἰρήνης τοῦ σύμπαντος κόσμου, εὐσταθείας τῶν ἁγίων τοῦ Θεοῦ Ἐκκλησιῶν, καὶ τῆς τῶν πάντων ἑνώσεως, τοῦ Κυρίου δεηθῶμεν.

Ὑπὲρ τοῦ ἁγίου Οἴκου τούτου, καὶ τῶν μετὰ πίστεως, εὐλαβείας καὶ φόβου Θεοῦ εἰσιόντων ἐν αὐτῷ, τοῦ Κυρίου δεηθῶμεν.

Ὑπὲρ τοῦ Ἀρχιεπισκόπου ἡμῶν (τοῦ δεῖνος), τοῦ τιμίου Πρεσβυτερίου, τῆς ἐν Χριστῷ Διακονίας, παντὸς τοῦ Κλήρου καὶ τοῦ Λαοῦ, τοῦ Κυρίου δεηθῶμεν.

Ὑπὲρ τοῦ δούλου τοῦ Θεοῦ (τοῦδε), καὶ τῆς δούλης τοῦ Θεοῦ (τῆσδε) τῶν νῦν μνηστευομένων ἀλλήλοις, καὶ τῆς σωτηρίας αὐτῶν, τοῦ Κυρίου δεηθῶμεν.

Ὑπὲρ τοῦ παρασχεθῆναι αὐτοῖς τέκνα εἰς διαδοχὴν γένους, καὶ πάντα τὰ πρὸς σωτηρίαν αἰτήματα, τοῦ Κυρίου δεηθῶμεν.

Ὑπὲρ τοῦ καταπεμφθῆναι αὐτοῖς ἀγάπην τελείαν, εἰρηνικήν, καὶ βοήθειαν, τοῦ Κυρίου δεηθῶμεν.

Ὑπὲρ τοῦ φυλαχθῆναι αὐτοὺς ἐν ὁμονοίᾳ καὶ βεβαίᾳ πίστει, τοῦ Κυρίου δεηθῶμεν.

Ὑπὲρ τοῦ εὐλογηθῆναι αὐτοὺς ἐν ὁμονοίᾳ καὶ βεβαίᾳ πίστει, τοῦ Κυρίου δεηθῶμεν.

Ὑπὲρ τοῦ διαφυλαχθῆναι αὐτοὺς ἐν ἀμέμπτῳ βιοτῇ καὶ πολιτείᾳ, τοῦ Κυρίου δεηθῶμεν.

Priest

Blessed is our God always, both now and ever, and to the ages of ages.

Choir: Amen.

Priest

In peace let us pray to the Lord.

Choir: Lord have mercy.

Priest

For the peace from above; for the salvation of our souls; let us pray to the Lord.

For the peace of the whole world; for the stability of the holy Churches of God; and for the union of all; let us pray to the Lord.

For this holy House, and for them that with faith, reverence, and the fear of God enter therein; let us pray to the Lord.

For our Most Reverend Archbishop (*Name*), for the venerable Priesthood, the Diaconate in Christ; for all the Clergy; and for all the people; let us pray to the Lord.

For the servant of God (*Name*) and the servant of God (*Name*) who now pledge themselves to one another, and for their salvation; let us pray to the Lord.

That there may be promised unto them children for the continuation of their race, granting unto them all their prayers unto salvation; let us pray to the Lord.

That He send down upon them love perfect and peaceful, and give them His protection; let us pray to the Lord.

That He may keep them in oneness of mind, and in steadfastness of the Faith; let us pray to the Lord.

That He may bless them in harmony and perfect trust; let us pray to the Lord.

That He may keep the course and manner of their life blameless; let us pray to the Lord.

Ὅπως Κύριος ὁ Θεὸς ἡμῶν χαρίσηται αὐτοῖς τίμιον τὸν γάμον, καὶ τὴν κοίτην ἀμίαντον, τοῦ Κυρίου δεηθῶμεν.

Ὑπὲρ τοῦ ρυσθῆναι ἡμᾶς ἀπὸ πάσης θλίψεως, ὀργῆς, κινδύνου καὶ ἀνάγκης, τοῦ Κυρίου δεηθῶμεν.

Ἀντιλαβοῦ, σῶσον, ἐλέησον, καὶ διαφύλαξον ἡμᾶς, ὁ Θεός, τῇ σῇ χάριτι.

Τῆς Παναγίας, ἀχράντου, ὑπερευλογημένης, ἐνδόξου, δεσποίνης ἡμῶν Θεοτόκου, καὶ ἀειπαρθένου Μαρίας, μετὰ πάντων τῶν ἁγίων μνημονεύσαντες, ἑαυτοὺς καὶ ἀλλήλους, καὶ πᾶσαν τὴν ζωὴν ἡμῶν Χριστῷ τῷ Θεῷ παραθώμεθα.

Ὁ Χορός· Σοί, Κύριε.

Ὁ Ἱερεύς, ἐκφώνως·

Ὅ;ι πρέπει σοι πᾶσα δόξα, τιμὴ καὶ προσκύνησις, τῷ Πατρὶ καὶ τῷ Υἱῷ καὶ τῷ Ἁγίῳ Πνεύματι, νῦν καὶ ἀεὶ καὶ εἰς τοὺς αἰῶνας τῶν αἰώνων.

Ὁ Χορός· Ἀμήν.

Ὁ Διάκονος
Τοῦ Κυρίου δεηθῶμεν.

Ὁ Χορός· Κύριε, ἐλέησον.

Ὁ Ἱερεὺς λέγει τὴν Εὐχὴν ταύτην μεγαλοφώνως·

Ο΄ Θεὸς ὁ αἰώνιος, ὁ τὰ διῃρημένα συναγαγὼν εἰς ἑνότητα καὶ σύνδεσμον διαθέσεως τιθεὶς ἄρρηκτον· ὁ εὐλογήσας Ἰσαὰκ καὶ Ῥεβέκκαν, καὶ κληρονόμους αὐτοὺς τῆς σῆς ἐπαγγελίας ἀναδείξας· αὐτὸς εὐλόγησον καὶ τοὺς δούλους σου τούτους, ὁδηγῶν αὐτοὺς ἐν παντὶ ἔργῳ ἀγαθῷ.

Ὅτι ἐλεήμων καὶ φιλάνθρωπος Θεὸς ὑπάρχεις, καὶ σοὶ τὴν δόξαν ἀναπέμπομεν, τῷ Πατρὶ καὶ τῷ Υἱῷ καὶ τῷ ἁγίῳ Πνεύματι, νῦν καὶ ἀεὶ καὶ εἰς τοὺς αἰῶνας τῶν αἰώνων.

Ὁ Χορός· Ἀμήν.

That the Lord God may grant unto them an honorable marriage and a bed undefiled; let us pray to the Lord.

That we may be delivered from all tribulation, wrath, danger and necessity; let us pray to the Lord.

Help us; save us; have mercy on us and keep us, O God, by Your Grace.

Calling to remembrance our all-holy, immaculate, exceedingly blessed glorious Lady Theotokos and Ever-Virgin Mary, with all the Saints, let us commend ourselves and one another and all our life to Christ our God.

Choir: To You, O God.

Priest (aloud)

For to You are due all Glory, honor, and worship, to the Father, and to the Son, and to the Holy Spirit, both now and ever, and to the ages of ages.

Choir: Amen.

Priest

Let us pray to the Lord.

Choir: Lord have mercy.

Priest (aloud)

O God eternal, Who has brought together into unity the things which before had been separate, and in so doing impose on them an indissoluble bond of love, Who did bless Isaac and Rebecca, declaring them to be the inheritors of Your promise: do You Yourself (+) bless these Your servants (*Name*) and (*Name*), directing them into every good work.

For You are a merciful and loving God, and to You do we send up all Glory: to the Father, and to the Son, and to the Holy Spirit, both now and ever, and to the ages of ages.

Choir: Amen.

Ὁ Ἱερεύς· **Εἰρήνη πᾶσι.**

Ὁ Διάκονος

Τὰς κεφαλὰς ὑμῶν τῷ Κυρίῳ κλίνατε.

Ὁ Ἱερεὺς ἐπεύχεται·

Κύριε ὁ Θεὸς ἡμῶν, ὁ τὴν ἐξ ἐθνῶν προμνηστευσά μενος Ἐκκλησίαν παρθένον ἁγνήν, εὐλόγησον τὰ μνῆστρα ταῦτα, καὶ ἕνωσον, καὶ διαφύλαξον τοὺς δούλους σου τούτους ἐν εἰρήνῃ καὶ ὁμονοίᾳ.

Ἐκφώνως

Σοὶ γὰρ πρέπει πᾶσα δόξα, τιμὴ καὶ προσκύ νησις, τῷ Πατρὶ καὶ τῷ Υἱῷ καὶ τῷ Ἁγίῳ Πνεύματι, νῦν καὶ ἀεὶ καὶ εἰς τοὺς αἰῶνας τῶν αἰώνων.

Ὁ Χορός· **Ἀμήν.**

Εἶτα, λαβὼν ὁ Ἱερεὺς τοὺς δακτυλίους τοὺς ἐν τῷ δισκελίῳ, ἐπιδίδωσι πρῶτον τῷ ἀνδρὶ τὸν χρυσοῦν καὶ λέγει αὐτῷ·

Ἀρραβωνίζεται ὁ δοῦλος τοῦ Θεοῦ (ὁ δεῖνα) **τὴν δούλην τοῦ Θεοῦ** (τὴν δεῖνα)**, εἰς τὸ ὄνομα τοῦ Πατρός, καὶ τοῦ Υἱοῦ, καὶ τοῦ Ἁγίου Πνεύματος. Ἀμὴν** (τρίς).

Καὶ ποιεῖ Σταυρὸν μετὰ τοῦ δακτυλίου ἐπὶ τὴν κεφαλὴν αὐτοῦ.

Εἶτα καὶ τῇ γυναικὶ λέγει, λαβὼν τὸν ἀργυροῦν·

Ἀρραβωνίζεται ἡ δούλη τοῦ Θεοῦ (ἡ δεῖνα)**, τὸν δοῦλον τοῦ Θεοῦ** (τὸν δεῖνα) **εἰς τὸ ὄνομα τοῦ Πατρός, καὶ τοῦ Υἱοῦ, καὶ τοῦ Ἁγίου Πνεύματος. Ἀμὴν** (τρίς).

Καὶ ὅταν εἴπῃ εἰς ἕκαστον τρίς, ποιεῖ Σταυρὸν μετὰ τοῦ δακτυλίου ἐπὶ τὰς κεφαλὰς αὐτῶν καὶ ἐπι τίθησιν αὐτοὺς ἐν τοῖς δεξιοῖς αὐτῶν δακτύλοις.

Priest: Peace be to all. (+) And to your spirit.

Let us bow our heads before the Lord. To You, O Lord.

O Lord our God, Who espoused the Church as a pure virgin called from out of the Gentiles, bless this Betrothal (+), uniting these Your servants, keeping them in peace and oneness of mind.

For to You are due all Glory, honor, and worship: to the Father, and to the Son, and to the Holy Spirit, both now and ever, and to the ages of ages.

Choir: Amen.

Then the Priest takes the rings, blesses them, makes with them the Sign of the Cross over the man's head, and says:

The servant of God (*Name*) is betrothed to the servant of God (*Name*), in the Name of the Father, and of the Son, and of the Holy Spirit. (*Thrice*) Amen.

Then with the rings the Priest makes the Sign of the Cross over the woman's head, saying:

The servant of God (*Name*) is betrothed to the servant of God (*Name*), in the Name of the Father, and of the Son, and of the Holy Spirit. (*Thrice*) Amen.

At the third time, the Priest puts the woman's ring on the man's right finger, and the man's ring on the woman's right finger.

Εἶτα ἀλλάσσει τοὺς δακτυλίους τῶν Νυμφίων ὁ Παράνυμφος.

Ὁ Διάκονος

Τοῦ Κυρίου δεηθῶμεν.

Ὁ Χορός· Κύριε, ἐλέησον.

Ὁ Ἱερεὺς λέγει τὴν Εὐχὴν ταύτην·

Κύριε ὁ Θεὸς ἡμῶν, ὁ τῷ παιδὶ τοῦ Πατριάρχου Ἀβραὰμ συμπορευθεὶς ἐν τῇ Μεσοποταμίᾳ, στελλομένῳ νυμφεύσασθαι τῷ κυρίῳ αὐτοῦ Ἰσαὰκ γυναῖκα, καὶ διὰ μεσιτείας ὑδρεύσεως ἀρραβωνίσασθαι τὴν Ῥεβέκκαν ἀποκαλύψας· Αὐτός, εὐλόγησον τὸν ἀρραβῶνα τῶν δούλων σου (τοῦδε) καὶ (τῆς δε) καὶ στήριξον τὸν παρ' αὐτοῖς λαληθέντα λόγον. Βεβαίωσον αὐτοὺς τῇ παρὰ σοῦ ἁγίᾳ ἑνότητι· σὺ γὰρ ἀπ' ἀρχῆς ἐδημιούργησας ἄρσεν καὶ θῆλυ, καὶ παρὰ σοῦ ἁρμόζεται ἀνδρὶ γυνὴ εἰς βοήθειαν καὶ διαδοχὴν τοῦ γένους τῶν ἀνθρώπων. Αὐτὸς οὖν, Κύριε ὁ Θεὸς ἡμῶν, ὁ ἐξαποστείλας τὴν ἀλήθειαν ἐπὶ τὴν κληρονομίαν σου, καὶ τὴν ἐπαγγελίαν σου ἐπὶ τοὺς δούλους σου, τοὺς πατέρας ἡμῶν, εἰς καθ' ἑκάστην γενεὰν καὶ γενεὰν τοὺς ἐκλεκτούς σου, ἐπίβλεψον ἐπὶ τὸν δοῦλόν σου (τόνδε), καὶ τὴν δούλην σου (τήνδε), καὶ στήριξον τὸν ἀρραβῶνα αὐτῶν ἐν πίστει καὶ ὁμονοίᾳ καὶ ἀληθείᾳ καὶ ἀγάπῃ· σὺ γάρ, Κύριε, ὑπέδειξας δίδοσθαι τὸν ἀρραβῶνα καὶ στηρίζεσθαι ἐν παντί. Διὰ δακτυλιδίου ἐδόθη ἡ ἐξουσία τῷ Ἰωσὴφ ἐν Αἰγύπτῳ· διὰ δακτυλιδίου ἐδοξάσθη Δανιὴλ ἐν χώρᾳ Βαβυλῶνος· διὰ δακτυλιδίου ἐφανερώθη ἡ ἀλήθεια τῆς Θάμαρ· διὰ δακτυλιδίου ὁ Πατὴρ ἡμῶν ὁ οὐράνιος οἰκτίρμων γέγονεν ἐπὶ τὸν ἄσωτον υἱόν· «Δότε γάρ, φησί, δακτύλιον εἰς τὴν χεῖρα αὐτοῦ καὶ ἐνέγκαντες τὸν μόσχον τὸν σιτευτὸν θύσατε, καὶ φαγόντες εὐφρανθῶμεν». Αὕτη ἡ δεξιά σου, Κύριε,

Then the Groomsman exchanges the rings thrice.

Priest

Let us pray to the Lord.

Choir: Lord have mercy.

Priest

O Lord our God, Who accompanied the servant of the patriarch Abraham to Mesopotamia, when he was sent to espouse a wife for his lord Isaac, and did reveal to him a sign by the drawing of water to betroth Rebecca; do You Yourself bless the betrothal of these Your servants (*Name*) and (*Name*) and confirm the word that has been spoken by them; for You, O Lord, from the beginning have created male and female, and by You is a woman joined to a man for assistance and for the continuation of the human race. Therefore, O Lord God, Who have sent forth Your truth to Your inheritance and Your promise to Your servants, our fathers, who were Your elect, do You give regard unto this Your servant (*Name*) and Your servant (*Name*), and seal their betrothal in faith, in oneness of mind, in truth and in love. For You, O Lord, have declared that a pledge is to be given and held inviolate in all things. By a ring Joseph was given might in Egypt; by a ring Daniel was exalted in Babylon; by a ring the truth of Thamar was made manifest; by a ring our heavenly Father showed compasssion upon His prodigal son, for He said, "Put a ring upon his right hand, kill the fatted calf, and let us eat and rejoice." Your own right hand, O Lord, armed

τὸν Μωϋσῆν ἐστρατοπέδευσεν ἐν Ἐρυθρᾷ θαλάσσῃ· διὰ γὰρ τοῦ λόγου σου τοῦ ἀληθινοῦ οἱ οὐρανοὶ ἐστερεώθησαν καὶ ἡ γῆ ἐθεμελιώθη· καὶ ἡ δεξιὰ τῶν δούλων σου εὐλογηθήσεται τῷ λόγῳ σου τῷ κραταιῷ καὶ τῷ βραχίονί σου τῷ ὑψηλῷ. Αὐτὸς οὖν καὶ νῦν, Δέσποτα, εὐλόγησον τὸ δακτυλοθέσιον τοῦτο εὐλογίαν οὐράνιον· καὶ Ἄγγελος Κυρίου προπορευέσθω ἔμπροσθεν αὐτῶν πάσας τὰς ἡμέρας τῆς ζωῆς αὐτῶν. Ὅτι σὺ εἶ ὁ εὐλογῶν καὶ ἁγιάζων τὰ σύμπαντα, καὶ σοὶ τὴν δόξαν ἀναπέμπομεν, τῷ Πατρὶ καὶ τῷ Υἱῷ καὶ τῷ Ἁγίῳ Πνεύματι, νῦν καὶ ἀεὶ καὶ εἰς τοὺς αἰῶνας τῶν αἰώνων.

Ὁ Χορός· Ἀμήν.

Moses in the Red Sea. Yea, by the word of Your truth were the Heavens established and the earth set upon her sure foundations; and the right hands of Your servants shall be blessed by Your mighty word, and by Your uplifted arm. Wherefore, O Sovereign Lord, do You Yourself bless this putting on of rings with Your heavenly benediction; and may Your Angel go before them all the days of their life, for You are He that blesses and sanctifies all things, and to You do we send up Glory: to the Father, and to the Son, and to the Holy Spirit, both now and ever, and to the ages of ages.

Choir: Amen.

ΑΚΟΛΟΥΘΙΑ
ΤΟΥ ΣΤΕΦΑΝΩΜΑΤΟΣ
ἤτοι
ΤΟΥ ΓΑΜΟΥ

—◦—

Εἰ μὲν βούλονται ἐν ταὐτῷ στεφανωθῆναι, παραμένουσιν ἐν τῷ Ναῷ καὶ ἄρχεται ἡ ἀκολουθία τοῦ στεφανώματος. Εἰ δὲ μεθ᾿ ἡμέρας βούλονται στεφανωθῆναι, εἰσέρχονται ἐν τῷ Ναῷ ἐκ τοῦ νάρθηκος μετὰ κηρῶν ἁπτομένων, προπορευομένου τοῦ Ἱερέως μετὰ τοῦ θυμιατοῦ, καὶ ψάλλοντος τὸν

ρκζ΄ (127) Ψαλμόν.

Μακάριοι πάντες οἱ φοβούμενοι τὸν Κύριον.

Ὁ Χορὸς ἐν ἑκάστῳ στίχῳ λέγει·

Δόξα σοι, ὁ Θεὸς ἡμῶν, δόξα οοι.

Οἱ πορευόμενοι ἐν ταῖς ὁδοῖς αὐτοῦ.

Δόξα σοι, ὁ Θεὸς ἡμῶν, δόξα σοι.

Τοὺς πόνους τῶν καρπῶν σου φάγεσαι.

Δόξα σοι, ὁ Θεὸς ἡμῶν, δόξα σοι.

Μακάριος εἶ, καὶ καλῶς σοι ἔσται.

Δόξα σοι, ὁ Θεὸς ἡμῶν, δόξα σοι.

THE SERVICE OF THE CROWNING
that is
OF MARRIAGE

If the Coronation follows the Betrothal immediately, then after the "Amen" of the Ekphonesis ("For You are He that blesses and sanctifies . . .), the Priest censes in front of the Altar, and goes out and censes the Ikonostasion. The Processional Psalm is then sung.

The Processional Psalm

Blessed is everyone that fears the Lord.

The Choir sings after each stikhos:

    Glory to You, O our God, Glory to You.

That walks in His ways,

    Glory to You, O our God, Glory to You.

For you shall eat the labor of your hands.

    Glory to You, O our God, Glory to You.

Blessed are you, and it shall be well with you.

    Glory to You, O our God, Glory to You.

Ἡ γυνή σου ὡς ἄμπελος εὐθηνοῦσα ἐν τοῖς κλίτεσι τῆς οἰκίας σου.

Δόξα σοι, ὁ Θεὸς ἡμῶν, δόξα σοι.

Οἱ υἱοί σου ὡς νεόφυτα ἐλαιῶν, κύκλῳ τῆς τραπέζης σου.

Δόξα σοι, ὁ Θεὸς ἡμῶν, δόξα σοι.

Ἰδοὺ οὕτως εὐλογηθήσεται ἄνθρωπος ὁ φοβούμενος τὸν Κύριον.

Δόξα σοι, ὁ Θεὸς ἡμῶν, δόξα σοι.

Εὐλογήσαι σε Κύριος ἐκ Σιών, καὶ ἴδοις τὰ ἀγαθὰ Ἱερουσαλὴμ πάσας τὰς ἡμέρας τῆς ζωῆς σου.

Δόξα σοι, ὁ Θεὸς ἡμῶν, δόξα σοι.

Καὶ ἴδοις υἱοὺς τῶν υἱῶν σου. Εἰρήνη ἐπὶ τὸν Ἰσραήλ.

Δόξα σοι, ὁ Θεὸς ἡμῶν, δόξα σοι.

Ὁ Ἱερεύς, στραφεὶς κατὰ ἀνατολὰς καὶ ὑψῶν, ὡς συνήθως, τὸ ἅγιον Εὐαγγέλιον, ἐκφωνεῖ·

Εὐλογημένη ἡ Βασιλεία τοῦ Πατρὸς καὶ τοῦ Υἱοῦ καὶ τοῦ Ἁγίου Πνεύματος, νῦν καὶ ἀεὶ καὶ εἰς τοὺς αἰῶνας τῶν αἰώνων.

Ὁ Χορός· Ἀμήν.

Κατὰ τὴν πασχάλιον περίοδον, ψάλλεται τὸ «Χριστὸς ἀνέστη» (γ΄).

Ὁ Διάκονος λέγει τὴν Συναπτήν, ὁ δὲ Χορὸς μεθ᾽ ἑκάστην Δέησιν λέγει τὸ Κύριε, ἐλέησον.

Your wife shall be as a fruitful vine on the sides of your house.

Glory to You, O our God, Glory to You.

Your children like young olive plants around your table.

Glory to You, O our God, Glory to You.

Behold! The man shall be blessed that fears the Lord.

Glory to You, O our God, Glory to You.

The Lord shall bless you out of Zion, and you shall see the good things of Jerusalem all the days of your life.

Glory to You, O our God, Glory to You.

Yea! You shall see your children's children, and peace be upon Israel.

Glory to You, O our God, Glory to You.

Turning towards the East and raising the Holy Gospel, the Priest says:

Blessed is the Kingdom of the Father, and of the Son, and of the Holy Spirit, both now and ever, and to the ages of ages.

Choir: **Amen.**

During the Easter season **"Christ is risen"** *is sung thrice.*

The Priest says the Synapte, and the Choir responds to each petition by singing "Lord have mercy."

Ὁ Διάκονος

Ἐν εἰρήνῃ τοῦ Κυρίου δεηθῶμεν.

Ὑπὲρ τῆς ἄνωθεν εἰρήνης, καὶ τῆς σωτηρίας τῶν ψυχῶν ἡμῶν, τοῦ Κυρίου δεηθῶμεν.

Ὑπὲρ τῆς εἰρήνης τοῦ σύμπαντος κόσμου, εὐσταθείας τῶν ἁγίων τοῦ Θεοῦ Ἐκκλησιῶν, καὶ τῆς τῶν πάντων ἑνώσεως, τοῦ Κυρίου δεηθῶμεν.

Ὑπὲρ τοῦ ἁγίου Οἴκου τούτου, καὶ τῶν μετὰ πίστεως, εὐλαβείας καὶ φόβου Θεοῦ εἰσιόντων ἐν αὐτῷ, τοῦ Κυρίου δεηθῶμεν.

Ὑπὲρ τοῦ Ἀρχιεπισκόπου ἡμῶν (τοῦ δεῖνος), τοῦ τιμίου πρεσβυτερίου, τῆς ἐν Χριστῷ διακονίας, παντὸς τοῦ κλήρου καὶ τοῦ λαοῦ, τοῦ Κυρίου δεηθῶμεν.

Ὑπὲρ τῶν δούλων τοῦ Θεοῦ (τοῦδε) καὶ (τῆς δε), τῶν νῦν συναπτομένων ἀλλήλοις εἰς γάμου κοινωνίαν, καὶ τῆς σωτηρίας αὐτῶν, τοῦ Κυρίου δεηθῶμεν.

Ὑπὲρ τοῦ εὐλογηθῆναι τὸν γάμον τοῦτον, ὡς τὸν ἐν Κανᾶ τῆς Γαλιλαίας, τοῦ Κυρίου δεηθῶμεν.

Ὑπὲρ τοῦ παρασχεθῆναι αὐτοῖς σωφροσύνην, καὶ καρπὸν κοιλίας πρὸς τὸ συμφέρον, τοῦ Κυρίου δεηθῶμεν.

Ὑπὲρ τοῦ εὐφρανθῆναι αὐτοὺς ἐν ὁράσει υἱῶν καὶ θυγατέρων, τοῦ Κυρίου δεηθῶμεν.

Ὑπὲρ τοῦ δωρηθῆναι αὐτοῖς εὐτεκνίας ἀπόλαυσιν, καὶ ἀκατάγνωστον διαγωγήν, τοῦ Κυρίου δεηθῶμεν.

Ὑπὲρ τοῦ δωρηθῆναι αὐτοῖς τε καὶ ἡμῖν πάντα τὰ πρὸς σωτηρίαν αἰτήματα, τοῦ Κυρίου δεηθῶμεν.

Ὑπὲρ τοῦ ῥυσθῆναι αὐτούς τε καὶ ἡμᾶς ἀπὸ πάσης θλίψεως, ὀργῆς, κινδύνου καὶ ἀνάγκης, τοῦ Κυρίου δεηθῶμεν.

Ἀντιλαβοῦ, σῶσον, ἐλέησον, καὶ διαφύλαξον ἡμᾶς, ὁ Θεός, τῇ σῇ χάριτι.

Priest

In peace let us pray to the Lord.

For the peace from above; for the salvation of our souls; let us pray to the Lord.

For the peace of the whole world; for the stability of the holy Churches of God; and for the union of all; let us pray to the Lord.

For this holy House; and for them that with faith, reverence, and the fear of God enter therein; let us pray to the Lord.

For our Most Reverend Archbishop (*Name*), for the venerable Priesthood, the Diaconate in Christ; for all the Clergy; and for all the people; let us pray to the Lord.

For the servants of God (*Name*) and (*Name*), who are now being joined to one another in the community of Marriage, and for their salvation; let us pray to the Lord.

That this marriage may be blessed as was that of Cana of Galilee; let us pray to the Lord.

That there may be given unto them soberness of life, and fruit of the womb as may be most expedient for them; let us pray to the Lord.

That they may rejoice in the beholding of sons and daughters; let us pray to the Lord.

That there may be granted unto them the happiness of abundant fertility, and a course of life blameless and unshamed; let us pray to the Lord.

That there may be granted unto them and unto us all prayers that tend unto salvation; let us pray to the Lord.

That both they and we may be delivered from tribulation, wrath, danger, and necessity; let us pray to the Lord.

Help us; save us; have mercy on us and keep us, O God by Your Grace.

Τῆς Παναγίας, ἀχράντου, ὑπερευλογημένης, ἐνδόξου, Δεσποίνης ἡμῶν Θεοτόκου, καὶ ἀειπαρθένου Μαρίας, μετὰ πάντων τῶν ἁγίων μνημονεύσαντες, ἑαυτοὺς καὶ ἀλλήλους, καὶ πᾶσαν τὴν ζωὴν ἡμῶν, Χριστῷ τῷ Θεῷ παραθώμεθα.

Ὁ Χορός· Σοί, Κύριε.

Ὁ Ἱερεύς, ἐκφώνως·

Ὅτι πρέπει σοι πᾶσα δόξα, τιμὴ καὶ προσκύνησις, τῷ Πατρὶ καὶ τῷ Υἱῷ καὶ τῷ Ἁγίῳ Πνεύματι, νῦν καὶ ἀεὶ καὶ εἰς τοὺς αἰῶνας τῶν αἰώνων.

Ὁ Χορός· Ἀμήν.

Ὁ Διάκονος
Τοῦ Κυρίου δεηθῶμεν.

Ὁ Χορός· Κύριε, ἐλέησον.

Καὶ ὁ Ἱερεὺς λέγει μεγαλοφώνως τὴν

Ε Υ Χ Η Ν

Ὁ Θεὸς ὁ ἄχραντος, καὶ πάσης κτίσεως δημιουργός, ὁ τὴν πλευρὰν τοῦ προπάτορος Ἀδὰμ διὰ τὴν σὴν φιλανθρωπίαν εἰς γυναῖκα μεταμορφώσας, καὶ εὐλογήσας αὐτούς, καὶ εἰπών· «Αὐξάνεσθε καὶ πληθύνεσθε, καὶ κατακυριεύσατε τῆς γῆς», καὶ ἀμφοτέρους αὐτοὺς ἓν μέλος ἀναδείξας διὰ τῆς συζυγίας· ἕνεκεν γὰρ τούτου καταλείψει ἄνθρωπος τὸν πατέρα αὐτοῦ καὶ τὴν μητέρα, καὶ προσκολληθήσεται τῇ ἰδίᾳ γυναικί, καὶ ἔσονται οἱ δύο εἰς σάρκα μίαν· καί, οὓς ὁ Θεὸς συνέζευξεν, ἄνθρωπος μὴ χωριζέτω· ὁ τὸν θεράποντά σου Ἀβραὰμ εὐλογήσας, καὶ διανοίξας τὴν μήτραν Σάρρας, καὶ πατέρα πλήθους ἐθνῶν ποιήσας· ὁ τὸν Ἰσαὰκ τῇ Ῥεβέκκᾳ χαρισάμενος, καὶ τὸν τόκον αὐτῆς εὐλογήσας· ὁ τὸν Ἰακὼβ τῇ Ῥαχὴλ συνάψας, καὶ ἐξ αὐτοῦ τοὺς δώδεκα Πατριάρχας ἀναδείξας· ὁ τὸν Ἰωσὴφ καὶ τὴν Ἀσυνὲθ συζεύξας, καρπὸν παιδοποιΐας αὐτοῖς τὸν Ἐφραίμ, καὶ τὸν

Calling to remembrance our all-holy, immaculate, exceedingly blessed glorious Lady Theotokos and Ever-Virgin Mary, with all the Saints; let us commend ourselves and one another and all our life to Christ our God.

Choir: To You, O God.

Priest

For to You are due all Glory, honor, and worship: to the Father, and to the Son, and to the Holy Spirit, both now and ever and to the ages of ages.

Choir: Amen.

Priest

Let us pray to the Lord.

Choir: Lord have mercy.

And the Priest says aloud the following:

O God most pure, Author of all creation, Who through Your manbefriending love transformed a rib of Adam the forefather into a woman, and blessed them and said, "Increase and multiply, and have dominion over the earth;" and, by the conjoining, declared them both to be one member, for because of this a man shall forsake his father and his mother, and shall cleave unto his wife, and the two shall be one flesh—and whom God has joined together let not man put asunder; Who did also bless Your servant Abraham, and opened the womb of Sara, and made him the father of many nations; Who bestowed Isaac upon Rebecca, and blessed her offspring; Who joined Jacob and Rachel, and from them made manifest the twelve patriarchs; Who yoked Joseph and Asenath together, and as the fruit of generation did bestow upon them Ephrem and Manasse; Who accepted Zacharias and Elizabeth, and declared their offspring the Forerunner; Who out of the root of Jesse, according to the flesh, produced the Ever-Virgin Mary, and from her were Incarnate—born

Μανασσῆν χαρισάμενος· ὁ τὸν Ζαχαρίαν καὶ τὴν Ἐλισάβετ προσδεξάμενος, καὶ Πρόδρομον τὸν τόκον αὐτῶν ἀναδείξας· ὁ ἐκ τῆς ῥίζης Ἰεσσαὶ τὸ κατὰ σάρκα βλαστήσας τὴν ἀειπάρθενον, καὶ ἐξ αὐτῆς σαρκωθεὶς καὶ τεχθεὶς εἰς σωτηρίαν τοῦ γένους τῶν ἀνθρώπων· ὁ διὰ τὴν ἄφραστόν σου δωρεὰν καὶ πολλὴν ἀγαθότητα παραγενόμενος ἐν Κανᾷ τῆς Γαλιλαίας καὶ τὸν ἐκεῖσε γάμον εὐλογήσας, ἵνα φανερώσῃς ὅτι σὸν θέλημά ἐστιν ἡ ἔννομος συζυγία καὶ ἡ ἐξ αὐτῆς παιδοποιΐα. Αὐτός, Δέσποτα Πανάγιε, πρόσδεξαι τὴν δέησιν ἡμῶν τῶν ἱκετῶν σου, ὡς ἐκεῖσε καὶ ἐνταῦθα παραγενόμενος τῇ ἀοράτῳ σου ἐπιστασίᾳ· εὐλόγησον τὸν γάμον τοῦτον, καὶ παράσχου τοῖς δούλοις σου τούτοις (τῷ δεῖνι) καὶ (τῇ δεῖνι) ζωὴν εἰρηνικήν, μακροημέρευσιν, σωφροσύνην, τὴν εἰς ἀλλήλους ἀγάπην ἐν τῷ συνδέσμῳ τῆς εἰρήνης, σπέρμα μακρόβιον, τὴν ἐπὶ τέκνοις χάριν, τὸν ἀμαράντινον τῆς δόξης στέφανον. Ἀξίωσον αὐτοὺς ἰδεῖν τέκνα τέκνων· τὴν κοίτην αὐτῶν ἀνεπιβούλευτον διατήρησον· καὶ δὸς αὐτοῖς ἀπὸ τῆς δρόσου τοῦ οὐρανοῦ ἄνωθεν, καὶ ἀπὸ τῆς πιότητος τῆς γῆς· ἔμπλησον τοὺς οἴκους αὐτῶν σίτου, οἴνου καὶ ἐλαίου καὶ πάσης ἀγαθωσύνης, ἵνα μεταδιδῶσι καὶ τοῖς χρείαν ἔχουσι, δωρούμενος ἅμα καὶ τοῖς συμπαροῦσι πάντα τὰ πρὸς σωτηρίαν αἰτήματα. Ὅτι Θεὸς ἐλέους, οἰκτιρμῶν καὶ φιλανθρωπίας ὑπάρχεις, καὶ σοὶ τὴν δόξαν ἀναπέμπομεν, σὺν τῷ ἀνάρχῳ σου Πατρί, καὶ τῷ παναγίῳ καὶ ἀγαθῷ καὶ ζωοποιῷ σου Πνεύματι, νῦν καὶ ἀεὶ καὶ εἰς τοὺς αἰῶνας τῶν αἰώνων.

Ὁ Χορός· Ἀμήν.

Τοῦ Κυρίου δεηθῶμεν.
Ὁ Χορός· Κύριε, ἐλέησον.

for the salvation of the human race; Who through Your unspeakable Grace and plentiful goodness were present in Cana of Galilee, and blessed the marriage there, that You might show a lawful union, and a generation therefrom, is according to Your Will; do You Yourself, O Most Holy Master, accept the prayer of us, Your servants; and as You were present there, be present also here with Your invisible protection. Bless (+) this marriage and grant unto these Your servants (*Name*) and (*Name*) a peaceful life, length of days, chastity, love for one another in a bond of peace, offspring long-lived, fair fame by reason of their children, and a crown of glory that does not fade away. Account them worthy to see their children's children. Keep their wedlock safe against every hostile scheme; give them of the dew from the Heavens above, and of the fatness of the earth. Fill their houses with bountiful food, and with every good thing, that they may have to give to them that are in need, bestowing also on them that are here assembled with us all their supplications that are unto salvation. For a God of mercy and of compassion, and of manbefriending love are You, and to You do we send up Glory: as to Your eternal Father and Your All-Holy, Good, and Life-creating Spirit, both now and ever, and to the ages of ages.

Choir: **Amen.**

Let us pray to the Lord.
Choir: **Lord have mercy.**

Ὁ δὲ Ἱερεὺς ἐκφώνως τὴν

ΕΥΧΗΝ

Εὐλογητὸς εἶ, Κύριε ὁ Θεὸς ἡμῶν, ὁ τοῦ μυστικοῦ καὶ ἀχράντου γάμου ἱερουργὸς καὶ τοῦ σωματικοῦ νομοθέτης, ὁ τῆς ἀφθαρσίας φύλαξ, καὶ τῶν βιοτικῶν ἀγαθὸς οἰκονόμος· αὐτὸς καὶ νῦν, Δέσποτα, ὁ ἐν ἀρχῇ πλάσας τὸν ἄνθρωπον, καὶ θέμενος αὐτὸν ὡς βασιλέα τῆς κτίσεως, καὶ εἰπών· «Οὐ καλὸν εἶναι τὸν ἄνθρωπον μόνον ἐπὶ τῆς γῆς· ποιήσωμεν αὐτῷ βοηθὸν κατ' αὐτόν»· καὶ λαβὼν μίαν τῶν πλευρῶν αὐτοῦ, ἔπλασας γυναῖκα, ἣν ἰδὼν Ἀδὰμ εἶπε· «Τοῦτο νῦν ὀστοῦν ἐκ τῶν ὀστῶν μου καὶ σὰρξ ἐκ τῆς σαρκός μου· αὕτη κληθήσεται γυνή, ὅτι ἐκ τοῦ ἀνδρὸς αὐτῆς ἐλήφθη αὕτη· ἕνεκεν τούτου καταλείψει ἄνθρωπος τὸν πατέρα αὐτοῦ καὶ τὴν μητέρα, καὶ προσκολληθήσεται πρὸς τὴν γυναῖκα αὐτοῦ, καὶ ἔσονται οἱ δύο εἰς σάρκα μίαν»· καὶ «οὓς ὁ Θεὸς συνέζευξεν, ἄνθρωπος μὴ χωριζέτω»· Αὐτὸς καὶ νῦν, Δέσποτα Κύριε, ὁ Θεὸς ἡμῶν, κατάπεμψον τὴν χάριν σου τὴν ἐπουράνιον ἐπὶ τοὺς δούλους σου τούτους (τὸν δεῖνα) καὶ (τὴν δεῖνα)· καὶ δὸς τῇ παιδίσκῃ ταύτῃ ἐν πᾶσιν ὑποταγῆναι τῷ ἀνδρί, καὶ τὸν δοῦλόν σου τοῦτον εἶναι εἰς κεφαλὴν τῆς γυναικός, ὅπως βιώσωσι κατὰ τὸ θέλημά σου. Εὐλόγησον αὐτούς, Κύριε, ὁ Θεὸς ἡμῶν, ὡς εὐλόγησας τὸν Ἀβραὰμ καὶ τὴν Σάρραν. Εὐλόγησον αὐτούς, Κύριε ὁ Θεὸς ἡμῶν, ὡς εὐλόγησας τὸν Ἰσαὰκ καὶ τὴν Ῥεβέκκαν. Εὐλόγησον αὐτοὺς Κύριε ὁ Θεὸς ἡμῶν, ὡς εὐλόγησας τὸν Ἰακὼβ καὶ πάντας τοὺς πατριάρχας. Εὐλόγησον αὐτούς, Κύριε ὁ Θεὸς ἡμῶν, ὡς εὐλόγησας τὸν Ἰωσὴφ καὶ τὴν Ἀσυνέθ. Εὐλόγησον αὐτούς, Κύριε ὁ Θεὸς ἡμῶν, ὡς εὐλόγησας Μωσέα καὶ Σεπφόραν. Εὐλόγησον αὐτούς, Κύριε ὁ Θεὸς ἡμῶν, ὡς εὐλόγησας Ἰωακεὶμ καὶ τὴν Ἄνναν. Εὐλόγησον αὐτούς, Κύριε ὁ Θεὸς

The Priest says aloud the following:

Prayer

Blessed are You, O Lord our God, Holy Celebrant of mystical and pure marriage, Maker of the laws that govern earthly bodies, Guardian of incorruption, Kindly protector of the means of life: do You Yourself now, O Master, Who in the beginning created man, and appointed him as the king of creation, and said, "It is not good for man to be alone upon the earth; let us make a helpmate for him;" then, taking one of his ribs, made woman, whom when Adam saw, he said, "This is now bone of my bones, and flesh of my flesh, for she was taken out of her man. For this cause shall a man forsake his father and his mother, and cleave unto his wife, and two shall be one flesh;" and "whom God has joined together, let no man put asunder." And now, O Master, Lord our God, send down Your heavenly Grace upon these Your servants, (*Name*) and (*Name*), and grant unto this woman to be in all things subject unto the man, and to this Your servant to be at the head of the woman, that they live according to Your Will. (+) Bless them, O Lord our God, as you blessed Abraham and Sara. (+) Bless them, O Lord our God, as You blessed Isaac and Rebecca. (+) Bless them, O Lord our God, as you blessed Jacob and all the Prophets. (+) Bless them, O Lord our God, as You blessed Joseph and Asenath. (+) Bless them, O Lord our God, as You blessed Moses and Zipporah. (+) Bless them, O Lord our God, as You blessed Joakim and Anna. (+) Bless them, O Lord our God, as You blessed

ἡμῶν, ὡς εὐλόγησας Ζαχαρίαν καὶ τὴν Ἐλισάβετ. Διαφύλαξον αὐτούς, Κύριε ὁ Θεὸς ἡμῶν, ὡς διεφύλαξας τὸν Νῶε ἐν τῇ Κιβωτῷ. Διαφύλαξον αὐτούς, Κύριε ὁ Θεὸς ἡμῶν, ὡς διεφύλαξας τὸν Ἰωνᾶν ἐν τῇ κοιλίᾳ τοῦ κήτους. Διαφύλαξον αὐτούς, Κύριε ὁ Θεὸς ἡμῶν, ὡς διεφύλαξας τοὺς ἁγίους τρεῖς Παῖδας ἐκ τοῦ πυρός, καταπέμψας αὐτοῖς δρόσον οὐρανόθεν· καὶ ἔλθοι ἐπ᾽ αὐτοὺς ἡ χαρὰ ἐκείνη, ἣν ἔσχεν ἡ μακαρία Ἑλένη, ὅτε εὖρε τὸν τίμιον Σταυρόν. Μνημόνευσον αὐτῶν, Κύριε ὁ Θεὸς ἡμῶν, ὡς ἐμνημόνευσας τοῦ Ἐνώχ, τοῦ Σήμ, τοῦ Ἠλία. Μνημόνευσον αὐτῶν, Κύριε ὁ Θεὸς ἡμῶν, ὡς ἐμνημόνευσας τῶν ἁγίων σου Τεσσαράκοντα Μαρτύρων, καταπέμψας αὐτοῖς οὐρανόθεν τοὺς στεφάνους. Μνημόνευσον, Κύριε ὁ Θεὸς ἡμῶν, καὶ τῶν ἀναθρεψάντων αὐτοὺς γονέων· ὅτι εὐχαὶ γονέων στηρίζουσι θεμέλια οἴκων. Μνημόνευσον, Κύριε ὁ Θεὸς ἡμῶν, τῶν δούλων σου τῶν Παρανύμφων, τῶν συνελθόντων εἰς τὴν χαρὰν ταύτην. Μνημόνευσον, Κύριε ὁ Θεὸς ἡμῶν, τοῦ δούλου σου (τοῦδε) καὶ τῆς δούλης σου (τῆσδε), καὶ εὐλόγησον αὐτούς. Δὸς αὐτοῖς καρπὸν κοιλίας, καλλιτεκνίαν, ὁμόνοιαν ψυχῶν καὶ σωμάτων. Ὕψωσον αὐτοὺς ὡς τὰς κέδρους τοῦ Λιβάνου, ὡς ἄμπελον εὐκληματοῦσαν. Δώρησαι αὐτοῖς σπέρμα στάχυος, ἵνα, πᾶσαν αὐτάρκειαν ἔχοντες, περισσεύσωσιν εἰς πᾶν ἔργον ἀγαθὸν καὶ σοὶ εὐάρεστον, καὶ ἴδωσιν υἱοὺς τῶν υἱῶν αὐτῶν, ὡς νεόφυτα ἐλαιῶν κύκλῳ τῆς τραπέζης αὐτῶν· καί, εὐαρεστήσαντες ἐνώπιόν σου, λάμψωσιν ὡς φωστῆρες ἐν οὐρανῷ, ἐν σοὶ τῷ Κυρίῳ ἡμῶν· ᾧ πρέπει πᾶσα δόξα, κράτος, τιμή, καὶ προσκύνησις, νῦν καὶ ἀεὶ καὶ εἰς τοὺς αἰῶνας τῶν αἰώνων.

Ὁ Χορός· Ἀμήν.

Zacharias and Elizabeth. Preserve them, O Lord our God, as You preserved Noah in the Ark. Preserve them, O Lord our God, as You preserved Jonah in the jaw of the seabeast. Preserve them, O Lord our God, as You preserved the holy Three Children from the fire, when You sent down upon them the dew of the Heavens. And may that joy come upon them which the blessed Helen had when she found the Precious Cross. Remember them, O Lord our God, as You remembered Enoch, Shem, and Elias. Remember them, O Lord our God, as You remembered Your holy Forty Martyrs, sending down upon them the crowns from the Heavens. Remember them, O Lord our God, and the parents who have reared them, for the prayers of parents confirm the foundation of houses. Remember, O Lord our God, the wedding company that here have come together, to be present at this rejoicing. Remember, O Lord our God, Your servant (*Name*) and Your servant (*Name*), and bless them. Give to them fruit of the womb, fair children, concord of soul and body. Exalt them as the cedars of Lebanon, and as well-cultured vine; bestow on them a rich store of sustenance, so that having a sufficiency of all things for themselves, they may abound in every good work that is good and acceptable before You. Let them behold their children's children as newly planted olive trees round about their table; and, being accepted before You, let them shine as stars in the Heavens, in You, our Lord, to Whom are due all Glory, honor, and worship, as to Your eternal Father, and Your All-Holy, Good, and Life-creating Spirit, both now and ever, and to the ages of ages.

Choir: **Amen.**

Ὁ Διάκονος
Τοῦ Κυρίου δεηθῶμεν.
Ὁ Χορός· Κύριε, ἐλέησον·
Καὶ πάλιν ὁ Ἱερεὺς τὴν Ε ὐ χ ὴ ν ταύτην ἐκφώνως·

Ο῾ Θεὸς ὁ ἅγιος, ὁ πλάσας ἐκ χοὸς τὸν ἄνθρωπον, καὶ ἐκ τῆς πλευρᾶς αὐτοῦ ἀνοικοδομήσας γυναῖκα, καὶ συζεύξας αὐτῷ βοηθὸν κατ᾽ αὐτόν, διὰ τὸ οὕτως ἀρέσαι τῇ σῇ μεγαλειότητι, μὴ μόνον εἶναι τὸν ἄνθρωπον ἐπὶ τῆς γῆς· αὐτὸς καὶ νῦν, Δέσποτα, ἐξαπόστειλον τὴν χεῖρά σου ἐξ ἁγίου κατοικητηρίου σου, καὶ ἅρμοσον* τὸν δοῦλον σου (τόνδε), καὶ τὴν δούλην σου (τήνδε), ὅτι παρὰ σοῦ ἁρμόζεται ἀνδρὶ γυνή. Σύζευξον αὐτοὺς ἐν ὁμοφροσύνῃ· στεφάνωσον αὐτοὺς εἰς σάρκα μίαν· χάρισαι αὐτοῖς καρπὸν κοιλίας, εὐτεκνίας ἀπόλαυσιν. Ὅτι σὸν τὸ κράτος, καὶ σοῦ ἐστιν ἡ βασιλεία καὶ ἡ δύναμις καὶ ἡ δόξα, τοῦ Πατρὸς καὶ τοῦ Υἱοῦ καὶ τοῦ Ἁγίου Πνεύματος, νῦν καὶ ἀεὶ καὶ εἰς τοὺς αἰῶνας τῶν αἰώνων.

Ὁ Χορός· Ἀμήν.

Καὶ λαβὼν ὁ Ἱερεὺς τὰ Στέφανα, στέφει πρῶτον τὸν Νυμφίον, λέγων·

Στέφεται ὁ δοῦλος τοῦ Θεοῦ (ὁ δεῖνα), τὴν δούλην τοῦ Θεοῦ (τήν δε), εἰς τὸ ὄνομα τοῦ Πατρός, καὶ τοῦ Υἱοῦ, καὶ τοῦ Ἁγίου Πνεύματος. Ἀμήν.

Τοῦτο δὲ λέγει ἐκ τρίτου, ποιῶν σχῆμα Σταυροῦ.

Εἶτα στέφει καὶ τὴν Νύμφην, λέγων.

Στέφεται ἡ δούλη τοῦ Θεοῦ (ἡ δεῖνα), τὸν δοῦλον τοῦ Θεοῦ (τόνδε), εἰς τὸ ὄνομα τοῦ Πατρός, καὶ τοῦ Υἱοῦ, καὶ τοῦ Ἁγίου Πνεύματος. Ἀμήν.

Καὶ τοῦτο τρίς, ὁμοίως.

---

* Τούτου λεγομένου, ὁ Ἱερεὺς ἁρμόζει τὰς δεξιὰς τῶν νυμφευομένων.

Priest

Let us pray to the Lord.

Choir: Lord have mercy.

Holy God, Who fashioned man from the dust, and from his rib fashioned woman, and joined her to him as a helpmate for him, for it was seemly unto Your Majesty for man not to be alone upon the earth, do You Yourself, O Sovereign Lord, stretch forth Your hand from Your holy dwelling place, and join* together this Your servant (*Name*) and Your servant (*Name*), for by You is a wife joined to her husband. Join them together in oneness of mind; crown them with wedlock into one flesh; grant to them the fruit of the womb, and the gain of well-favored children, for Yours is the dominion, and Yours is the Kingdom, and the Power, and the Glory: of the Father, and of the Son, and of the Holy Spirit, both now and ever, and to the ages of ages.

Choir: Amen.

After the Amen, the Priest, taking up the Crowns, crowns first the Bridegroom, saying:

The servant of God (*Name*) is crowned for the servant of God (*Name*), in the Name of the Father, and of the Son, and of the Holy Spirit. Amen. (*Thrice*)

And he crowns the Bride, saying:

The servant of God (*Name*) is crowned for the servant of God (*Name*), in the Name of the Father, and of the Son, and of the Holy Spirit. Amen. (*Thrice*)

When this is said, the priest joins their right hands.

Εἶτα τίθησι τὰ Στέφανα ἐπὶ τὰς κεφαλὰς τῶν Νυμφίων, ψάλλων ἐκ τρίτου.

Κύριε ὁ Θεὸς ἡμῶν, δόξῃ καὶ τιμῇ στεφάνωσον αὐτούς.

Ὁ Διάκονος· Πρόσχωμεν.

Ὁ Ἀναγνώστης
Προκείμενον, Ἦχος πλ. δ΄.
Ἔθηκας ἐπὶ τὴν κεφαλὴν αὐτῶν στεφάνους ἐκ λίθων τιμίων.
Στίχ. Ζωὴν ᾐτήσαντό σε, καὶ ἔδωκας αὐτοῖς μακρότητα ἡμερῶν.

Ὁ Διάκονος· Σοφία.

Ὁ Ἀναγνώστης
Πρὸς Ἐφεσίους Ἐπιστολῆς Παύλου τὸ Ἀνάγνωσμα
(Κεφ. ε΄ 20-33).

Ὁ Διάκονος· Πρόσχωμεν.

Ὁ Ἀναγνώστης
Ἀδελφοί, εὐχαριστεῖτε πάντοτε ὑπὲρ πάντων, ἐν ὀνόματι τοῦ Κυρίου ἡμῶν Ἰησοῦ Χριστοῦ τῷ Θεῷ καὶ Πατρί, ὑποτασσόμενοι ἀλλήλοις ἐν φόβῳ Χριστοῦ. Αἱ γυναῖκες τοῖς ἰδίοις ἀνδράσιν ὑποτάσσεσθε ὡς τῷ Κυρίῳ, ὅτι ὁ ἀνήρ ἐστι κεφαλὴ τῆς γυναικός, ὡς καὶ ὁ Χριστὸς κεφαλὴ τῆς Ἐκκλησίας, καὶ αὐτός ἐστι σωτὴρ τοῦ σώματος. Ἀλλ᾽ ὥσπερ ἡ Ἐκκλησία ὑποτάσσεται τῷ Χριστῷ, οὕτω καὶ αἱ γυναῖκες τοῖς ἰδίοις ἀνδράσιν ἐν παντί. Οἱ ἄνδρες ἀγαπᾶτε τὰς γυναῖκας ἑαυτῶν, καθὼς καὶ ὁ Χριστὸς ἠγάπησε τὴν Ἐκκλησίαν καὶ ἑαυτὸν παρέδωκεν ὑπὲρ αὐτῆς, ἵνα αὐτὴν ἁγιάσῃ, καθαρίσας τῷ λουτρῷ τοῦ ὕδατος ἐν ῥήματι, ἵνα παραστήσῃ αὐτὴν ἑαυτῷ ἔνδοξον τὴν Ἐκκλησίαν, μὴ ἔχουσαν σπίλον ἢ ῥυτίδα ἤ τι τῶν τοιούτων, ἀλλ᾽ ἵνα ᾖ ἁγία καὶ ἄμωμος. Οὕτως ὀφείλουσιν οἱ ἄνδρες ἀγαπᾶν τὰς ἑαυ-

The Priest takes the Crown of the Groom in his right hand, and the Crown of the Bride in his left, and places them on their heads while he intones:

O Lord, our God, crown them with glory and honor.

Let us attend.

Reader

Prokeimenon, in Tone 8

You have set upon their heads crowns of precious stones.

They asked life of You, and You gave it to them.

Priest: Wisdom!

Reader

The Reading from the Epistle of the holy Apostle Paul to the Ephesians. (5:20-33)

Priest: Let us attend.

Reader

Brethren, give thanks always for all things in the name of our Lord Jesus Christ to God the Father. Be subject to one another out of reverence for Christ. Wives, be subject to your husbands, as to the Lord. For the husband is the head of the wife as Christ is the head of the church, his body, and is himself its Savior. As the church is subject to Christ, so let wives be also subject in everything to their husbands. Husbands, love your wives, as Christ loved the church and gave himself up for her, that he might sanctify her, having cleansed her by the washing of water with the word, that he might present the church to himself in splendor, without spot or wrinkle or any such thing, that she might be holy and without blemish. Even so husbands should love their wives as their own

τῶν γυναῖκας, ὡς τὰ ἑαυτῶν σώματα· ὁ ἀγαπῶν τὴν ἑαυτοῦ γυναῖκα ἑαυτὸν ἀγαπᾷ· οὐδεὶς γάρ ποτε τὴν ἑαυτοῦ σάρκα ἐμίσησεν, ἀλλ' ἐκτρέφει καὶ θάλπει αὐτήν, καθὼς καὶ ὁ Κύριος τὴν Ἐκκλησίαν· ὅτι μέλη ἐσμὲν τοῦ σώματος αὐτοῦ, ἐκ τῆς σαρκὸς αὐτοῦ καὶ ἐκ τῶν ὀστέων αὐτοῦ· ἀντὶ τούτου καταλείψει ἄνθρωπος τὸν πατέρα αὐτοῦ καὶ τὴν μητέρα καὶ προσκολληθήσεται πρὸς τὴν γυναῖκα αὐτοῦ, καὶ ἔσονται οἱ δύο εἰς σάρκα μίαν. Τὸ μυστήριον τοῦτο μέγα ἐστίν, ἐγὼ δὲ λέγω εἰς Χριστὸν καὶ εἰς τὴν Ἐκκλησίαν. Πλὴν καὶ ὑμεῖς οἱ καθ' ἕνα, ἕκαστος τὴν ἑαυτοῦ γυναῖκα οὕτως ἀγαπάτω ὡς ἑαυτόν, ἡ δὲ γυνὴ ἵνα φοβῆται τὸν ἄνδρα.

Ὁ Ἱερεὺς

Εἰρήνη σοι τῷ ἀναγινώσκοντι.

Ὁ Χορὸς

Ἦχος πλ. α΄.

Ἀλληλούϊα, ἀλληλούϊα, ἀλληλούϊα.

Στίχ. Σύ, Κύριε, φυλάξαις ἡμᾶς καὶ διατηρήσαις ἡμᾶς.

Ὁ Διάκονος

Σοφία· ὀρθοί· ἀκούσωμεν τοῦ ἁγίου Εὐαγγελίου.

Ὁ Ἱερεύς· Εἰρήνη πᾶσι.

Ὁ Χορός· Καὶ τῷ πνεύματί σου.

Ὁ Ἱερεὺς

Ἐκ τοῦ κατὰ Ἰωάννην ἁγίου Εὐαγγελίου
τὸ Ἀνάγνωσμα.

(Κεφ. β΄ 1-11)

Ὁ Διάκονος· Πρόσχωμεν

Ὁ Ἱερεὺς

Τῷ καιρῷ ἐκείνῳ, γάμος ἐγένετο ἐν Κανᾷ τῆς Γαλιλαίας, καὶ ἦν ἡ μήτηρ τοῦ Ἰησοῦ ἐκεῖ· ἐκλήθη δὲ καὶ ὁ Ἰησοῦς καὶ οἱ μαθηταὶ αὐτοῦ εἰς

bodies. He who loves his wife loves himself. For no man ever hates his own flesh, but nourishes and cherishes it, as Christ does the church, because we are members of his body. "For this reason a man shall leave his father and his mother and shall be joined to his wife, and the two shall become one." This is a great mystery, and I take it to mean Christ and the church; however, let each one of you love his wife as himself, and let the wife see that she respects her husband.

Priest

Peace be to you who read.

Choir

Allelluia, alleluia, alleluia.

O Lord, You shall keep us and You shall preserve us from this generation forth and forever.

Priest

Wisdom! Let us attend! Let us hear the Holy Gospel.

Peace be to all. (+)

Choir: And to your spirit.

Priest

The Reading from the Holy Gospel according to St. John.
(John 2:1-11)

Choir: Glory to You, O Lord, Glory to You.

Priest

At that time there was a marriage at Cana in Galilee, and the mother of Jesus was there; Jesus also was invited to the marriage, with his disciples. When the wine failed, the

τὸν γάμον. Καὶ ὑστερήσαντος οἴνου, λέγει ἡ μήτηρ τοῦ Ἰησοῦ πρὸς αὐτόν· Οἶνον οὐκ ἔχουσι. Λέγει αὐτῇ ὁ Ἰησοῦς· Τί ἐμοὶ καὶ σοί, γύναι; οὔπω ἥκει ἡ ὥρα μου. Λέγει ἡ μήτηρ αὐτοῦ τοῖς διακόνοις· Ὅ,τι ἂν λέγῃ ὑμῖν, ποιήσατε. Ἦσαν δὲ ἐκεῖ ὑδρίαι λίθιναι ἓξ κείμεναι κατὰ τὸν καθαρισμὸν τῶν Ἰουδαίων, χωροῦσαι ἀνὰ μετρητὰς δύο ἢ τρεῖς. Λέγει αὐτοῖς ὁ Ἰησοῦς· Γεμίσατε τὰς ὑδρίας ὕδατος. Καὶ ἐγέμισαν αὐτὰς ἕως ἄνω. Καὶ λέγει αὐτοῖς· Ἀντλήσατε νῦν καὶ φέρετε τῷ ἀρχιτρικλίνῳ. Καὶ ἤνεγκαν. Ὡς δὲ ἐγεύσατο ὁ ἀρχιτρίκλινος τὸ ὕδωρ οἶνον γεγενημένον (καὶ οὐκ ᾔδει πόθεν ἐστίν· οἱ δὲ διάκονοι ᾔδεισαν οἱ ἠντληκότες τὸ ὕδωρ) φωνεῖ τὸν νυμφίον ὁ ἀρχιτρίκλινος καὶ λέγει αὐτῷ· Πᾶς ἄνθρωπος πρῶτον τὸν καλὸν οἶνον τίθησι, καὶ ὅταν μεθυσθῶσι, τότε τὸν ἐλάσσω· σὺ δὲ τετήρηκας τὸν καλὸν οἶνον ἕως ἄρτι. Ταύτην ἐποίησε τὴν ἀρχὴν τῶν σημείων ὁ Ἰησοῦς ἐν Κανᾷ τῆς Γαλιλαίας καὶ ἐφανέρωσε τὴν δόξαν αὐτοῦ, καὶ ἐπίστευσαν εἰς αὐτὸν οἱ Μαθηταὶ αὐτοῦ.

Ὁ Χορός· **Δόξά σοι, Κύριε, δόξα σοι.**

Καὶ εὐθύς, ὁ Διάκονος, τὴν Ἐκτενῆ·

Εἴπωμεν πάντες ἐξ ὅλης τῆς ψυχῆς, καὶ ἐξ ὅλης τῆς διανοίας ἡμῶν εἴπωμεν.

Κύριε Παντοκράτορ, ὁ Θεὸς τῶν Πατέρων ἡμῶν, δεόμεθά σου ἐπάκουσον, καὶ ἐλέησον.

Ἐλέησον ἡμᾶς ὁ Θεός, κατὰ τὸ μέγα ἔλεός σου· δεόμεθά σου ἐπάκουσον καὶ ἐλέησον.

Ἔτι δεόμεθα ὑπὲρ ἐλέους, ζωῆς, εἰρήνης, ὑγίειας καὶ σωτηρίας τῶν δούλων σου (τοῦ δεῖνος) καὶ (τῆς δεῖνος) καὶ ὑπὲρ τοῦ περιεστῶτος λαοῦ, τῶν ἀπεκδεχομένων τὸ παρὰ σοῦ πλούσιον ἔλεος.

mother of Jesus said to him, "They have no wine." And Jesus said to her, "O woman, what have you to do with me? My hour has not yet come." His mother said to the servants, "Do whatever he tells you." Now six stone jars were standing there, for the Jewish rites of purification, each holding twenty or thirty gallons. Jesus said to them, "Fill the jars with water." And they filled them up to the brim. He said to them, "Now draw some out, and take it to the steward of the feast." So they took it. When the steward of the feast tasted the water now become wine, and did not know where it came from (though the servants who had drawn the water knew), the steward of the feast called the bridegroom and said to him, "Every man serves the good wine first; and when men have drunk freely, then the poor wine; but you have kept the good wine until now." This, the first of his signs, Jesus did at Cana in Galilee, and manifested his glory; and his disciples believed in him.

Choir: Glory to You, O Lord, Glory to You.

The Priest gives the Book of the Gospels to the Bride and the Groom to be kissed, and then continues with the following petitions. After each, the Choir responds thrice with "Lord have mercy."

Let us say with all our soul and all our mind, let us say:

O Lord Almighty, God of our fathers, we pray You, listen and have mercy.

Have mercy on us, O God, according to Your great mercy; we pray You, listen and have mercy.

Again let us pray for the servants of God, (*Name*) and (*Name*), that they may have mercy, life, health, peace, safety, salvation, pardon and remission of their sins.

Ὁ Ἱερεύς, ἐκφώνως·

Ὅτι ἐλεήμων, καὶ φιλάνθρωπος Θεὸς ὑπάρχεις, καὶ σοὶ τὴν δόξαν ἀναπέμπομεν, τῷ Πατρὶ καὶ τῷ Υἱῷ καὶ τῷ Ἁγίῳ Πνεύματι, νῦν καὶ ἀεὶ καὶ εἰς τοὺς αἰῶνας τῶν αἰώνων.

Ὁ Χορός· Ἀμήν.

Ὁ Διάκονος

Τοῦ Κυρίου δεηθῶμεν.

Ὁ Χορός· Κύριε, ἐλέησον.

Καὶ ὁ Ἱερεὺς τὴν Εὐχὴν ταύτην·

Κύριε ὁ Θεὸς ἡμῶν, ὁ ἐν τῇ σωτηριώδει σου οἰκονομίᾳ καταξιώσας ἐν Κανᾶ τῆς Γαλιλαίας τίμιον ἀναδεῖξαι τὸν γάμον, διὰ τῆς σῆς παρουσίας, αὐτὸς καὶ νῦν τοὺς δούλους σου (τὸν δεῖνα) καὶ (τὴν δεῖνα), οὓς ηὐδόκησας συναφθῆναι ἀλλήλοις, ἐν εἰρήνῃ καὶ ὁμονοίᾳ διαφύλαξον. Τίμιον αὐτοῖς τὸν γάμον ἀνάδειξον· ἀμίαντον αὐτῶν τὴν κοίτην διατήρησον· ἀκηλίδωτον αὐτῶν τὴν συμβίωσιν διαμεῖναι εὐδόκησον· καὶ καταξίωσον αὐτοὺς ἐν γήρει πίονι καταντῆσαι, ἐν καθαρᾷ τῇ καρδίᾳ ἐργαζομένους τὰς ἐντολάς σου.

Σὺ γὰρ εἶ ὁ Θεὸς ἡμῶν, Θεὸς τοῦ ἐλεεῖν καὶ σῴζειν, καὶ σοὶ τὴν δόξαν ἀναπέμπομεν, σὺν τῷ ἀνάρχῳ σου Πατρί, καὶ τῷ παναγίῳ καὶ ἀγαθῷ καὶ ζωοποιῷ σου Πνεύματι, νῦν καὶ ἀεὶ καὶ εἰς τοὺς αἰῶνας τῶν αἰώνων.

Ὁ Χορός· Ἀμήν.

Ὁ Διάκονος

Ἀντιλαβοῦ, σῶσον, ἐλέησον καὶ διαφύλαξον ἡμᾶς, ὁ Θεός, τῇ σῇ χάριτι.

Ὁ Χορός· Κύριε ἐλέησον.

Priest

For You are a merciful and loving God, and to You do we send up Glory: to the Father, and to the Son, and to the Holy Spirit, both now and ever, and to the ages of ages.

Choir: Amen.

Priest

Let us pray to the Lord.

Choir: Lord have mercy.

Priest (facing the married couple)

O Lord our God, Who in Your saving Providence did promise in Cana of Galilee to declare marriage honorable by Your presence, do You Yourself preserve in peace and oneness of mind these Your servants (*Name*) and (*Name*), whom You are well pleased should be joined to one another. Declare their marriage honorable. Preserve their bed undefiled. Grant that their life together be with-be without spot of sin. And assure that they may be worthy to attain unto a ripe old age, keeping Your commandments in a pure heart.

For You are our God, the God to have mercy and save, and to You do we send up all Glory, as to Your Eternal Father, and Your All-Holy, Good, and Life-creating Spirit, both now and ever, and to the ages of ages.

Choir: Amen.

Priest

Help us; save us; have mercy on us, and keep us, O God, by Your Grace.

Choir: Lord have mercy.

Ὁ Διάκονος

Τὴν ἡμέραν πᾶσαν, τελείαν, ἁγίαν, εἰρηνικὴν καὶ ἀναμάρτητον παρὰ τοῦ Κυρίου αἰτησώμεθα.

Ὁ Χορός, μεθ᾽ ἑκάστην Δέησιν·

Παράσχου, Κύριε.

Ὁ Διάκονος

Ἄγγελον εἰρήνης, πιστὸν ὁδηγόν, φύλακα τῶν ψυχῶν καὶ τῶν σωμάτων ἡμῶν, παρὰ τοῦ Κυρίου αἰτησώμεθα.

Συγγνώμην καὶ ἄφεσιν τῶν ἁμαρτιῶν καὶ τῶν πλημμελημάτων ἡμῶν, παρὰ τοῦ Κυρίου αἰτησώμεθα

Τὰ καλὰ καὶ συμφέροντα ταῖς ψυχαῖς ἡμῶν, καὶ εἰρήνην τῷ κόσμῳ, παρὰ τοῦ Κυρίου αἰτησώμεθα.

Τὸν ὑπόλοιπον χρόνον τῆς ζωῆς ἡμῶν, ἐν εἰρήνῃ καὶ μετανοίᾳ ἐκτελέσαι, παρὰ τοῦ Κυρίου αἰτησώμεθα.

Τὴν ἑνότητα τῆς πίστεως, καὶ τὴν κοινωνίαν τοῦ Ἁγίου Πνεύματος αἰτησάμενοι, ἑαυτοὺς καὶ ἀλλήλους καὶ πᾶσαν τὴν ζωὴν ἡμῶν Χριστῷ τῷ Θεῷ παραθώμεθα.

Ὁ Ἱερεύς, ἐκφώνως·

Καὶ καταξίωσον ἡμᾶς, Δέσποτα, μετὰ παρρησίας, ἀκατακρίτως, τολμᾶν ἐπικαλεῖσθαί σε τὸν ἐπουράνιον Θεὸν Πατέρα, καὶ λέγειν.

Ὁ Ἀναγνώστης τὸ

Πάτερ ἡμῶν ὁ ἐν τοῖς οὐρανοῖς· ἁγιασθήτω τὸ ὄνομά σου· ἐλθέτω ἡ βασιλεία σου· γενηθήτω τὸ θέλημά σου, ὡς ἐν οὐρανῷ καὶ ἐπὶ τῆς γῆς· τὸν ἄρτον ἡμῶν τὸν ἐπιούσιον δὸς ἡμῖν σήμερον· καὶ ἄφες ἡμῖν τὰ ὀφειλήματα ἡμῶν, ὡς καὶ

Priest

That the whole day may be kept perfect, holy, peaceful, and sinless; let us ask of the Lord.

Choir responds to each petition saying:

O Lord, grant this prayer.

An Angel of Peace, a faithful Guide, a Guardian of our souls and bodies; let us ask of the Lord.

Pardon and remission of our sins and offenses; let us ask of the Lord.

All things that are good and profitable for our souls, and peace for the whole world; let us ask of the Lord.

That we may complete the remaining time of our life in peace and repentance; let us ask of the Lord.

A Christian ending to our life, painless, without shame, peaceful; and a good defense before the dread Judgment Seat of Christ; let us ask of the Lord.

Asking for the unity of the Faith and the Communion of the Holy Spirit, let us commend ourselves and one another and all our life to Christ our God.

And account us worthy, O Sovereign Lord, with boldness and without condemnation to dare call on You, the Heavenly God, as Father, and to say:

Our Father, Who are in Heaven,
Hallowed be Your Name; Your Kingdom come.
Your Will be done on earth as it is in Heaven.
Give us this day our daily bread;
And forgive us our trespasses,

ἡμεῖς ἀφίεμεν τοῖς ὀφειλέταις ἡμῶν· καὶ μὴ εἰσενέγκῃς ἡμᾶς εἰς πειρασμόν, ἀλλὰ ῥῦσαι ἡμᾶς ἀπὸ τοῦ πονηροῦ.

Ὁ Ἱερεύς, ἐκφώνως·

Ὅτι σοῦ ἐστιν ἡ βασιλεία καὶ ἡ δύναμις καὶ ἡ δόξα, τοῦ Πατρὸς καὶ τοῦ Υἱοῦ καὶ τοῦ Ἁγίου Πνεύματος, νῦν καὶ ἀεὶ καὶ εἰς τοὺς αἰῶνας τῶν αἰώνων.

Ὁ Χορός· Ἀμήν.

Ὁ Ἱερεύς· Εἰρήνη πᾶσι.

Ὁ Χορός· Καὶ τῷ πνεύματί σου.

Ὁ Διάκονος

Τὰς κεφαλὰς ἡμῶν τῷ Κυρίῳ κλίνωμεν.

Ὁ Χορός· Σοί, Κύριε.

Εἶτα προσφέρεται τὸ κοινὸν ποτήριον.

Ὁ Διάκονος

Τοῦ Κυρίου δεηθῶμεν.

Ὁ Χορός· Κύριε, ἐλέησον.

Ὁ Ἱερεύς, εὐλογῶν τὸ ποτήριον, λέγει τὴν Εὐχὴν ταύτην·

Ὁ Θεός, ὁ πάντα ποιήσας τῇ ἰσχύϊ σου, καὶ στερεώσας τὴν οἰκουμένην, καὶ κοσμήσας τὸν στέφανον πάντων τῶν πεποιημένων ὑπὸ σοῦ, καὶ τὸ ποτήριον τὸ κοινὸν τοῦτο παρεχόμενος τοῖς συναφθεῖσι πρὸς γάμου κοινωνίαν, εὐλόγησον εὐλογίᾳ πνευματικῇ.

Ὅτι ηὐλόγηταί σου τὸ ὄνομα, καὶ δεδόξασταί σου ἡ βασιλεία τοῦ Πατρὸς καὶ τοῦ Υἱοῦ καὶ τοῦ Ἁγίου Πνεύματος, νῦν καὶ ἀεὶ καὶ εἰς τοὺς αἰῶνας τῶν αἰώνων.

Ὁ Χορός· Ἀμήν.

As we forgive those who trespass against us
And lead us not into temptation.
But deliver us from evil.

Priest

For Yours is the Kingdom and the Power and the Glory,
of the Father, and of the Son, and of the Holy Spirit,
both now and ever, and to the ages of ages.

Choir: Amen.

Priest: Peace (+) be to all.

Choir: And to your spirit.

Priest

Let us bow our heads before the Lord.

Choir: To You, O Lord.

Then the common cup is offered.

Priest

Let us pray to the Lord. Lord have mercy.

The Priest blesses the cup saying this prayer:

O God, Who by Your might create all things, and confirm the universe, and adorn the crown of all things created
by You, do You, with Your spiritual blessing (+), bless
also this common cup given to them that are joined in
the community of marriage.

For blessed is Your Holy Name, and glorified is the
Kingdom of the Father, and of the Son, and of the Holy
Spirit, both now and ever, and to the ages of ages.

Choir: Amen.

Εἶτα, λαβὼν ὁ Ἱερεὺς ἐπὶ χεῖρας τὸ κοινὸν ποτήριον, μεταδίδωσιν αὐτοῖς ἐκ γʹ, πρῶτον τῷ ἀνδρί, καὶ αὖθις τῇ γυναικί, ψάλλων εἰς ἦχον αʹ.

Π οτήριον σωτηρίου λήψομαι, καὶ τὸ ὄνομα Κυρίου ἐπικαλέσομαι.

Καὶ εὐθέως λαβὼν αὐτοὺς ὁ Ἱερεύς, τοῦ Παρανύμφου κρατοῦντος ὄπισθεν τοὺς στεφάνους, στρέφει ὡς ἐν σχήματι κύκλου περὶ τὸ ἐν τῷ μέσῳ τραπεζίδιον ἐκ τρίτου.

Καὶ ψάλλει ὁ Ἱερεὺς ἢ ὁ Χορὸς τὰ Τροπάρια·

Ἦχος πλ. αʹ.

Η σαΐα χόρευε· ἡ Παρθένος ἔσχεν ἐν γαστρί, καὶ ἔτεκεν Υἱὸν τὸν Ἐμμανουήλ, Θεόν τε καὶ ἄνθρωπον· Ἀνατολὴ ὄνομα αὐτῷ· ὃν μεγαλύνοντες, τὴν Παρθένον μακαρίζομεν.

Ἦχος βαρύς.

Α γιοι Μάρτυρες, οἱ καλῶς ἀθλήσαντες καὶ στεφανωθέντες, πρεσβεύσατε πρὸς Κύριον, ἐλεηθῆναι τὰς ψυχὰς ἡμῶν.

Δ όξα σοι Χριστὲ ὁ Θεός, Ἀποστόλων καύχημα, Μαρτύρων ἀγαλλίαμα, ὧν τὸ κήρυγμα· Τριὰς ἡ ὁμοούσιος.

Εἶτα ὁ Ἱερεὺς ἐπαίρει τοὺς στεφάνους· καὶ ἐπάρας τὸν στέφανον τοῦ Νυμφίου, λέγει·

Μεγαλύνθητι, Νυμφίε, ὡς ὁ Ἀβραάμ, καὶ εὐλογήθητι ὡς ὁ Ἰσαάκ, καὶ πληθύνθητι ὡς ὁ Ἰακώβ, πορευόμενος ἐν εἰρήνῃ καὶ ἐργαζόμενος ἐν δικαιοσύνῃ τὰς ἐντολὰς τοῦ Θεοῦ.

Καὶ ἐν τῷ τῆς Νύμφης λέγει·

Καὶ σύ, Νύμφη, μεγαλύνθητι ὡς ἡ Σάρρα, καὶ εὐφράνθητι ὡς ἡ Ρεβέκκα, καὶ πληθύνθητι ὡς ἡ

Then the Priest gives them to drink thrice from the cup, first to the man, then to the woman, chanting:

I will drink from the cup of salvation; I will call upon the name of the Lord.

Then he takes the Bridal Pair, while the Groomsman holds the Crowns behind and above them, and leads them in a circle around the Analogion thrice. The people sing:

Tone 5

O Isaiah, dance your joy, for the Virgin was indeed with child; and brought to birth a Son, that Emmanuel, Who came as both God and man; Day-at-the-Dawn is the Name He bears, and by extolling Him, We hail the Virgin as blessed.

Hear us, you martyred Saints, who fought the good fight, gaining crowns: entreat the Lord to shed His tender mercy on our souls.

Glory to You, O Christ our God, Your Apostles' proudest boast and treasure of Your Martyrs' joy, Who to all proclaimed the Consubstantial Trinity.

Then the Priest removes the Crowns, taking first that of the Groom and saying:

Be magnified, O Bridegroom, as Abraham, and blessed as Isaac, and increased as was Jacob. Go your way in peace, performing in righteousness the commandments of God.

He takes the Crown of the Bride and says:

And you, O Bride, be magnified as was Sarah, and rejoiced as was Rebecca, and increased as Rachel, being

Ῥαχήλ, εὐφραινομένη τῷ ἰδίῳ ἀνδρί, φυλάττουσα τοὺς ὅρους τοῦ νόμου, ὅτι οὕτως ηὐδόκησεν ὁ Θεός.

Εἶτα λέγει ὁ Διάκονος·

Τοῦ Κυρίου δεηθῶμεν.

Ὁ Χορός· **Κύριε, ἐλέησον.**

Καὶ ὁ Ἱερεὺς τὴν Ε ὐ χ ὴ ν ταύτην·

Ο῾ Θεός, ὁ Θεὸς ἡμῶν, ὁ παραγενόμενος ἐν Κανᾶ τῆς Γαλιλαίας, καὶ τὸν ἐκεῖσε γάμον εὐλογήσας, εὐλόγησον καὶ τοὺς δούλους σου τούτους, τοὺς τῇ σῇ προνοίᾳ πρὸς γάμου κοινωνίαν συναφθέντας. Εὐλόγησον αὐτῶν εἰσόδους καὶ ἐξόδους· πλήθυνον ἐν ἀγαθοῖς τὴν ζωὴν αὐτῶν· ἀνάλαβε* τοὺς στεφάνους αὐτῶν ἐν τῇ Βασιλείᾳ σου, ἀσπίλους καὶ ἀμώμους καὶ ἀνεπιβουλεύτους διατηρῶν εἰς τοὺς αἰῶνας τῶν αἰώνων.

Ὁ Χορός· **Ἀμήν.**

Ὁ Ἱερεύς· **Εἰρήνη πᾶσι.**

Ὁ Χορός· **Καὶ τῷ πνεύματί σου.**

Ὁ Διάκονος

Τὰς κεφαλὰς ὑμῶν τῷ Κυρίῳ κλίνατε.

Ὁ Χορός· **Σοί, Κύριε.**

Καὶ εὔχεται ὁ Ἱερεὺς

Ο῾ Πατήρ, ὁ Υἱὸς καὶ τὸ Ἅγιον Πνεῦμα, ἡ παναγία καὶ ὁμοούσιος καὶ ζωαρχικὴ Τριάς, ἡ μία Θεότης καὶ Βασιλεία, εὐλογήσαι ὑμᾶς, καὶ παράσχοι

---

* Ἐνταῦθα ὁ Ἱερεὺς αἴρει τοὺς στεφάνους ἀπὸ τῶν κεφαλῶν τῶν Νυμφίων, καὶ τίθησιν αὐτοὺς ἐπὶ τῆς τραπέζης.

glad in your husband, keeping the paths of the Law, for so God is well pleased.

Priest

Let us pray to the Lord.

Choir: Lord have mercy.

Now the Priest says this prayer:

O God our God, Who was present in Cana of Galilee, and blèssed the marriage there, do You (+) also bless these Your servants, who, by Your Providence, are joined in the community of marriage. Bless their comings-in and their goings-out. Replenish their life with all good things. Accept* their crowns in Your Kingdom unsoiled and undefiled; and preserve them without offense to the ages of ages.

Choir: Amen.

Priest: Peace be to all. (+)

Choir: And to your spirit.

Priest

Let us bow our heads before the Lord.

Choir: To You, O Lord.

Priest

The Father, the Son, and the Holy Spirit; the All-Holy, Consubstantial and Life-creating Trinity; One Godhead and Kingdom; bless (+) you; grant to you long life, well-

* *Here the priest lifts the crowns from the heads of the bride and groom and places them on the table.*

ὑμῖν μακροζωΐαν, εὐτεκνίαν, προκοπὴν βίου καὶ πίστεως, καὶ ἐμπλῆσαι ὑμᾶς πάντων τῶν ἐπὶ γῆς ἀγαθῶν, ἀξιῶσαι δὲ ὑμᾶς καὶ τῶν ἐπηγγελμένων ἀγαθῶν τῆς ἀπολαύσεως, πρεσβείαις τῆς ἁγίας Θεοτόκου, καὶ πάντων τῶν Ἁγίων.

Ὁ Χορός· Ἀμήν.

Ὁ Ἱερεύς

Δόξα σοι, ὁ Θεός, ἡ ἐλπὶς ἡμῶν, δόξα σοι.

Ὁ Διάκονος

Δόξα, Καὶ νῦν. Κύριε, ἐλέησον (γ΄). Πάτερ ἅγιε, εὐλόγησον.

Ὁ Ἱερεύς

Ο ´ διὰ τῆς ἐν Κανᾶ ἐπιδημίας τίμιον ἀναδείξας τὸν γάμον, Χριστὸς ὁ ἀληθινὸς Θεὸς ἡμῶν. ταῖς πρεσβείαις τῆς παναχράντου αὐτοῦ Μητρός, τῶν ἁγίων ἐνδόξων καὶ πανευφήμων Ἀποστόλων, τῶν ἁγίων θεοστέπτων βασιλέων καὶ ἰσαποστόλων Κωνσταντίνου καὶ Ἑλένης, τοῦ ἁγίου μεγαλομάρτυρος Προκοπίcυ, καὶ πάντων τῶν Ἁγίων, ἐλεήσαι καὶ σώσαι ἡμᾶς ὡς ἀγαθὸς καὶ φιλάνθρωπος καὶ ἐλεήμων Θεός.

Δι᾿ εὐχῶν τῶν ἁγίων Πατέρων...

Ὁ Χορός· Ἀμήν.

favored children, progress in life and in Faith; replenish you with all the good things of the earth, and count you worthy of the promised blessings, through the intercessions of the holy Theotokos, and of all the Saints.

Choir: Amen.

Priest

Glory to You, O Christ our God and our hope; glory to You.

Glory to the Father and to the Son and to the Holy Spirit, both now and ever, and to the ages of ages. Amen. Lord have mercy; Lord have mercy; Lord have mercy.

He, Who by His presence in Cana of Galilee declared marriage to be honorable, Christ our true God, through the intercessions of His all-pure Mother, of the holy, glorious, and all-praiseworthy Apostles, of the holy, God-crowned and Equal-to-the-Apostles Constantine and Helen, of the Holy, great Martyr Procopios, and of all the holy Saints, have mercy on us and save us, as our good and loving Lord.

Through the prayers of our holy Fathers ...

Choir: Amen.

ΑΚΟΛΟΥΘΙΑ ΝΕΚΡΩΣΙΜΟΣ
ἤτοι
ΕΙΣ ΚΕΚΟΙΜΗΜΕΝΟΥΣ

«Πάντες γὰρ ὑμεῖς εἷς ἐστε ἐν Χριστῷ Ἰησοῦ»
(Γαλ. γ΄, 28)

Ἰστέον ὅτι ἡ κατωτέρω τάξις τῆς Νεκρωσίμου Ἀκολουθίας ψάλλεται εἰς ἅπαντας τοὺς κεκοιμημένους βασιλεῖς τε καὶ πατριάρχας, καὶ ἀρχιερεῖς, καὶ ἱερεῖς, εἰς ἄνδρας τε καὶ γυναῖκας, μικρούς τε καὶ μεγάλους, πλὴν τῶν νηπίων, ὧν ἡ Νεκρώσιμος Ἀκολουθία καταχωρίζεται ἐν σελ.126-132.

*

Τελευτήσαντός τινος τῶν εὐσεβῶν Ὀρθοδόξων, εὐθὺς προσκαλεῖται παρὰ τῶν συγγενῶν αὐτοῦ ὁ Ἱερὸς Κλῆρος. Ἐλθόντες δὲ εἰς τὸν οἶκον, ἐν ᾧ τὸ λείψανον κεῖται, οἱ μὲν Ἱερεῖς βάλλουσιν Ἐπιτραχήλιον καὶ Φελώνιον λευκόν, οἱ δὲ Διάκονοι ἐνδύονται Στιχάριον καὶ Ὀράριον, κρατοῦντες θυμιατά. Τότε εἷς Ἱερεὺς μετὰ Διακόνου εἰσέρχονται, ὅπου ὁ νεκρὸς κεῖται.

97

FUNERAL SERVICE
that is
THE SERVICE FOR THOSE
WHO HAVE FALLEN ASLEEP

"For you are all one in Jesus Christ."

Galatians 3:28

The Funeral Service below is sung for all those who have fallen asleep: kings and patriarchs, bishops and priests, men and women, young and old, except for infants, whose Funeral Service can be found on pages 126-132.

When a pious Orthodox Christian dies, the Clergy are invited by one of his (her) relatives. Coming to the place, where the deceased lies, the Clergy put on their vestments, take up the censer, and begin.

Ὁ Ἱερεὺς

Εὐλογητὸς ὁ Θεὸς ἡμῶν, πάντοτε, νῦν καὶ ἀεὶ καὶ εἰς τοὺς αἰῶνας τῶν αἰώνων.

Ὁ Διάκονος

Ἀμήν. Ἅγιος ὁ Θεός, Ἅγιος Ἰσχυρός, Ἅγιος Ἀθάνατος, ἐλέησον ἡμᾶς (γ΄).

Δόξα Πατρὶ καὶ Υἱῷ καὶ Ἁγίῳ Πνεύματι. Καὶ νῦν καὶ ἀεὶ καὶ εἰς τοὺς αἰῶνας τῶν αἰώνων. Ἀμήν.

Παναγία Τριάς, ἐλέησον ἡμᾶς. Κύριε, ἱλάσθητι ταῖς ἁμαρτίαις ἡμῶν. Δέσποτα, συγχώρησον τὰς ἀνομίας ἡμῖν. Ἅγιε, ἐπίσκεψαι καὶ ἴασαι τὰς ἀσθενείας ἡμῶν, ἕνεκεν τοῦ ὀνόματός σου.

Κύριε, ἐλέησον·Κύριε, ἐλέησον·Κύριε, ἐλέησον.

Δόξα Πατρὶ καὶ Υἱῷ καὶ Ἁγίῳ Πνεύματι. Καὶ νῦν καὶ ἀεὶ καὶ εἰς τοὺς αἰῶνας τῶν αἰώνων. Ἀμήν.

Πάτερ ἡμῶν ὁ ἐν τοῖς οὐρανοῖς· ἁγιασθήτω τὸ ὄνομά σου· ἐλθέτω ἡ βασιλεία σου· γενηθήτω τὸ θέλημά σου, ὡς ἐν οὐρανῷ καὶ ἐπὶ τῆς γῆς· τὸν ἄρτον ἡμῶν τὸν ἐπιούσιον δὸς ἡμῖν σήμερον· καὶ ἄφες ἡμῖν τὰ ὀφειλήματα ἡμῶν, ὡς καὶ ἡμεῖς ἀφίεμεν τοῖς ὀφειλέταις ἡμῶν· καὶ μὴ εἰσενέγκῃς ἡμᾶς εἰς πειρασμόν, ἀλλὰ ῥῦσαι ἡμᾶς ἀπὸ τοῦ πονηροῦ.

Ὁ Ἱερεὺς

Ὅτι σοῦ ἐστιν ἡ Βασιλεία καὶ ἡ δύναμις καὶ ἡ δόξα τοῦ Πατρὸς καὶ τοῦ Υἱοῦ καὶ τοῦ Ἁγίου Πνεύματος, νῦν καὶ ἀεὶ καὶ εἰς τοὺς αἰῶνας τῶν αἰώνων. Ἀμήν.

THE TRISAGION FOR THE DEAD

Blessed is our God always, both now and ever, and to the ages of ages.

Reader

Amen. Holy God, Holy Mighty, Holy Immortal, have mercy on us. (3)

Glory to the Father and to the Son and to the Holy Spirit, now and ever, and to the ages of ages. Amen.

All-Holy Trinity, have mercy on us. Lord, be gracious unto our sins. Master, pardon our transgressions. Holy One, visit and heal our infirmities, for Your Name's sake.

Lord have mercy; Lord have mercy; Lord have mercy.

Glory to the Father and to the Son and to the Holy Spirit, now and ever, and to the ages of ages. Amen.

Our Father, Who are in Heaven,
Hallowed be Your Name; Your Kingdom come.
Your Will be done on earth as it is in Heaven.
Give us this day our daily bread;
And forgive us our trespasses,
As we forgive those who trespass against us.
And lead us not into temptation,
But deliver us from evil.

Priest

For Yours is the Kingdom and the Power and the Glory, of the Father, and of the Son, and of the Holy Spirit; both now and ever, and to the ages of ages. Amen.

Ἦχος δ΄.

Μετὰ πνευμάτων δικαίων τετελειωμένων, τὴν ψυχὴν τοῦ δούλου σου, Σῶτερ, ἀνάπαυσον, φυλάττων αὐτὴν εἰς τὴν μακαρίαν ζωήν, τὴν παρὰ σοί, φιλάνθρωπε.

Εἰς τὴν κατάπαυσίν σου, Κύριε, ὅπου πάντες οἱ Ἅγιοί σου ἀναπαύονται, ἀνάπαυσον καὶ τὴν ψυχὴν τοῦ δούλου σου, ὅτι μόνος ὑπάρχεις ἀθάνατος.

Δόξα Πατρί.

Σὺ εἶ ὁ Θεὸς ἡμῶν, ὁ καταβὰς εἰς Ἅδην, καὶ τὰς ὀδύνας λύσας τῶν πεπεδημένων· αὐτὸς καὶ τὴν ψυχὴν τοῦ δούλου σου, Σῶτερ, ἀνάπαυσον.

Καὶ νῦν.

Ἡ μόνη ἁγνὴ καὶ ἄχραντος Παρθένος, ἡ Θεὸν ἀφράστως κυήσασα, πρέσβευε ὑπὲρ τοῦ σωθῆναι τὴν ψυχὴν τοῦ δούλου σου.

Ὁ Διάκονος

Ἐλέησον ἡμᾶς ὁ Θεός, κατὰ τὸ μέγα ἔλεός σου, δεόμεθά σου, ἐπάκουσον καὶ ἐλέησον.

Ἔτι δεόμεθα ὑπὲρ ἀναπαύσεως τῆς ψυχῆς τοῦ κεκοιμημένου δούλου τοῦ Θεοῦ* (τοῦδε), καὶ ὑπὲρ τοῦ συγχωρηθῆναι αὐτῷ πᾶν πλημμέλημα ἑκούσιόν τε καὶ ἀκούσιον.

Ὅπως Κύριος ὁ Θεὸς τάξῃ τὴν ψυχὴν αὐτοῦ ἔνθα οἱ Δίκαιοι ἀναπαύονται· τὰ ἐλέη τοῦ Θεοῦ, τὴν βασιλείαν τῶν οὐρανῶν, καὶ ἄφεσιν τῶν αὐτοῦ

Troparia, Tone 4

With the spirits of the righteous made perfect
Give rest to the soul of Your servant, O Savior;
And keep it safe in that life of blessedness
That is lived with You, O Friend of Man.

In the place of Your rest, O Lord,
Where all Your Saints repose,
Give rest also to the soul of Your servant,
For You alone are immortal.

Glory to the Father and to the Son and to the Holy Spirit.

You are our God Who went down to Hades
To loose the pains of the dead that were there;
Give rest also to the soul of Your servant, O Savior.

Both now and ever, and to the ages of ages. Amen.

O Virgin, alone pure and immaculate that in maiden-motherhood brought forth God, intercede for the salvation of the soul of your servant.

Priest

Have mercy on us. O God, according to Your great mercy; we pray You, listen and have mercy.
Lord have mercy.
Again we pray for the repose of the soul of the servant of God (*Name*), departed this life, and for the forgiveness of his (her) every transgression, voluntary and involuntary.
Lord have mercy.
Let the Lord God establish his (her) soul where the Just repose; the mercies of God, the Kingdom of the Heavens, and the remission of his (her) sins, let us ask

ἁμαρτιῶν, παρὰ Χριστῷ τῷ ἀθανάτῳ Βασιλεῖ καὶ Θεῷ ἡμῶν αἰτησώμεθα.

Τοῦ Κυρίου δεηθῶμεν.

Ὁ Ἱερεὺς

Ὁ Θεὸς τῶν πνευμάτων καὶ πάσης σαρκός, ὁ τὸν θάνατον καταπατήσας, τὸν δὲ διάβολον καταργήσας, καὶ ζωὴν τῷ κόσμῳ σου δωρησάμενος· αὐτός, Κύριε, ἀνάπαυσον τὴν ψυχὴν τοῦ κεκοιμημένου δούλου σου (τοῦδε) ἐν τόπῳ φωτεινῷ, ἐν τόπῳ χλοερῷ, ἐν τόπῳ ἀναψύξεως, ἔνθα ἀπέδρα ὀδύνη, λύπη καὶ στεναγμός. Πᾶν ἁμάρτημα τὸ παρ' αὐτοῦ πραχθὲν ἐν λόγῳ ἢ ἔργῳ ἢ διανοίᾳ, ὡς ἀγαθὸς καὶ φιλάνθρωπος Θεός, συγχώρησον· ὅτι οὐκ ἔστιν ἄνθρωπος, ὃς ζήσεται καὶ οὐχ ἁμαρτήσει· σὺ γὰρ μόνος ἐκτὸς ἁμαρτίας ὑπάρχεις· ἡ δικαιοσύνη σου δικαιοσύνη εἰς τὸν αἰῶνα, καὶ ὁ νόμος σου ἀλήθεια. Ὅτι σὺ εἶ ἡ ἀνάστασις, ἡ ζωή, καὶ ἡ ἀνάπαυσις τοῦ κεκοιμημένου δούλου σου (τοῦδε), Χριστὲ ὁ Θεὸς ἡμῶν, καὶ σοὶ τὴν δόξαν ἀναπέμπομεν, σὺν τῷ ἀνάρχῳ σου Πατρί, καὶ τῷ παναγίῳ καὶ ἀγαθῷ καὶ ζωοποιῷ σου Πνεύματι, νῦν καὶ ἀεὶ καὶ εἰς τοὺς αἰῶνας τῶν αἰώνων. Ἀμήν.

Καὶ ἡ ἀπόλυσις οὕτω·

Ὁ Διάκονος

Δόξα. Καὶ νῦν. Κύριε, ἐλέησον· (γ'), Πάτερ ἅγιε, εὐλόγησον.

Ὁ Ἱερεὺς

Δόξα σοι, ὁ Θεός, ἡ ἐλπὶς ἡμῶν, δόξα σοι.

Ὁ καὶ νεκρῶν καὶ ζώντων τὴν ἐξουσίαν ἔχων, ὡς ἀθάνατος Βασιλεύς, καὶ ἀναστὰς ἐκ νεκρῶν, Χριστὸς ὁ ἀληθινὸς Θεὸς ἡμῶν, ταῖς πρεσβείαις

of Christ, our immortal King and our God.

Let us pray to the Lord. Lord have mercy.

Priest

O God of all spirits and of every flesh, Who did trod down death and overcome the devil, bestowing life on this Your world, to the soul of this Your servant (*Name*), departed this life, do You Yourself, O Lord, give rest in a place of light, in a place of green pasture, in a place of refreshment, from.where pain and sorrow and mourning have fled away. Every sin by him (her) committed in thought, word, or deed, do You as our Good and Loving God forgive; seeing that there is no man who shall live and sin not, for You alone are without sin. Your righteousness is an everlasting righteousness, and Your Law is truth; for You are the Resurrection, the Life, and the Repose of Your servant (*Name*), departed this life, O Christ our God; and to You do we send up glory, with Your Eternal Father and Your All-Holy, Good and Life-creating Spirit; both now and ever, and to the ages of ages. Amen.

Reader

Glory to the Father and to the Son and to the Holy Spirit, both now and ever, and to the ages of ages. Amen.
Lord have mercy; Lord have mercy; Lord have mercy.

Priest

Glory to You, O Christ our God and our Hope; glory to You.

May Christ our true God, Who rose from the dead, have mercy on us; He Who as Immortal King has authority over both the dead and the living. Through the intercessions

τῆς παναχράντου ἁγίας αὐτοῦ Μητρός· τῶν ἁγίων ἐνδόξων καὶ πανευφήμων Ἀποστόλων· τῶν ὁσίων καὶ θεοφόρων Πατέρων ἡμῶν· τῶν ἁγίων ἐνδόξων προπατόρων Ἀβραάμ, Ἰσαὰκ καὶ Ἰακώβ· τοῦ ἁγίου καὶ δικαίου φίλου αὐτοῦ Λαζάρου τοῦ τετραημέρου, καὶ πάντων τῶν Ἁγίων, τὴν ψυχὴν τοῦ ἐξ ἡμῶν μεταστάντος δούλου αὐτοῦ ἐν σκηναῖς Δικαίων τάξαι, ἐν κόλποις Ἀβραὰμ ἀναπαῦσαι, καὶ μετὰ Δικαίων συναριθμῆσαι, ἡμᾶς δὲ ἐλεῆσαι ὡς ἀγαθὸς καὶ φιλάνθρωπος

Αἰωνία σου ἡ μνήμη, ἀξιομακάριστε καὶ ἀείμνηστε ἀδελφὲ ἡμῶν.

Ἐπὶ δὲ γυναικός·

Αἰωνία σου ἡ μνήμη, ἀξιομακάριστος καὶ ἀείμνηστος ἀδελφὴ ἡμῶν.

Δι' εὐχῶν τῶν ἁγίων Πατέρων ἡμῶν, Κύριε, Ἰησοῦ Χριστὲ ὁ Θεὸς ἡμῶν, ἐλέησον καὶ σῶσον ἡμᾶς. Ἀμήν.

Καὶ εἰ μὲν ἕτοιμά ἐστιν ἅπαντα τὰ τοῦ ἐξοδίου, εὐλογεῖ αὖθις ὁ Ἰερεύς, καὶ ἀρχόμεθα ψάλλειν, μετὰ φόβου καὶ πάσης κατανύξεως, (καθ' ὁδὸν) τό,

Ἅγιος ὁ Θεός, Ἅγιος Ἰσχυρός, Ἅγιος Ἀθάνατος, ἐλέησον ἡμᾶς.

Ἄραντες δὲ τὸ λείψανον, ἀπερχόμεθα εἰς τὸν Ναόν, προπορευομένων τῶν Ἰερέων μετὰ λαμπάδων καὶ τῶν Διακόνων ἔμπροσθεν μετὰ θυμιατῶν. Ὅταν δὲ ἔλθωμεν εἰς τὸν Ναόν, ἀποτίθεται τὸ λείψανον ἐν τῷ μέσῳ.

of His spotless, pure and holy Mother; of the holy, glorious, and all-praiseworthy Apostles; of our venerable and God-bearing Fathers; of the holy and glorious forefathers Abraham, Isaac and Jacob; of His holy and just friend Lazaros, who lay in the grave four days; and of all the Saints; establish the soul of His servant (*Name*), departed from us, in the tentings of the Just; give him (her) rest in the bosom of Abraham; and number him (her) among the Just, through His goodness and compassion as our merciful God.

Everlasting be your memory, O our brother, who are worthy of blessedness and eternal memory. (3)

For women:

Everlasting be your memory, O our sister, who are worthy of blessedness and eternal memory.

Through the prayers of our holy Fathers, Lord, Jesus Christ our God, have mercy and save us. Amen.

When all things are ready for the funeral, the priest blesses again, and we begin to sing the Trisagion.

Holy God, Holy Mighty, Holy Immortal, have mercy on us.

Taking up the body, we take it to the church, where it is placed on the solea. The priest leads the way, singing the Trisagion and holding the censer.

Ἐν τῷ Ναῷ.

Ο Ἱερεύς

Εὐλογητὸς ὁ Θεὸς ἡμῶν, πάντοτε, νῦν καὶ ἀεὶ καὶ εἰς τοὺς αἰῶνας τῶν αἰώνων.

Ὁ Χορός· Ἀμήν.

Καὶ εὐθὺς οἱ Χοροὶ ἄρχονται ψάλλοντες (ἐναλλὰξ) ἐκ τοῦ ριη΄ (118) Ψαλμοῦ.

ΣΤΑΣΙΣ Α΄.

Ἦχος πλ. β΄.

Ἄμωμοι ἐν ὁδῷ, Ἀλληλούϊα. Εὐλογητὸς εἶ Κύριε, δίδαξόν με τὰ δικαιώματά σου. Ἀλληλούϊα.

Ἐπεπόθησεν ἡ ψυχή μου τοῦ ἐπιθυμῆσαι τὰ κρίματά σου ἐν παντὶ καιρῷ. Ἀλληλούϊα.

Ἐνύσταξεν ἡ ψυχή μου ἀπὸ ἀκηδίας, βεβαίωσόν με ἐν τοῖς λόγοις σου. Ἀλληλούϊα.

Κλῖνον τὴν καρδίαν μου εἰς τὰ μαρτύριά σου, καὶ μὴ εἰς πλεονεξίαν. Ἀλληλούϊα.

Ἀθυμία κατέσχε με ἀπὸ ἁμαρτωλῶν, τῶν ἐγκαταλιμπανόντων τὸν νόμον σου. Ἀλληλούϊα.

Μέτοχος ἐγώ εἰμι πάντων τῶν φοβουμένων σε, καὶ τῶν φυλασσόντων τὰς ἐντολάς σου. Ἀλληλούϊα. Ὁ α΄ Χορός· Δόξα... Ὁ β΄ Χορός Καὶ νῦν... Ὁ α΄ Χορός· Ἀλληλούϊα.

Ὁ Διάκονος

Ἐλέησον ἡμᾶς, ὁ Θεός, κατὰ τὸ μέγα ἔλεός σου, δεόμεθά σου, ἐπάκουσον καὶ ἐλέησον.

Ἔτι δεόμεθα ὑπὲρ ἀναπαύσεως τῆς ψυχῆς τοῦ κεκοιμημένου δούλου τοῦ Θεοῦ (τοῦδε), καὶ ὑπὲρ τοῦ συγχωρηθῆναι αὐτῷ πᾶν πλημμέλημα ἑκούσιόν τε καὶ ἀκούσιον.

THE FUNERAL SERVICE

Priest

Blessed is our Lord God, always; both now and ever, and to the ages of ages.

Choir: Amen.

The First Stasis, in Tone 6

Ah, the blameless in the way. Alleluia. Blessed are You, O Lord, teach me Your statutes. Alleluia.

My soul is worn with endless longing for Your judgments at all times. Alleluia.

My soul has slumbered from sorrow; strengthen me with Your words. Alleluia.

Incline my heart unto Your testimonies, and not unto covetousness. Alleluia.

Despair took hold on me because of sinners that forsake Your Law. Alleluia.

I am a partaker with all that fear You, and with them that keep Your commandments. Alleluia.

Glory to the Father and to the Son and to the Holy Spirit, both now and ever, and to the ages of ages. Amen. Alleluia.

Priest

Have mercy on us, O God, according to Your great mercy; listen, and have mercy.

Again we pray for the repose of the soul of the servant of God (*Name*), departed this life; and for the forgiveness of his (her) every transgression, voluntary and involuntary.

Ὅπως, Κύριος ὁ Θεός, τάξῃ τὴν ψυχὴν αὐτοῦ ἔνθα οἱ Δίκαιοι ἀναπαύονται· τὰ ἐλέη τοῦ Θεοῦ, τὴν βασιλείαν τῶν οὐρανῶν, καὶ ἄφεσιν τῶν αὐτοῦ ἁμαρτιῶν, παρὰ Χριστῷ τῷ ἀθανάτῳ Βασιλεῖ καὶ Θεῷ ἡμῶν αἰτησώμεθα.

Τοῦ Κυρίου δεηθῶμεν.

Ὁ Ἱερεύς, ἐκφωνεῖ·

Ὅτι σὺ εἶ ἡ ἀνάστασις, ἡ ζωή, καὶ ἡ ἀνάπαυσις τοῦ κεκοιμημένου δούλου σου (τοῦδε), Χριστὲ ὁ Θεὸς ἡμῶν, καὶ σοὶ τὴν δόξαν ἀναπέμπομεν, σὺν τῷ ἀνάρχῳ σου Πατρί, καὶ τῷ παναγίῳ, καὶ ἀγαθῷ, καὶ ζωοποιῷ σου Πνεύματι, νῦν καὶ ἀεὶ καὶ εἰς τοὺς αἰῶνας τῶν αἰώνων.

Ὁ Χορός· Ἀμήν.

ΣΤΑΣΙΣ Β΄.

Ἦχος πλ. α΄.

Αἱ χεῖρές σου ἐποίησάν με καὶ ἔπλασάν με, συνέτισόν με, καὶ μαθήσομαι τὰς ἐντολάς σου. Ἐλέησόν με, Κύριε.

Ὅτι ἐγενήθην ὡς ἀσκὸς ἐν πάχνῃ, τὰ δικαιώματά σου οὐκ ἐπελαθόμην. Ἐλέησόν με, Κύριε.

Σός εἰμι ἐγώ, σῶσόν με, ὅτι τὰ δικαιώματά σου ἐξεζήτησα. Ἐλέησόν με, Κύριε.

Ἀπὸ τῶν κριμάτων σου οὐκ ἐξέκλινα, ὅτι σὺ ἐνομοθέτησάς με. Ἐλέησόν με, Κύριε.

Ἔκλινα τὴν καρδίαν μου, τοῦ ποιῆσαι τὰ δικαιώματά σου εἰς τὸν αἰῶνα δι᾽ ἀντάμειψιν. Ἐλέησόν με, Κύριε.

Καιρὸς τοῦ ποιῆσαι τῷ Κυρίῳ· διεσκέδασαν τὸν νόμον σου. Ἐλέησόν με, Κύριε.

Δόξα. Καὶ νῦν. Ἐλέησόν με Κύριε, Κύριε.

Let the Lord establish his (her) soul where the Just repose; the mercies of God, the Kingdom of the Heavens, and the remission of his (her) sins; let us ask of Christ our immortal King and our God.

Let us pray to the Lord. Lord have mercy.

Priest

For You are the Resurrection, the Life, and the Repose of Your servant *(Name)*, O Christ our God; and to You do we send up glory, with Your Eternal Father, and Your All-Holy, Good and Life-creating Spirit, both now and ever, and to the ages of ages.

Choir: Amen.

The Second Stasis, in Tone 5

Your hands have made and fashioned me; give me understanding, and I will learn Your commandments. Have mercy on me, O Lord.

For I am become as a bottle in the frost; yet Your statutes have not forgotten. Have mercy on me, O Lord.

I am Yours, O save me; for after Your statutes have I sought. Have mercy on me, O Lord.

From Your judgments I have not declined, for You have set a Law for me. Have mercy on me, O Lord.

I have inclined my heart to perform Your statutes, forever, in return for Your mercies. Have mercy on me, O Lord.

It is time to serve the Lord; but they have violated Your law.
Have mercy on me, O Lord.
Glory . . . Both now . . . Have mercy on me Lord.

Ὁ Διάκονος

Τοῦ Κυρίου δεηθῶμεν.

Ὁ β΄ Ἱερεύς, ἐκφωνεῖ·

Ὅτι σὺ εἶ ἡ ἀνάστασις, ἡ ζωή, καὶ ἡ ἀνάπαυσις τοῦ κεκοιμημένου δούλου σου (τοῦδε), Χριστὲ ὁ Θεὸς ἡμῶν, καὶ σοὶ τὴν δόξαν ἀναπέμπομεν, σὺν τῷ ἀνάρχῳ σου Πατρί, καὶ τῷ παναγίῳ, καὶ ἀγαθῷ, καὶ ζωοποιῷ σου Πνεύματι, νῦν καὶ ἀεὶ καὶ εἰς τοὺς αἰῶνας τῶν αἰώνων. Ἀμήν.

Ἦχος πλ. δ΄.

Καὶ ἐλέησόν με. Ἀλληλούϊα.

Ἐπίβλεψον ἐπ᾽ ἐμὲ καὶ ἐλέησόν με, κατὰ τὸ κρῖμα τῶν ἀγαπώντων τὸ ὄνομά σου. Ἀλληλούϊα.

Νεώτερος ἐγώ εἰμι, καὶ ἐξουδενωμένος, τὰ δικαιώματά σου οὐκ ἐπελαθόμην. Ἀλληλούϊα.

Τῆς φωνῆς μου ἄκουσον, Κύριε, κατὰ τὸ ἔλεός σου, κατὰ τὸ κρῖμά σου ζῆσόν με. Ἀλληλούϊα.

Ἄρχοντες κατεδίωξάν με δωρεάν, καὶ ἀπὸ τῶν λόγων σου ἐδειλίασεν ἡ καρδία μου. Ἀλληλούϊα.

Ζήσεται ἡ ψυχή μου καὶ αἰνέσει σε, καὶ τὰ κρίματά σου βοηθήσει μοι.

Ἐπλανήθην ὡς πρόβατον ἀπολωλός· ζήτησον τὸν δοῦλόν σου, ὅτι τὰς ἐντολάς σου οὐκ ἐπελαθόμην.

Ὁ Διάκονος

Τοῦ Κυρίου δεηθῶμεν.

Ὁ Ἱερεύς, ἐκφωνεῖ·

Ὅτι σὺ εἶ ἡ ἀνάστασις, ἡ ζωή, καὶ ἡ ἀνάπαυσις τοῦ κεκοιμημένου δούλου σου (τοῦδε), Χριστὲ ὁ Θεὸς ἡμῶν, καὶ σοὶ τὴν δόξαν ἀναπέμπομεν, σὺν

Priest

Let us pray to the Lord. Lord have mercy.

Priest

For You are the Resurrection, the Life, and the repose of Your servant (*Name*), O Christ our God; and to You do we send up glory, with Your Eternal Father, and Your All-Holy, Good and Life-creating Spirit, both now and ever, and to the ages of ages. Amen.

Tone 8

And have mercy upon me. Alleluia.

Look upon me, and have mercy on me.

According to the judgment of them that love Your Name. Alleluia.

I am young and accounted as nothing.

Your statutes have I not forgotten.

Hear my voice, O Lord, according to Your mercy; According to Your judgments quicken me. Alleluia.

Princes have persecuted me without a cause, and because of Your words my heart has been afraid. Alleluia.

My soul shall live, and shall praise You, And Your judgments will help me. Alleluia.

I have gone astray like a sheep that is lost.

Seek Your servant, for I have not forgotten Your commandments.

Priest

Let us pray to the Lord. Lord have mercy.

For You are the Resurrection and the Life and the Repose of Your servant (*Name*), O Christ our God; and   to You do we send up glory, with Your Eternal Father, and

τῷ ἀνάρχῳ σου Πατρί, καὶ τῷ παναγίῳ, καὶ ἀγαθῷ, καὶ ζωοποιῷ σου Πνεύματι, νῦν καὶ ἀεὶ καὶ εἰς τοὺς αἰῶνας τῶν αἰώνων.

Ὁ Χορός Ἀμήν.

Ἦχος πλ. α΄.

Εὐλογητὸς εἶ, Κύριε, δίδαξόν με τὰ δικαιώματά σου.

Τῶν Ἁγίων ὁ χορός, εὗρε πηγὴν τῆς ζωῆς καὶ θύραν Παραδείσου· εὕρω κἀγώ, τὴν ὁδὸν διὰ τῆς μετανοίας· τὸ ἀπολωλὸς πρόβατον ἐγώ εἰμι· ἀνακάλεσαί με, Σωτήρ, καὶ σῶσόν με.

Ἐὰν ὦσι πλείονες τῶν τριῶν Ἱερεῖς, εἰς τὸ τέλος ἑκάστου Τροπαρίου ὁ Διάκονος ἐκφωνεῖ· Τοῦ Κυρίου δεηθῶμεν, οἱ δὲ Ἱερεῖς κατὰ τὴν τῶν πρεσβείων σειρὰν ἕκαστος ἐκ τῶν μὴ ἐκφωνησάντων· Ὅτι σὺ εἶ ἡ ἀνάστασις..., ἤτοι αἱ ἐκφωνήσεις γίνονται κατὰ τὸν ἀριθμὸν τῶν Ἱερέων.

Εὐλογητὸς εἶ, Κύριε, δίδαξόν με τὰ δικαιώματά σου.

Ὁ πάλαι μέν, ἐκ μὴ ὄντων πλάσας με, καὶ εἰκόνι σου θεία τιμήσας, παραβάσει ἐντολῆς δὲ πάλιν με ἐπιστρέψας, εἰς γῆν ἐξ ἧς ἐλήφθην, εἰς τὸ καθ' ὁμοίωσιν ἐπανάγαγε, τὸ ἀρχαῖον κάλλος ἀναμορφώσασθαι.

Εὐλογητός εἶ, Κύριε, δίδαξόν με τὰ δικαιώματά σου.

Εἰκών εἰμι, τῆς ἀρρήτου δόξης σου, εἰ καὶ στίγματα φέρω πταισμάτων· οἰκτείρησον τὸ σὸν πλάσμα Δέσποτα, καὶ καθάρισον σῇ εὐσπλαγχνίᾳ· καὶ τὴν ποθεινὴν πατρίδα παράσχου μοι, Παραδείσου πάλιν ποιῶν πολίτην με.

Εὐλογητὸς εἶ, Κύριε, δίδαξόν με τὰ δικαιώματά σου.

Your All-Holy, Good and Life-creating Spirit, both now and ever, and to the ages of ages:

Choir: Amen.

Eulogetaria for the Dead

Blessed are You, O Lord; teach me Your statutes.

The Choir of the Saints has found the Fountain of Life, and the Door of Paradise. May I also find the way through repentance: the sheep that was lost am I; call me up to You, O Savior, and save me.

If there are more than three priests, each repeats after each "troparion": **"Let us pray to the Lord,"** *followed by* **"For You are the Resurrection and the Life."**

Blessed are You, O Lord; teach me Your statutes.

You Who of old did fashion me out of nothingness, and with Your Image divine did honor me; but because of transgression of Your commandments did return me again to the earth where I was taken; lead me back to be refashioned into that ancient beauty of Your Likeness.

Blessed are You, O Lord; teach me Your statutes.

Image am I of Your unutterable glory, though I bear the scars of my stumblings. Have compassion on me, the work of Your hands, O Sovereign Lord, and cleanse me through Your loving kindness; and the homeland of my heart's desire bestow on me by making me a citizen of Paradise.

Blessed are You, O Lord; teach me Your statutes.

Ἀνάπαυσον, ὁ Θεὸς τὸν δοῦλόν σου, καὶ κατάταξον αὐτὸν ἐν Παραδείσῳ, ὅπου χοροὶ τῶν Ἁγίων Κύριε, καὶ οἱ Δίκαιοι ἐκλάμψουσιν ὡς φωστῆρες· τὸν κεκοιμημένον δοῦλόν σου ἀνάπαυσον, παρορῶν αὐτοῦ πάντα τὰ ἐγκλήματα.

Δόξα. Τριαδικόν.

Τὸ τριλαμπές, τῆς μιᾶς Θεότητος, εὐσεβῶς ὑμνήσωμεν βοῶντες· Ἅγιος εἶ, ὁ Πατὴρ ὁ ἄναρχος, ὁ συνάναρχος Υἱὸς καὶ τὸ θεῖον Πνεῦμα· φώτισον ἡμᾶς, πίστει σοι λατρεύοντας, καὶ τοῦ αἰωνίου πυρὸς ἐξάρπασον.

Καὶ νῦν. Θεοτοκίον.

Χαῖρε σεμνή, ἡ Θεὸν σαρκὶ τεκοῦσα, εἰς πάντων σωτηρίαν, δι᾿ ἧς γένος τῶν ἀνθρώπων εὕρατο τὴν σωτηρίαν· διὰ σοῦ εὕροιμεν Παράδεισον, Θεοτόκε, ἁγνὴ εὐλογημένη.

Ἀλληλούϊα, Ἀλληλούϊα, Ἀλληλούϊα, Δόξα σοι ὁ Θεὸς (ἐκ γ´).

Ἦχος πλ. δ´.

Μετὰ τῶν Ἁγίων ἀνάπαυσον, Χριστέ, τὴν ψυχὴν τοῦ δούλου σου, ἔνθα οὐκ ἔστι πόνος, οὐ λύπη, οὐ στεναγμός, ἀλλὰ ζωὴ ἀτελεύτητος.

(Ἰωάννου Μοναχοῦ, τοῦ Δαμασκηνοῦ).

Ἦχος α´.

Ποία τοῦ βίου τρυφὴ διαμένει λύπης ἀμέτοχος; Ποία δόξα ἔστηκεν ἐπὶ γῆς ἀμετάθετος; Πάντα σκιᾶς ἀσθενέστερα, πάντα ὀνείρων ἀπατηλότερα· μία ῥοπή, καὶ ταῦτα πάντα θάνατος διαδέχεται. Ἀλλ᾿ ἐν τῷ φωτί, Χριστέ, τοῦ προσώπου σου, καὶ τῷ γλυκασμῷ τῆς σῆς ὡραιότητος, ὃν ἐξελέξω ἀνάπαυσον, ὡς φιλάνθρωπος.

Give rest, O God, unto Your servant, and appoint for him (her) a place in Paradise; where the choirs of the Saints, O Lord, and the just will shine forth like stars; to Your servant that is sleeping now do You give rest, overlooking all his (her) offenses.

Glory to the Father and to the Son and to the Holy Spirit.

The Trinal Radiance of One Godhead with reverent song acclaiming let us cry; Holy are You, O Eternal Father, and Son also Eternal, and Spirit Divine; shine with Your Light on us who with faith adore You; and from the fire eternal rescue us.

Both now and ever and to the ages of ages. Amen.

Hail, O Gracious Lady, that in the flesh bears God for salvation of all; and through whom the human race has found salvation: through You may we find Paradise, Theotokos, our Lady pure and blessed.

Alleluia, Alleluia, Alleluia; Glory to You, O God.

Tone 8

With the Saints give rest, O Christ, to the soul of Your servant where there is not pain, nor any sorrow, nor any sighing, but Life everlasting.

(Composed by St. John of Damascus)
Tone 1

Where is the pleasure in life which is unmixed with sorrow? Where the glory which on earth has stood firm and unchanged? All things are weaker than shadow, all more illusive than dreams; comes one fell stroke, and Death in turn, prevails over all these vanities. Wherefore in the Light, O Christ, of Your countenance, and in the sweetness of Your beauty, to him (her) whom You have chosen grant repose, for You are the Friend of Mankind.

Ἦχος β΄.

Ὡς ἄνθος μαραίνεται, καὶ ὡς ὄναρ παρέρχεται, καὶ διαλύεται πᾶς ἄνθρωπος· πάλιν δὲ ἠχούσης τῆς σάλπιγγος, νεκροί, ὡς ἐν συσσεισμῷ, πάντες ἀναστήσονται πρὸς τὴν σὴν ὑπάντησιν, Χριστὲ ὁ Θεός· τότε, Δέσποτα, ὃν μετέστησας ἐξ ἡμῶν, ἐν ταῖς τῶν Ἁγίων σου κατάταξον σκηναῖς, τὸ πνεῦμα τοῦ σοῦ δούλου, Χριστέ.

Ἕτερον ἐκτὸς Τυπικοῦ. Ἦχος ὁ αὐτός.

Οἴμοι, οἷον ἀγῶνα ἔχει ἡ ψυχή, χωριζομένη ἐκ τοῦ σώματος! Οἴμοι, πόσα δακρύει τότε, καὶ οὐχ ὑπάρχει ὁ ἐλεῶν αὐτήν! Πρὸς τοὺς Ἀγγέλους τὰ ὄμματα ῥέπουσα, ἄπρακτα καθικετεύει· πρὸς τοὺς ἀνθρώπους τὰς χεῖρας ἐκτείνουσα, οὐκ ἔχει τὸν βοηθοῦντα. Διό, ἀγαπητοί μου ἀδελφοί, ἐννοήσαντες ἡμῶν τὸ βραχὺ τῆς ζωῆς, τῷ μεταστάντι τὴν ἀνάπαυσιν, παρὰ Χριστοῦ αἰτησώμεθα, καὶ ταῖς ψυχαῖς ἡμῶν τὸ μέγα ἔλεος.

Ἦχος γ΄.

Πάντα ματαιότης τὰ ἀνθρώπινα, ὅσα οὐχ ὑπάρχει μετὰ θάνατον· οὐ παραμένει ὁ πλοῦτος, οὐ συνοδεύει ἡ δόξα· ἐπελθὼν γὰρ ὁ θάνατος, ταῦτα πάντα ἐξηφάνισται. Διὸ Χριστῷ τῷ ἀθανάτῳ Βασιλεῖ βοήσωμεν· Τὸν μεταστάντα ἐξ ἡμῶν ἀνάπαυσον, ἔνθα πάντων ἐστὶν εὐφραινομένων ἡ κατοικία.

Ἦχος δ΄.

Ὄντως φοβερώτατον, τὸ τοῦ θανάτου μυστήριον, πῶς ψυχὴ ἐκ τοῦ σώματος, βιαίως χωρίζεται ἐκ τῆς ἁρμονίας, καὶ τῆς συμφυῖας ὁ φυσικώτατος δεσμός, θείῳ βουλήματι ἀποτέμνεται. Διό σε ἱκετεύομεν· Τὸν μεταστάντα ἀνάπαυσον, ἐν σκηναῖς τῶν Δικαίων σου, Ζωοδότα Φιλάνθρωπε.

Tone 2

Like a blossom that wastes away, and like a dream that passes and is gone, so is every mortal into dust resolved; but again, when the trumpet sounds its call, as though at a quaking of the earth, all the dead shall arise and go forth to meet You, O Christ our God: on that day, O Lord, for him (her) whom You have withdrawn from among us appoint a place in the tentings of Your Saints—yea, for the spirit of Your servant, O Christ.

Another in Tone 2

Alas! What an agony the soul endures when from the body it is parting; how many are her tears for weeping, but there is none that will show compassion: unto the angels she turns with downcast eyes; useless are her supplications; and unto men she extends her imploring hands, but finds none to bring her rescue. Thus, my beloved brethren, let us all ponder well how brief is the span of our life; and peaceful rest for him (her) that now is gone, let us ask of Christ, and also His abundant mercy for our souls.

Tone 3

Vanity are all the works and quests of man, and they have no being after death has come; our wealth is with us no longer. How can our glory go with us? For when death has come all these things are vanished clean away. Wherefore to Christ the Immortal King let us cry, "To him (her) that has departed grant repose where a home is prepared for all those whose hearts You have filled with gladness."

Tone 4

Terror truly past compare is by the mystery of death inspired; now the soul and the body part, disjoined by resistless might, and their concord is broken; and the bond of nature which made them live and grow as one, now by the edict of God is rest in twain. Wherefore now we implore Your aid: grant that Your servant now gone to rest where the just that are Yours abide, Life-bestower and Friend of Mankind.

Ἕτερον ἐκτὸς Τυπικοῦ. Ἦχος ὁ αὐτός.

Ποῦ ἐστιν ἡ τοῦ κόσμου προσπάθεια; Ποῦ ἐστιν ἡ τῶν προσκαίρων φαντασία; Ποῦ ἐστιν ὁ χρυσὸς καὶ ὁ ἄργυρος; Ποῦ ἐστι τῶν οἰκετῶν ἡ πλημμύρα καὶ ὁ θόρυβος; Πάντα κόνις, πάντα τέφρα, πάντα σκιά. Ἀλλὰ δεῦτε βοήσωμεν τῷ ἀθανάτῳ Βασιλεῖ· Κύριε, τῶν αἰωνίων σου ἀγαθῶν ἀξίωσον, τὸν μεταστάντα ἐξ ἡμῶν, ἀναπαύων αὐτὸν ἐν τῇ ἀγήρῳ μακαριότητι.

Ἦχος πλ. α΄.

Ἐμνήσθην τοῦ Προφήτου βοῶντος· Ἐγώ εἰμι γῆ καὶ σποδός· καὶ πάλιν κατενόησα ἐν τοῖς μνήμασι καὶ εἶδον τὰ ὀστᾶ τὰ γεγυμνωμένα καὶ εἶπον· ἆρα τίς ἐστι, βασιλεὺς ἢ στρατιώτης, ἢ πλούσιος ἢ πένης, ἢ δίκαιος ἢ ἁμαρτωλός; Ἀλλὰ ἀνάπαυσον, Κύριε, μετὰ Δικαίων τὸν δοῦλόν σου, ὡς φιλάνθρωπος.

Ἦχος πλ. β΄.

Ἀρχή μοι καὶ ὑπόστασις, τὸ πλαστουργόν σου γέγονε πρόσταγμα· βουληθεὶς γὰρ ἐξ ἀοράτου τε, καὶ ὁρατῆς με ζῷον συμπῆξαι φύσεως, γῆθέν μου τὸ σῶμα διέπλασας, δέδωκας δέ μοι ψυχήν, τῇ θείᾳ σου καὶ ζωοποιῷ ἐμπνεύσει. Διό, Χριστέ, τὸν δοῦλόν σου, ἐν χώρᾳ ζώντων, ἐν σκηναῖς Δικαίων ἀνάπαυσον.

Ἦχος βαρύς.

Ἀνάπαυσον, Σωτὴρ ἡμῶν ζωοδότα, ὃν μετέστησας ἀδελφὸν ἡμῶν ἐκ τῶν προσκαίρων, κράζοντα δόξα σοι

Ἕτερον ἐκτὸς Τυπικοῦ. Ἦχος ὁ αὐτός.

Κατ᾽ εἰκόνα σὴν καὶ ὁμοίωσιν, πλαστουργήσας κατ᾽ ἀρχὰς τὸν ἄνθρωπον, ἐν Παραδείσῳ τέθεικας, κατάρχειν σου τῶν κτισμάτων· φθόνῳ δὲ

Tone 4

Where is now our affection for earthly things? Where is now the alluring pomp of transient questing? Where is now our gold, and our silver? Where is now the surging crowd of domestics, and their busy cries? All is dust, all is ashes, all is shadow. Wherefore draw near that we may cry to our immortal King, "Lord, Your everlasting blessings vouchsafe unto him (her) that now has gone away. bringing him (her) to repose in that blessedness which never grows old."

Tone 5

I called to mind the Prophet who shouted, "I am but earth and ash." And once again I looked with attention on the tombs, and I saw the bones therein which of flesh were naked; and I said, "Which indeed is he that is king? Or which is soldier? Which is the wealthy, which the needy? Which the righteous, or which the sinner?" But to Your servant, O Lord, grant that with the righteous he (she) may repose.

Tone 6

My beginning and foundation was the form-bestowing Word of Your commandment; for it pleased You to make me by compounding visible and invisible nature into a living thing. out of earth was my body formed and made, but a soul You gave me by the Divine and Life-creating In-breathing. Wherefore, O Christ, to Your servant in the land of the living, in the courts of the righteous, do You grant repose.

Tone 7

Bring to his (her) rest, O our Savior, You giver of life, our brother (sister) whom You have withdrawn from this transient world, for he (she) lifts up his (her) voice to cry: "Glory to You."

Another in Tone 7

When in Your own image and likeness You in the beginning did create and fashion man, You gave him a home in Paradise, and made him the chief of your creation. But by

διαβόλου ἀπατηθείς, τῆς βρώσεως μετέσχε, τῶν ἐντολῶν σου παραβάτης γεγονώς· διὸ πάλιν εἰς γῆν ἐξ ἧς ἐλήφθη, κατεδίκασας ἐπιστρέφειν, Κύριε, καὶ αἰτεῖσθαι τὴν ἀνάπαυσιν.

Ἦχος πλ. δ΄.

Θρηνῶ καὶ ὀδύρομαι, ὅταν ἐννοήσω τὸν θάνατον, καὶ ἴδω ἐν τοῖς τάφοις κειμένην τὴν κατ᾽ εἰκόνα Θεοῦ, πλασθεῖσαν ἡμῖν ὡραιότητα, ἄμορφον, ἄδοξον, μὴ ἔχουσαν εἶδος. Ὦ τοῦ θαύματος! Τί τὸ περὶ ἡμᾶς τοῦτο γέγονε μυστήριον; Πῶς παρεδόθημεν τῇ φθορᾷ, καὶ συνεζεύχθημεν τῷ θανάτῳ; Ὄντως Θεοῦ προστάξει, ὡς γέγραπται, τοῦ παρέχοντος τοῖς μεταστᾶσι τὴν ἀνάπαυσιν.

Δόξα Πατρί. Ὁ αὐτός.

Ὁ θάνατός σου, Κύριε, ἀθανασίας γέγονε πρόξενος· εἰ μὴ γὰρ ἐν μνήματι κατετέθης, οὐκ ἂν ὁ Παράδεισος ἠνέῳκτο· διὸ τὸν μεταστάντα ἀνάπαυσον ὡς φιλάνθρωπος.

Καὶ νῦν. Ὁ αὐτός.

Ἀγνὴ Παρθένε, τοῦ Λόγου Πύλη, τοῦ Θεοῦ ἡμῶν Μήτηρ, ἱκέτευε ἐλεηθῆναι τὴν ψυχὴν αὐτοῦ.

Προκείμενον. Ἦχος γ΄.

Μακαρία ἡ ὁδός, ᾗ πορεύει σήμερον, ὅτι ἡτοιμάσθη σοι τόπος ἀναπαύσεως (γ΄).

Στίχ. Πρὸς σέ, Κύριε, κεκράξομαι, ὁ Θεός μου.

Ὁ Ἀναγνώστης

Πρὸς Θεσσαλονικεῖς Α΄ Ἐπιστολῆς Παύλου τὸ Ἀνάγνωσμα.

(Κεφ. δ΄, 13-17).

Πρόσχωμεν. Σοφία. Πρόσχωμεν.

the devil's envy, alas, beguiled to eat the fruit forbidden, transgressor then of Your commandments he became; wherefore back to earth, from which he first was taken, You did sentence him to return again, O Lord, and to pray You to give him rest.

I weep, and with tears lament when with understanding I think on death, and see how in the graves there sleeps the beauty which once for us was fashioned in the image of God, but now is shapeless, ignoble, and bare of all the graces. O how strange a thing; what is this mystery which concerns us humans? Why were we given up to decay? And why to death united in wedlock? Truly, as it is written, these things come to pass by ordinance of God, Who to him (her) now gone gives rest.

Glory to the Father and to the Son and to the Holy Spirit.

The death which You have endured, O Lord, is become the harbinger of deathlessness; if You had not been laid in Your tomb, then would not the gates of Paradise have been opened; wherefore to him (her) now gone from us give rest, for You are the Friend of Mankind.

Both now and ever and to the ages of ages. Amen.

Virgin chaste and holy, Gateway of the Word, Mother of our God, make supplication that his (her) soul find mercy.

Prokeimenon, Tone 3

Blessed is the way wherein you walk today, for there is prepared for you a place of rest. (3)

Unto You , O Lord, will I cry.

Priest: Wisdom!

The reading from the First Epistle of the Holy Apostle Paul to the Thessalonians. (1 Thess. 4:13-18)

Priest: Wisdom. Let us attend.

Ὁ Ἀναγνώστης

Ἀδελφοί, οὐ θέλω ὑμᾶς ἀγνοεῖν περὶ τῶν κεκοιμημένων, ἵνα μὴ λυπῆσθε καθὼς καὶ οἱ λοιποὶ οἱ μὴ ἔχοντες ἐλπίδα. Εἰ γὰρ πιστεύομεν ὅτι Ἰησοῦς ἀπέθανε καὶ ἀνέστη, οὕτω καὶ ὁ Θεὸς τοὺς κοιμηθέντας διὰ τοῦ Ἰησοῦ ἄξει σὺν αὐτῷ. Τοῦτο γὰρ ὑμῖν λέγομεν ἐν λόγῳ Κυρίου, ὅτι ἡμεῖς οἱ ζῶντες, οἱ περιλειπόμενοι εἰς τὴν παρουσίαν τοῦ Κυρίου, οὐ μὴ φθάσωμεν τοὺς κοιμηθέντας· ὅτι αὐτὸς ὁ Κύριος ἐν κελεύσματι, ἐν φωνῇ ἀρχαγγέλου καὶ ἐν σάλπιγγι Θεοῦ καταβήσεται ἀπ' οὐρανοῦ, καὶ οἱ νεκροὶ ἐν Χριστῷ ἀναστήσονται πρῶτον, ἔπειτα ἡμεῖς οἱ ζῶντες οἱ περιλειπόμενοι, ἅμα σὺν αὐτοῖς ἁρπαγησόμεθα ἐν νεφέλαις, εἰς ἀπάντησιν τοῦ Κυρίου εἰς ἀέρα, καὶ οὕτω πάντοτε σὺν Κυρίῳ ἐσόμεθα.

Ὁ Ἱερεύς· Εἰρήνη σοι τῷ ἀναγινώσκοντι.

Ὁ Χορός

Ἀλληλούϊα· Ἀλληλούϊα· Ἀλληλούϊα.

Ὁ Διάκονος

Σοφία· ὀρθοί· ἀκούσωμεν τοῦ ἁγίου Εὐαγγελίου.

Ὁ Ἱερεύς· Εἰρήνη πᾶσι.

Ὁ Χορός· Καὶ τῷ πνεύματί σου.

Ὁ Ἱερεύς

Ἐκ τοῦ κατὰ Ἰωάννην ἁγίου Εὐαγγελίου
τὸ Ἀνάγνωσμα.
(Κεφ. ε', 24-30).

Ὁ Διάκονος· Πρόσχωμεν.

Ὁ Χορός· Δόξα σοι, Κύριε, δόξα σοι.

Ὁ Ἱερεύς

Εἶπεν ὁ Κύριος πρὸς τοὺς ἐληλυθότας πρὸς αὐτὸν Ἰουδαίους. Ἀμὴν ἀμὴν λέγω ὑμῖν ὅτι ὁ

Reader

Brethren, we would not have you ignorant concerning those who are asleep, that you may not grieve as others do who have no hope. For since we believe that Jesus died and rose again, even so, through Jesus, God will bring with him those who have fallen asleep. For this we declare to you by the word of the Lord, that we who are alive, who are left until the coming of the Lord, shall not precede those who have fallen asleep. For the Lord himself will descend from heaven with a cry of command, with the archangel's call, and with the sound of the trumpet of God. And the dead in Christ will rise first; then we who are alive, who are left, shall be caught up together with them in the clouds to meet the Lord in the air, and we shall always be with the Lord. Therefore comfort one another with these words.

Priest: Peace be to you who read. And with your spirit.

Choir:

Alleluia, Alleluia, Alleluia.

Priest

Wisdom! Attend! Let us hear the Holy Gospel. Peace be to all.

Choir: And with your spirit.

Priest

The reading from the Holy Gospel of St. John. (John 5:24-30) Let us attend.

Choir: Glory to You, O Lord, glory to You.

Priest

The Lord said to those Jews which had come to him: Truly, truly, I say to you, he who hears my word and

τὸν λόγον μου ἀκούων καὶ πιστεύων τῷ πέμψαντί με, ἔχει ζωὴν αἰώνιον, καὶ εἰς κρίσιν οὐκ ἔρχεται, ἀλλὰ μεταβέβηκεν ἐκ τοῦ θανάτου εἰς τὴν ζωήν. Ἀμὴν ἀμὴν λέγω ὑμῖν ὅτι ἔρχεται ὥρα, καὶ νῦν ἐστιν, ὅτε οἱ νεκροὶ ἀκούσονται τῆς φωνῆς τοῦ Υἱοῦ τοῦ Θεοῦ, καὶ οἱ ἀκούσαντες ζήσονται. Ὥσπερ γὰρ ὁ Πατὴρ ἔχει ζωὴν ἐν ἑαυτῷ· οὕτως ἔδωκε καὶ τῷ Υἱῷ ζωὴν ἔχειν ἐν ἑαυτῷ καὶ ἐξουσίαν ἔδωκεν αὐτῷ καὶ κρίσιν ποιεῖν, ὅτι υἱὸς ἀνθρώπου ἐστί. Μὴ θαυμάζετε τοῦτο· ὅτι ἔρχεται ὥρα, ἐν ᾗ πάντες οἱ ἐν τοῖς μνημείοις ἀκούσονται τῆς φωνῆς αὐτοῦ, καὶ ἐκπορεύσονται οἱ τὰ ἀγαθὰ ποιήσαντες εἰς ἀνάστασιν ζωῆς, οἱ δὲ τὰ φαῦλα πράξαντες εἰς ἀνάστασιν κρίσεως. Οὐ δύναμαι ἐγὼ ποιεῖν ἀπ' ἐμαυτοῦ οὐδέν. Καθὼς ἀκούω κρίνω, καὶ ἡ κρίσις ἡ ἐμὴ δικαία ἐστίν· ὅτι οὐ ζητῶ τὸ θέλημα τὸ ἐμόν, ἀλλὰ τὸ θέλημα τοῦ πέμψαντός με Πατρός.

Ὁ Χορός· Δόξα σοι, Κύριε, δόξα σοι.

Ὁ Διάκονος

Ἐλέησον ἡμᾶς, ὁ Θεός, κατὰ τὸ μέγα ἔλεός σου, δεόμεθά σου ἐπάκουσον, καὶ ἐλέησον.

Ἔτι δεόμεθα ὑπὲρ ἀναπαύσεως τῆς ψυχῆς τοῦ κεκοιμημένου δούλου τοῦ Θεοῦ (τοῦδε), καὶ ὑπὲρ τοῦ συγχωρηθῆναι αὐτῷ πᾶν πλημμέλημα ἑκούσιόν τε καὶ ἀκούσιον.

Ὅπως Κύριος ὁ Θεὸς τάξῃ τὴν ψυχὴν αὐτοῦ, ἔνθα οἱ δίκαιοι ἀναπαύονται· τὰ ἐλέη τοῦ Θεοῦ, τὴν βασιλείαν τῶν οὐρανῶν καὶ ἄφεσιν τῶν αὐτοῦ ἁμαρτιῶν, παρὰ Χριστῷ τῷ ἀθανάτῳ Βασιλεῖ καὶ Θεῷ ἡμῶν αἰτησώμεθα.

Τοῦ Κυρίου δεηθῶμεν.

Ὁ πρῶτος τῇ τάξει τῶν Ἱερέων, πλησίον τοῦ λειψάνου ἀπελθών, λέγει μεγαλοφώνως τὴν Εὐχήν· ὡσαύτως καὶ οἱ συμπαρόντες Ἱερεῖς ἅπαντες μυστικῶς.

believes him who sent me, has eternal life; he does not come into judgment, but has passed from death to life. Truly, truly, I say to you, the hour is coming, and now is, when the dead will hear the voice of the Son of God, and those who hear will live. For as the Father has life in himself, so he has granted the Son also to have life in himself, and has given him the authority to execute judgment, because he is the Son of man. Do not marvel at this; for the hour is coming when all who are in the tombs will hear his voice and come forth, those who have done good, to the resurrection of life, and those who have done evil, to the resurrection of judgment. I can do nothing on my own authority; as I hear, I judge; and my judgment is just, because I seek not my own will but the will of him who sent me.

Choir

Glory to You, O Lord, glory to You.

Priest

Have mercy on us, O God, according to Your great mercy; we pray You listen and have mercy.   (Lord have mercy.)

Again we pray for the repose of the soul of the servant of God (*Name*) departed this life; and for the forgiveness of his (her) every transgression, voluntary and involuntary. (Lord have mercy.)

Let the Lord God establish his (her) soul where the just repose; the mercies of God, the Kingdom of the Heavens, and remission of his (her) sins: let us ask of Christ our Immortal King and our God.   (Lord have mercy.)

Let us pray to the Lord.

Lord have mercy.

The first-ranking priest approaches the deceased and says the following prayer in a loud voice; the other priests present simultaneously say the same prayer inaudibly.

111

Ο Θεὸς τῶν πνευμάτων καὶ πάσης σαρκός, ὁ τὸν θάνατον καταπατήσας, τὸν δὲ διάβολον καταργήσας καὶ ζωὴν τῷ κόσμῳ σου δωρησάμενος· αὐτός, Κύριε, ἀνάπαυσον τὴν ψυχὴν τοῦ κεκοιμημένου δούλου σου (τοῦδε), ἐν τόπῳ φωτεινῷ, ἐν τόπῳ χλοερῷ, ἐν τόπῳ ἀναψύξεως, ἔνθα ἀπέδρα ὀδύνη, λύπη καὶ στεναγμός. Πᾶν ἁμάρτημα τὸ παρ᾽ αὐτοῦ πραχθὲν ἐν λόγῳ ἢ ἔργῳ ἢ διανοίᾳ, ὡς ἀγαθὸς καὶ φιλάνθρωπος Θεὸς συγχώρησον·ὅτι οὐκ ἔστιν ἄνθρωπος, ὃς ζήσεται καὶ οὐχ ἁμαρτήσει· σὺ γὰρ μόνος ἐκτὸς ἁμαρτίας ὑπάρχεις· ἡ δικαιοσύνη σου, δικαιοσύνη εἰς τὸν αἰῶνα, καὶ ὁ νόμος σου ἀλήθεια.

Ὅτι σὺ εἶ ἡ ἀνάστασις, ἡ ζωὴ καὶ ἡ ἀνάπαυσις τοῦ κεκοιμημένου δούλου σου (τοῦδε). Χριστὲ ὁ Θεὸς ἡμῶν, καὶ σοὶ τὴν δόξαν ἀναπέμπομεν, σὺν τῷ ἀνάρχῳ σου Πατρί, καὶ τῷ παναγίῳ, καὶ ἀγαθῷ, καὶ ζωοποιῷ σου Πνεύματι, νῦν καὶ ἀεὶ καὶ εἰς τοὺς αἰῶνας τῶν αἰώνων. Ἀμήν.

Ὁ Διάκονος

Τοῦ Κυρίου δεηθῶμεν.

καὶ ἕκαστος τῶν Ἱερέων κατὰ σ ε ι ρ ά ν, εὐλογῶν τὸ λείψανον, ἐκφωνεῖ·

Ὅτι σὺ εἶ ἡ ἀνάστασις, ἡ ζωή, καὶ ἡ ἀνάπαυσις τοῦ κεκοιμημένου δούλου σου (τοῦδε) Χριστὲ ὁ Θεὸς ἡμῶν, καὶ σοὶ τὴν δόξαν ἀναπέμπομεν, σὺν τῷ ἀνάρχῳ σου Πατρί, καὶ τῷ παναγίῳ, καὶ ἀγαθῷ, καὶ ζωοποιῷ σου Πνεύματι, νῦν καὶ ἀεὶ καὶ εἰς τοὺς αἰῶνας τῶν αἰώνων. Ἀμήν.

Εἰ δὲ τῆς Νεκρωσίμου Ἀκολουθίας προΐσταται Ἀρχιερεύς, λέγει καὶ μίαν τῶν κατωτέρω Συγχωρητικῶν Ε ὐ χ ῶ ν.

O God of all spirits and flesh, Who has trodden down death, destroying the power of the devil, bestowing life on Your world: to the soul of Your servant (*Name*) departed this life, do You Yourself, O Lord, give rest in a place of light, in a place of green pasture, in a place of refreshment, from where pain and sorrow and mourning are fled away. Every sin by him (her) committed in thought, word, or deed, do You as our good and loving God forgive, seeing that there is no man that shall live and sin not, for You alone are without sin: Your righteousness, and Your law is truth.

For You are the Resurrection, the Life, and the Repose of Your servant (*Name*), O Christ our God; and to You do we send up Glory, as to Your Eternal Father and Your All-Holy, Good, and Life-creating Spirit, both now and ever, and to the ages of ages. Amen.

Priest

Let us pray to the Lord. Lord have mercy.

Each of the priests in turn blesses the deceased and says:

For You are the Resurrection, the Life, and the Repose of Your servant (*Name*), O Christ our God; and to You do we send up Glory, as to Your Eternal Father and Your All-Holy, Good, and Life-creating Spirit, both now and ever and to the ages of ages. Amen.

If the Funeral Service is presided over by a Bishop, he then says the following Prayer of Absolution.

ΕΥΧΑΙ ΣΥΓΧΩΡΗΤΙΚΑΙ

εἰς πᾶσαν ὥρὰν καὶ ἀφορισμόν, εἰς τεθνεῶτα, ἀναγινωσκόμεναι παρὰ τοῦ Ἀρχιερέως.

Ὁ Διάκονος· Τοῦ Κυρίου δεηθῶμεν.

Ὁ Ἀρχιερεύς

Κ ύριε ὁ Θεὸς ἡμῶν, ὁ τῇ σῇ ἀρρήτῳ σοφίᾳ δη- μιουργήσας τὸν ἄνθρωπον ἐκ τοῦ χοός, καὶ τοῦτον ἀναμορφώσας εἰς εἶδος καὶ κάλλος, καὶ ἐξωραΐσας, ὡς τίμιον καὶ οὐράνιον κτῆμα, εἰς δο- ξολογίαν καὶ εὐπρέπειαν τῆς σῆς δόξης καὶ βασι- λείας, διὰ τὸ κατ᾽ εἰκόνα καὶ καθ᾽ ὁμοίωσιν τοῦτον παραγαγεῖν· τὴν ἐντολὴν δὲ παραβάντα τοῦ σοῦ προστάγματος, καὶ μεταλαβόντα τῆς εἰκόνος, καὶ μὴ φυλάξαντα· καὶ διὰ τοῦτο, ἵνα μὴ τὸ κακὸν ἀθά- νατον γένηται, φιλανθρώπως κελεύσας τὴν κρᾶ- σιν, καὶ μῖξιν ταύτην, καὶ τὸν ἄρρηκτόν σου, τοῦτον δεσμόν, ὡς Θεὸς τῶν Πατέρων ἡμῶν, τῷ θείῳ βου- λήματι ἀποτέμνεσθαι καὶ διαλύεσθαι· ὥστε τὴν μὲν ψυχὴν ἐκεῖσε χωρεῖν, ἔνθα καὶ τὸ εἶναι προσε- λάβετο, μέχρι τῆς κοινῆς ἀναστάσεως, τὸ δὲ σῶμα εἰς τὰ ἐξ ὧν συνετέθη ἀναλύεσθαι· διὰ τοῦτο δεό- μεθα σοῦ τοῦ ἀνάρχου Πατρός, καὶ τοῦ μονογε- νοῦς σου Υἱοῦ, καὶ τοῦ παναγίου, καὶ ὁμοουσίου καὶ ζωοποιοῦ σου Πνεύματος, ἵνα μὴ παρίδῃς τὸ σὸν πλάσμα καταποθῆναι τῇ ἀπωλείᾳ· ἀλλὰ τὸ μὲν σῶμα διαλυθῆναι εἰς τὰ ἐξ ὧν συνετέθη, τὴν δὲ ψυ- χὴν καταταγῆναι ἐν τῷ χορῷ τῶν δικαίων. Ναί, Κύριε ὁ Θεὸς ἡμῶν, νικησάτω σου τὸ ἄμετρον ἔλεος, καὶ ἡ φιλανθρωπία ἡ ἀνείκαστος· καὶ εἴτε ὑπὸ κατάραν πατρὸς ἢ μητρός, εἴτε τῷ ἰδίῳ ἀνα- θέματι ὑπέπεσεν ὁ δοῦλός σου οὗτος, εἴτε τινὰ τῶν ἱερωμένων παρεπίκρανε, καὶ παρ᾽ αὐτοῦ δεσμὸν ἄλυτον ἐδέξατο, εἴτε ὑπὸ Ἀρχιερέως βαρυτάτῳ

PRAYERS OF ABSOLUTION

For the loosing from every curse and interdict, read for the deceased person by the Bishop.

Priest: Let us pray to the Lord, Lord have mercy.

O Lord our God, Who by Your unutterable wisdom have fashioned man out of the dust and transformed him into comeliness and beauty; and have adorned him, as a precious and heavenly creature, for doxology and magnificence of Your glory and Kingdom, in that You brought him into existence as a being fashioned according to Your image and likeness; and Who, when he had transgressed the commandment of Your ordinance, and kept it not, although he participated in Your image, gave command for this reason, as God of our fathers, to prevent evil from becoming immortal, decreeing that his composite and mixture, this bond which You made for joining body and soul unbreakably, should be sundered by Your divine Will, and be dissolved; so that the soul would withdraw where it had required existence, and there abide until the general Resurrection; whereas the body would break up into the elements out of which it had first been compounded; for this reason we pray You, the beginningless Father, and Your Only-Begotten Son, and Your All-Holy, Consubstantial and Life-creating Spirit, that endured not to see the work of Your fashioning swallowed up by destruction, but rather let the body indeed be dissolved into the elements, and let the soul be appointed a place in the Choir of the Just: Yea, O Lord our God, let Your immeasurable mercy prevail, and Your manbefriending love which is beyond compare; and if this servant has incurred the curse of father or mother, or a ban invoked upon himself (herself); or if he (she) has provoked any priest to bitter severity, and from him has incurred a ban unbreakable; or if he (she) has incurred a Bishop's

ἀφορισμῷ περιέπεσε, καὶ ἀμελείᾳ καὶ ῥαθυμίᾳ χρησάμενος, οὐκ ἔτυχε συγχωρήσεως, συγχώρησον
αὐτῷ δι᾽ ἐμοῦ τοῦ ἁμαρτωλοῦ καὶ ἀναξίου δούλου
σου· καὶ τὸ μὲν σῶμα αὐτοῦ εἰς τὰ ἐξ ὧν συνετέθη
διάλυσον, τὴν δὲ ψυχὴν αὐτοῦ ἐν σκηναῖς Ἁγίων
κατάταξον. Ναί, Κύριε ὁ Θεὸς ἡμῶν, ὁ τοῖς ἁγίοις
σου Μαθηταῖς καὶ Ἀποστόλοις τὴν ἐξουσίαν ταύτην δούς, ὥστε τῶν ἁμαρτημάτων διδόναι τὴν ἄφεσιν, καὶ εἰπών· Ὅσα ἂν δήσητε καὶ λύσητε, ἵνα
ὦσι δεδεμένα, καὶ λελυμένα· δι᾽ αὐτῶν δὲ καὶ εἰς
ἡμᾶς, εἰ καὶ ἀναξίους, ὡσαύτως τὴν τηλικαύτην
δωρεὰν φιλανθρώπως διαβιβάσας, λῦσον τὸν κοιμηθέντα δοῦλόν σου (τὸν δεῖνα) τοῦ ψυχικοῦ καὶ σωματικοῦ ἁμαρτήματος, καὶ ἔστω συγκεχωρημένος,
καὶ ἐν τῷ νῦν αἰῶνι καὶ ἐν τῷ μέλλοντι· πρεσβείαις
τῆς παναχράντου καὶ ἀειπαρθένου σου Μητρός,
καὶ πάντων σου τῶν Ἁγίων. Ἀμήν.

*

Εὐχὴ ἑτέρα.

Τοῦ Κυρίου δεηθῶμεν.

Δέσποτα πολυέλεε, Κύριε Ἰησοῦ Χριστὲ ὁ
Θεὸς ἡμῶν, ὁ τὰς κλεῖς τῆς τῶν οὐρανῶν Βασιλείας, καὶ τῇ σῇ χάριτι τὴν τοῦ δεσμεῖν τε καὶ
λύειν τὰς τῶν ἀνθρώπων ἁμαρτίας, μετὰ τὴν ἁγίαν
σου ἐκ νεκρῶν τριήμερον ἐξανάστασιν, τοῖς σοῖς
ἁγίοις Μαθηταῖς καὶ ἱεροῖς Ἀποστόλοις δωρησάμενος ἐξουσίαν, ὥστε δεδεμένα εἶναι καὶ ἐν τῷ
οὐρανῷ ὅσα δι᾽ αὐτῶν ἐν γῇ δέδενται, καὶ λελυμένα
ὡσαύτως ἐν τῷ οὐρανῷ ὅσα δι᾽ αὐτῶν ἐν γῇ λέ-
λυνται, διαδόχους δὲ ἡμᾶς τοὺς εὐτελεῖς καὶ ἀναξίους δούλους σου τῆς αὐτῆς ταύτης παρὰ σοῦ
ὑπεραγίας δωρεᾶς τε καὶ χάριτος τῇ ἀφάτῳ σου φιλανθρωπίᾳ καταξιώσας γενέσθαι, ὥστε καὶ ἡμᾶς

very grievous interdict, but through thoughtlessness and needlessness has failed to obtain forgiveness; do You forgive him (her) through me, Your sinful and unworthy servant; and let his (her) body indeed dissolve into its elements, but his (her) soul do You appoint to dwell in the tentings of the Saints. Yea, O Lord our God, Who to Your holy Disciples and Apostles gave this authority for granting remission of sins, and did say that whatsoever things they would bind and loose, those things would be bound and would be loosed; and Who through them in Your manbefriending love has caused to be transmitted to us also, unworthy though we be, the same gift in equal measure; loose this Your servant (*Name*), now fallen asleep from sin of soul and body, and make him (her) to be now forgiven in this present world and in the world to come; through the intercessions of Your all-pure and Ever Virgin Mother, and of all the Saints. Amen.

Second Prayer of Absolution

Let us pray to the Lord. Lord have mercy.

Greatly merciful Sovereign Lord Jesus Christ our God, Who after Your holy, third-day resurrection from the dead gave to Your holy Disciples and Apostles the Keys of the Kingdom of Heaven, and also the authority of Your Grace both to bind and to loose the sins of men, so that bound in Heaven would be whatsoever things through them might be bound on earth, and likewise loosed in Heaven whatsoever things through them might be loosed; and gave also that as their successors, we, Your deficient and unworthy servants, should have, by Your unutterable and manbefriending love, this same exceedingly holy Gift and Grace from You, so that we in like manner should

οὕτω δεσμεῖν τε καὶ λύειν τὰ ἐν τῷ λαῷ σου συμβαίνοντα· αὐτός, πανάγαθε Βασιλεῦ, δι᾽ ἐμοῦ τοῦ ταπεινοῦ καὶ ἀναξίου δούλου σου, συγχώρησον τῷ δούλῳ σου (τῷ δεῖνι) εἴτι ἐν τῷ παρόντι βίῳ ὡς ἄνθρωπος ἐπλημμέλησε· καὶ ἄφες αὐτῷ ὅσα ἐν λόγῳ ἢ ἔργῳ ἢ κατὰ διάνοιαν ἥμαρτε, λύσας αὐτοῦ καὶ τὸν ἐπικείμενον, μεθ᾽ οἱωνδήποτε τρόπων, δεσμόν, ὃν αὐτὸς καθ᾽ ἑαυτὸν ἐκ συναρπαγῆς ἢ ἄλλης τινὸς αἰτίας ἔδησεν, εἴτε ὑπὸ Ἀρχιερέως εἴτε παρ᾽ ἄλλου τινός, φθόνῳ καὶ συνεργείᾳ τοῦ πονηροῦ, τοιοῦτον ὑπέστη ὀλίσθημα· εὐδόκησον, ὡς μόνος ἀγαθὸς καὶ πολυέλεος, τὴν μὲν ψυχὴν αὐτοῦ μετὰ τῶν Ἁγίων ταχθῆναι τῶν ἀπ᾽ αἰῶνός σοι εὐαρεστησάντων, τὸ δὲ σῶμα τῇ παρὰ σοῦ δημιουργηθείσῃ φύσει δοθῆναι. Ὅτι εὐλογητὸς καὶ δεδοξασμένος ὑπάρχεις εἰς τοὺς αἰῶνας. Ἀμήν.

Ὁ Διάκονος

Δόξα... Καὶ νῦν... Κύριε, ἐλέησον (γ´). Πάτερ ἅγιε, εὐλόγησον.

Εἶτα παρὰ τοῦ Ἀρχιερέως ἢ τοῦ πρώτου τῇ τάξει Ἱερέως ἡ νεκρώσιμος Ἀπόλυσις οὕτως·

Δόξα σοι ὁ Θεός, ἡ ἐλπὶς ἡμῶν, δόξα σοι.

Ὁ καὶ νεκρῶν καὶ ζώντων τὴν ἐξουσίαν ἔχων, ὡς ἀθάνατος Βασιλεύς, καὶ ἀναστὰς ἐκ νεκρῶν, Χριστὸς ὁ ἀληθινὸς Θεὸς ἡμῶν, ταῖς πρεσβείαις τῆς παναχράντου ἁγίας αὐτοῦ Μητρός, τῶν ἁγίων ἐνδόξων καὶ πανευφήμων Ἀποστόλων, τῶν ὁσίων καὶ θεοφόρων Πατέρων ἡμῶν, τῶν ἁγίων καὶ ἐνδόξων προπατόρων Ἀβραάμ, Ἰσαάκ, καὶ Ἰακώβ, τοῦ ἁγίου καὶ δικαίου φίλου αὐτοῦ Λαζάρου τοῦ τετραημέρου καὶ πάντων τῶν Ἁγίων, τὴν ψυχὴν τοῦ ἐξ ἡμῶν μεταστάντος δούλου αὐτοῦ (τοῦ δεῖνος) ἐν σκηναῖς δικαίων τάξαι, ἐν κόλποις Ἀ-

both bind and loose the   things that happen to be done among Your people; Yourself, All-Good King, through me, Your humble and unprofitable servant, forgive this Your servant whatsoever mistakes as a human being he (she) has made in this present life: remit for him (her) whatsoever sins he (she) has committed in word, deed, and thought: and loose him (her) also from any ban which in any wise whatsoever has come upon him (her), whether he (she) himself (herself) out of recklessness or by some other fault has bound it upon himself (herself); or, by a Bishop or another, when, because of the envy and cooperation of the Evil One, he (she) stumbled into so grievous a state: be well pleased, as alone Good and greatly merciful, that his (her) soul be appointed a place with the Saints which from everlasting have been well pleasing to You, but that his (her) body be given to the nature which You have fashioned; for blessed and glorified are You to the ages. Amen.

Priest

Glory to the Father and to the Son and to the Holy Spirit both now and ever and to the ages of ages. Amen. Lord have mercy; Lord have mercy; Lord have mercy.

Glory to You, O Christ our God and our Hope; glory to You.

May Christ our true God, Who rose from the dead, have mercy on us; He Who as Immortal King has authority over both the dead and the living. Through the intercessions of His spotless, pure, and holy Mother; of His holy and just friend Lazaros, who lay in the grave four days; of the holy and glorious forefathers, Abraham, Isaac, and Jacob; may He give rest to our brother (sister), who has departed from us, and number him (her) among the just and holy, through His goodness and compassion, as our merciful God.

βραὰμ ἀναπαύσαι, καὶ μετὰ ἁγίων συναριθμῆσαι, ἡμᾶς δὲ ἐλεῆσαι ὡς ἀγαθὸς καὶ φιλάνθρωπος.

Αἰωνία σου ἡ μνήμη, ἀξιομακάριστε καὶ ἀείμνηστε ἀδελφὲ ἡμῶν (ἐκ γ΄).

'Επὶ δὲ γυναικῶν

Αἰωνία σου ἡ μνήμη, ἀξιομακάριστος καὶ ἀείμνηστος ἀδελφὴ ἡμῶν.

Μετὰ δὲ τὴν ἀπόλυσιν γίνεται ὁ τελευταῖος ἀσπασμὸς τοῦ λειψάνου, ψαλλομένου τοῦ ἑξῆς Στιχηροῦ Προσομοίου.

῏Ηχος β΄. ῞Οτε ἐκ τοῦ ξύλου σε νεκρόν.

Δεῦτε τελευταῖον ἀσπασμόν, δῶμεν ἀδελφοὶ τῷ θανόντι, εὐχαριστοῦντες Θεῷ· οὗτος γὰρ ἐξέλιπε τῆς συγγενείας αὐτοῦ, καὶ πρὸς τάφον ἐπείγεται, οὐκ ἔτι φροντίζων, τὰ τῆς ματαιότητος, καὶ πολυμόχθου σαρκός. Ποῦ νῦν συγγενεῖς τε καὶ φίλοι; ῎Αρτι χωριζόμεθα, ὅνπερ ἀναπαῦσαι Κύριος εὐξώμεθα.

῏Ηχος ὁ αὐτός.

Ποῖος χωρισμός, ὦ ἀδελφοί, ποῖος κοπετός, ποῖος θρῆνος, ἐν τῇ παρούσῃ ῥοπῇ! Δεῦτε οὖν ἀσπάσασθε τὸν πρὸ μικροῦ μεθ' ἡμῶν· παραδίδοται τάφῳ γάρ, καλύπτεται λίθῳ, σκότει κατοικίζεται, νεκροῖς συνθάπτεται· πάντες συγγενεῖς τε καὶ φίλοι, ἄρτι χωριζόμεθα, ὅνπερ ἀναπαῦσαι Κύριος εὐξώμεθα.

Θεοτοκίον

Σῶζε τοὺς ἐλπίζοντας εἰς σέ, Μήτηρ τοῦ ἀδύτου 'Ηλίου, Θεογεννήτρια· αἴτησαι πρεσβείαις σου

Everlasting be your memory, O our brother, who are worthy of blessedness and eternal memory. (3)

For women:

Everlasting be your memory, O our sister, who are worthy of blessedness and eternal memory. (3)

And the Choir begins the Stikhera of the Last Kiss, singing as many as may be needed to fill up the time until all have said Farewell.

Tone 2

Brethren, come, and let us a farewell kiss give to him (her) whom death has taken, and offer thanks to God. For he (she) has departed from the bosom of his (her) kin; and he (she) hastens to burial, no longer remembering vanity, nor yet the flesh which is often sore distressed. Where are now his (her) kindred and comrades? Now is come the hour of partings: let us pray to the Lord to bring him (her) to his (her) rest.

Tone 2

Brethren, what at this last moment means your distress of parting, your wailing? What means your funeral dirge? Come, and give a kiss to him (her) so lately with us: for consigned to the grave is he (she); with stone is he (she) to be covered. Darkness is his (her) dwelling place; he (she) with the dead is entombed. Come, all you his (her) kindred and comrades: now is come the hour of parting. let us pray to the Lord to bring him (her) to his (her) rest.

Theotokion

Mother of the never setting Sun, Parent of our God, O preserve them that set their hope on you; intercede,

τὸν Ὑπεράγαθον, ἀναπαῦσαι δεόμεθα, τὸν νῦν μεταστάντα, ἔνθα ἀναπαύονται αἱ τῶν δικαίων ψυχαί·
θείων ἀγαθῶν κληρονόμον, δεῖξον ἐν αὐλαῖς τῶν
δικαίων εἰς μνημόσυνον, Πανάμωμε, αἰώνιον.

Δόξα. Ἦχος πλ. β΄.

Ο ῥῶντές με ἄφωνον καὶ ἄπνουν προκείμενον,
κλαύσατε πάντες ἐπ᾽ ἐμοί, ἀδελφοὶ καὶ φίλοι,
συγγενεῖς καὶ γνωστοί· τὴν γὰρ χθὲς ἡμέραν μεθ᾽
ὑμῶν ἐλάλουν, καὶ ἄφνω ἐπῆλθέ μοι ἡ φοβερὰ ὥρα
τοῦ θανάτου. Ἀλλὰ δεῦτε πάντες οἱ ποθούμενοί με,
καὶ ἀσπάσασθέ με τὸν τελευταῖον ἀσπασμόν· οὐκ
ἔτι γὰρ μεθ᾽ ὑμῶν πορεύσομαι, ἢ συλλαλήσω τοῦ
λοιποῦ· εἰς κριτὴν γὰρ ἀπέρχομαι, ἔνθα προσωπο-
ληψία οὐκ ἔστι· δοῦλος γὰρ καὶ δεσπότης ὁμοῦ
παρίστανται, βασιλεὺς καὶ στρατιώτης, πλούσιος
καὶ πένης, ἐν ἀξιώματι ἴσῳ· ἕκαστος γὰρ ἐκ τῶν
ἰδίων ἔργων ἢ δοξασθήσεται ἢ αἰσχυνθήσεται.
Ἀλλ᾽ αἰτῶ πάντας καὶ δυσωπῶ, ἀδιαλείπτως ὑπὲρ
ἐμοῦ προσεύχεσθαι Χριστῷ τῷ Θεῷ, ἵνα μὴ κατα-
ταγῶ διὰ τὰς ἁμαρτίας μου, εἰς τὸν τόπον τῆς βα-
σάνου, ἀλλ᾽ ἵνα με κατατάξῃ, ὅπου τὸ φῶς τῆς
ζωῆς.

Καὶ νῦν. Θεοτοκίον. Ὁ αὐτός.

Π ρεσβείαις τῆς τεκούσης σε, Χριστέ, καὶ τῶν
Μαρτύρων σου, Ἀποστόλων, Προφητῶν, Ἱεραρχῶν, Ὁσίων καὶ Δικαίων, καὶ πάντων τῶν Ἁ-
γίων, τὸν κοιμηθέντα δοῦλόν σου ἀνάπαυσον.

Ὁ Ἱερεὺς

Δ ι᾽ εὐχῶν τῶν ἁγίων Πατέρων ἡμῶν, Κύριε Ἰησοῦ
Χριστέ, ὁ Θεὸς ἡμῶν, ἐλέησον καὶ σῶσον ἡμᾶς.

Ὁ Χορός· Ἀμήν.

117

we pray you, with our greatly gracious Lord, that repose may be granted him (her) that now is departed. in that habitation where repose the souls of the Just: and unto everlasting remembrance set him (her) in the courts of the Righteous, Maid All-Blameless, as the heir of blessings divine.

Glory to the Father and to the Son and to the Holy Spirit.

Looking on me as I lie here prone before you, voiceless and unbreathing, mourn for me, everyone—brethren and friends, kindred, and you who knew me well; for but yesterday with you I was talking, and suddenly there came upon me the fearful hour of death: therefore come, all you that long for me, and kiss me with the last kiss of parting. For no longer shall I walk with you, nor talk with you henceforth: for to the Judge I go, where no person is valued for his (her) earthly station: Yea, slave and master together stand before Him, king and soldier, rich man and poor man, all accounted of equal rank: for each one, according to his (her) own deeds shall be glorified, or shall be put to shame. Therefore I beg you all, and implore you, to offer prayer unceasingly for me to Christ our God, that I be not assigned for my sins to the place of torment; but that He assign me to the place where there is Light of Life.

Both now and ever and to the ages of ages. Amen.

Theotokion, Tone 6

Through the prayers of her that gave You birth, O Christ, and the prayers of Your Forerunner, of Apostles, Prophets, Hierarchs, Ascetics, and of the Righteous, and of all the Saints, to Your sleeping servant do You grant repose.

Priest

Through the prayers of our Holy Fathers, Lord Jesus Christ, have mercy and save us.

Choir: Amen.

Εἰ δὲ προΐσταται Ἀρχιερεύς, λέγει οὗτος.
Δι' εὐχῶν τῶν ἁγίων Πατέρων ἡμῶν...

Ὁ Ἱερεὺς

Δι' εὐχῶν τοῦ ἁγίου Δεσπότου ἡμῶν...

Μετὰ τὸ πέρας τοῦ ἀσπασμοῦ ἄραντες τὸ λείψανον, ἀπερχόμεθα εἰς τὸν τάφον ψάλλοντες τό·
Θρηνῶ καὶ ὀδύρομαι... (σελ. 78).

Ἐπὶ τοῦ τάφου.

Καὶ ἐν τῷ κατατεθεῖναι τὸν νεκρὸν ἐν τῷ μνη-
μείῳ, ὁ Ἱερεὺς ἀναγινώσκει τὸ «Νεκρώσιμον Τρισάγιον», ὡς ἐν τῷ ο ἴ κ ῳ (βλέπε, σελ. 98 -101).

Μετὰ ταῦτα καταβιβάζεται ὁ νεκρὸς ἐν τῷ τάφῳ,
ὁπότε ὁ Ἱερεὺς ῥαντίζει αὐτὸν σταυροειδῶς διὰ
τοῦ ἐλαίου τῆς κανδήλας λέγων·

Ρ῾αντιεῖς με ὑσσώπῳ καὶ καθαρισθήσομαι, πλυνεῖς με, καὶ ὑπὲρ χιόνα λευκανθήσομαι.

Εἶτα ἄρας χοῦν διὰ τοῦ πτύου, ῥίπτει αὐτὸν σταυροειδῶς ἐπὶ τοῦ νεκροῦ λέγων·

Τοῦ Κυρίου ἡ γῆ καὶ τὸ πλήρωμα αὐτῆς, ἡ οἰ-
κουμένη καὶ πάντες οἱ κατοικοῦντες ἐν αὐτῇ.
Γῆ εἶ καὶ εἰς γῆν ἀπελεύσει.

Ἀ π ό λ υ σ ι ς.

If a Bishop is presiding, he says:
Through the prayers of our holy Fathers . . .

Priest

Through the prayers of our holy Bishop . . .

After the last farewell has been given we proceed to the grave, singing:

I weep, and with tears lament . . .*(see page 78).*

THE BURIAL

At the gravesite the Trisagion is sung (see pages 98-101).

Then the Priest sprinkles the deceased in the form of the Cross with oil, saying:

You shall sprinkle me with hyssop and I shall be clean. You shall wash me and I shall be whiter than snow.

Then the priest spinkles the deceased in the form of the Cross with earth, saying:

The earth is the Lord's, and the fullness thereof; the world, and all that dwell therein. You are dust, and to dust you will return.

Through the prayers of our holy Fathers . . .

ΕΠΙΚΗΔΕΙΟΣ ΑΚΟΛΟΥΘΙΑ
ΕΝ ΤΗ ΔΙΑΚΑΙΝΗΣΙΜΩ ΕΒΔΟΜΑΔΙ

—◦—

Δεῖ γινώσκειν, ὅτι ἐὰν γένηταί τινα ἀδελφὸν ἐκδημῆσαι πρὸς Κύριον ἐν τῇ ἁγίᾳ ἑβδομάδι τῆς Διακαινησίμου, οὐ ψάλλομεν ἐπ' αὐτοῦ τὴν συνειθισμένην Ἀκολουθίαν τῶν κεκοιμημένων, ἀλλὰ πᾶσαν τὴν Ἀναστάσιμον Ἀκολουθίαν. Ἡ αὐτὴ Ἀκολουθία τελεῖται καὶ τῇ ἡμέρᾳ τῆς ἀποδόσεως τοῦ ἁγίου Πάσχα. Καθ' ὅλην δὲ τὴν μέχρι ταύτης χρονικὴν περίοδον ψάλλεται ἡ συνήθης Νεκρώσιμος Ἀκολουθία, ἀντικαθισταμένου τοῦ **Ἅγιος ὁ Θεὸς** διὰ τοῦ **Χριστὸς ἀνέστη.** Μέχρι τοῦ Ναοῦ ψάλλομεν ἐπίσης τὸ **Χριστὸς ἀνέστη.** Ἀντὶ δὲ **Δεῦτε τελευταῖον ἀσπασμόν...** ψάλλομεν τὸ **Ἀναστάσεως ἡμέρα...** Τὸ αὐτὸ ψάλλομεν καὶ μέχρι τοῦ τάφου).

Ὁ Ἱερεὺς

Εὐλογητὸς ὁ Θεὸς ἡμῶν, πάντοτε· νῦν καὶ ἀεὶ καὶ εἰς τοὺς αἰῶνας τῶν αἰώνων. Ἀμήν.

Χριστὸς ἀνέστη ἐκ νεκρῶν, θανάτῳ θάνατον πατήσας, καὶ τοῖς ἐν τοῖς μνήμασι ζωὴν χαρισάμενος (ἐκ γ').

FUNERAL SERVICE
DURING RENEWAL WEEK

If any of the brethren dies during the holy week of Renewal, we do not sing the customary Funeral Service but that of the Resurrection. This same service is also sung on the Apodosis of Easter. Meanwhile, during the period between the end of Renewal Week and the Apodosis, the regular service is sung except that instead of Holy God *we sing* Christ is risen. *On the way to the church we also sing* Christ is risen. *Instead of* Brethren, come and let us a farewell kiss, *we sing* Resurrection Day is dawning.

Priest

Blessed is our God always, both now and ever, and to the ages of ages. Amen.

Christ is risen from the dead, by death trampling upon Death, and upon those in the tombs bestowing life. (3).

Ἀναστὰς ὁ Ἰησοῦς ἀπὸ τοῦ τάφου καθὼς προεῖπεν, ἔδωκεν ἡμῖν τὴν αἰώνιον ζωὴν καὶ μέγα ἔλεος.

Ὁ Διάκονος

Ἐλέησον ἡμᾶς ὁ Θεός, κατὰ τὸ μέγα ἔλεός σου δεόμεθά σου, ἐπάκουσον καὶ ἐλέησον.

Ἔτι δεόμεθα ὑπὲρ ἀναπαύσεως τῆς ψυχῆς τοῦ κεκοιμημένου δούλου τοῦ Θεοῦ (τοῦ δεῖνος), καὶ ὑπὲρ τοῦ συγχωρηθῆναι αὐτῷ πᾶν πλημμέλημα ἑκούσιόν τε καὶ ἀκούσιον.

Ὅπως Κύριος ὁ Θεὸς τάξῃ τὴν ψυχὴν αὐτοῦ ἔνθα οἱ Δίκαιοι ἀναπαύονται· τὰ ἐλέη τοῦ Θεοῦ, τὴν βασιλείαν τῶν οὐρανῶν, καὶ ἄφεσιν τῶν αὐτοῦ ἁμαρτιῶν παρὰ Χριστῷ τῷ ἀθανάτῳ Βασιλεῖ καὶ Θεῷ ἡμῶν αἰτησώμεθα.

Τοῦ Κυρίου δεηθῶμεν.

Ὁ Ἱερεύς

Ὁ Θεὸς τῶν πνευμάτων... (βλέπε σελ. 100).

Ὅτι σὺ εἶ ἡ ἀνάστασις...

Ἡ Ἀπόλυσις.

Δόξα σοι ὁ Θεός, ἡ ἐλπὶς ἡμῶν, δόξα σοι. Ὁ ἀναστὰς ἐκ νεκρῶν...

Αἰωνία σου ἡ μνήμη, ἀξιομακάριστε καὶ ἀείμνηστε ἀδελφὲ ἡμῶν (ἐκ γ΄).

Χριστὸς ἀνέστη...

*

Καθ' ὁδὸν μέχρι τοῦ Ναοῦ οἱ ψάλται ψάλλουσιν ἀργῶς τό·

Χριστὸς ἀνέστη ἐκ νεκρῶν, θανάτῳ θάνατον πατήσας, καὶ τοῖς ἐν τοῖς μνήμασι ζωὴν χαρισάμενος.

Jesus, having risen from the grave, as He foretold, has given us Eternal Life and great Mercy.

Priest

Have mercy on us, O God, according to Your great Mercy; we pray You, listen and have mercy.

Again we pray for the repose of the soul of the servant of God (*Name*), departed this life, and for the forgiveness of his (her) every transgression, voluntary and involuntary.

Let the Lord God establish his (her) soul where the Just repose; the mercies of God, the Kingdom of the Heavens, and the remission of his (her) sins, let us ask of Christ, our immortal King and our God.

Let us pray to the Lord. Lord have mercy.

Priest

O God of all spirits . . . *(see page 100)*.

For You are the Resurrection . . .

Apolysis

Glory to You, O God our hope, glory to You. Christ our true God, Who rose from the dead . . . *(see pp. 100-101)*.

Everlasting be your memory, O our brother (sister), who are worthy of blessedness and eternal memory. (3)

Christ is risen . . .

Christ is risen from the dead, by death trampling upon Death, and upon those in the tombs bestowing life.

Ἐν τῷ Ναῷ.

Ὁ Ἱερεύς

Εὐλογητὸς ὁ Θεὸς ἡμῶν, πάντοτε· νῦν καὶ ἀεὶ καὶ εἰς τοὺς αἰῶνας τῶν αἰώνων. Ἀμήν.
καὶ ψάλλει ἅπαξ τό·

Χριστὸς ἀνέστη ἐκ νεκρῶν, θανάτῳ θάνατον πατήσας, καὶ τοῖς ἐν τοῖς μνήμασι ζωὴν χαρισάμενος.

Ὁ Χορὸς

Χριστὸς ἀνέστη ἐκ νεκρῶν, θανάτῳ θάνατον πατήσας καὶ τοῖς ἐν τοῖς μνήμασι ζωὴν χαρισάμενος (δίς).

Ὁ Διάκονος

Ἐλέησον ἡμᾶς, ὁ Θεός... Ἔτι δεόμεθα ὑπὲρ ἀναπαύσεως... Ὅπως, Κύριος ὁ Θεός...

Τοῦ Κυρίου δεηθῶμεν.

Ὁ Ἱερεύς· Ὅτι σὺ εἶ ἡ ἀνάστασις...

Εἶτα ψάλλονται αἱ Καταβασίαι τοῦ Πάσχα ὡς ἑξῆς.

Ὠδὴ α΄. Ἦχος α΄.

Ἀναστάσεως ἡμέρα λαμπρυνθῶμεν λαοί, Πάσχα Κυρίου Πάσχα· ἐκ γὰρ θανάτου πρὸς ζωὴν καὶ ἐκ γῆς πρὸς οὐρανὸν Χριστὸς ὁ Θεός, ἡμᾶς διεβίβασεν ἐπινίκιον ᾄδοντας.

Χριστὸς ἀνέστη ἐκ νεκρῶν, θανάτῳ θάνατον πατήσας, καὶ τοῖς ἐν τοῖς μνήμασι ζωὴν χαρισάμενος.
(γ΄) καὶ τό

Ἀναστὰς ὁ Ἰησοῦς ἀπὸ τοῦ τάφου καθὼς προεῖπεν, ἔδωκεν ἡμῖν τὴν αἰώνιον ζωὴν καὶ μέγα ἔλεος.

In the church

Priest

Blessed is our God always, both now and ever, and to the ages of ages. Amen.

And then is sung:

Christ is risen from the dead, by death trampling upon Death , and upon those in the tombs bestowing life.

Choir

Christ is risen from the dead, by death trampling upon Death, and upon those in the tombs bestowing life.   (2).

Priest

Have mercy on us, O God . . . Again we pray for the repose . . . That the Lord God establish . . . *(see page 99)*.

Let us pray to the Lord. Lord have mercy.

Priest: For You are the Resurrection . . .*(see pp. 104)*.

Then the katavasia of Easter are sung as follows:

Ode 1, Tone 1

Resurrection Day is dawning! Let us shine forth with its light! Pascha, the Lord's own Pascha! For out of death into life, and from earth into His Heaven has Christ our God taken us, in safety singing our triumphal song.

Christ is risen from the dead, by death trampling upon Death, and upon those in the tombs bestowing life.

Jesus, having risen from the grave, as He foretold, has given us Eternal Life and great Mercy.

Ὁ Διάκονος· **Τοῦ Κυρίου δεηθῶμεν.**

Ὁ Ἱερεὺς
Ὅτι σὺ εἶ ἡ ἀνάστασις...

Ἐὰν ὦσι πλείονες Ἱερεῖς, εἰς τὸ τέλος ἑκάστης ᾠδῆς ὁ Διάκονος ἐκφωνεῖ· **Τοῦ Κυρίου δεηθῶμεν.** Οἱ δὲ Ἱερεῖς κατὰ τὴν τῶν πρεσβείων σειρὰν ἕκαστος ἐκ τῶν μὴ ἐκφωνησάντων. **Ὅτι σὺ εἶ ἡ ἀνάστασις...** Ἤτοι αἱ ἐκφωνήσεις γίνονται κατὰ τὸν ἀριθμὸν τῶν Ἱερέων.

Ὠδὴ γ΄. Ἦχος ὁ αὐτός.

Δεῦτε πόμα πίωμεν καινόν, οὐκ ἐκ πέτρας ἀγόνου τερατουργούμενον, ἀλλ᾽ ἀφθαρσίας πηγήν, ἐκ τάφου ὀμβρήσαντος Χριστοῦ, ἐν ᾧ στερεούμεθα.

Χριστὸς ἀνέστη... (τρίς). **Ἀναστὰς ὁ Ἰησοῦς...**

Ὁ Διάκονος
Τοῦ Κυρίου δεηθῶμεν.

Ὁ Ἱερεὺς
Ὅτι σὺ εἶ ἡ ἀνάστασις...

Ὠδὴ δ΄. Ἦχος ὁ αὐτός.

Ἐπὶ τῆς θείας φυλακῆς, ὁ θεηγόρος Ἀββακοὺμ στήτω μεθ᾽ ἡμῶν καὶ δεικνύτω, φαεσφόρον Ἄγγελον, διαπρυσίως λέγοντα· Σήμερον σωτηρία τῷ κόσμῳ, ὅτι ἀνέστη Χριστὸς ὡς παντοδύναμος.

Χριστὸς ἀνέστη... (τρίς). **Ἀναστὰς ὁ Ἰησοῦς...**

Ὠδὴ ε΄. Ἦχος ὁ αὐτός.

Ὀρθρίσωμεν ὄρθρου βαθέως, καὶ ἀντὶ μύρου, τὸν ὕμνον προσοίσωμεν τῷ Δεσπότῃ, καὶ Χριστὸν ὀψόμεθα, δικαιοσύνης ἥλιον, πᾶσι ζωὴν ἀνατέλλοντα.

Priest

Let us pray to the Lord. Lord have mercy.

For You are the Resurrection and the Life and the repose of Your servant, O Christ our God; and to You do we send up glory, with Your Eternal Father, and Your All-Holy, Good, and Life-creating Spirit, both now and ever, and to the ages of ages. Amen.

Ode 3

Come, of this new drink let us drink deeply. Not such water as Prophet once drew from sterile rock, but life immortal which is Christ abundantly pours forth from His grave; in Him we have our strength.

Christ is risen (3) . . . Jesus, having risen . . .

Priest

Let us pray to the Lord. Lord have mercy.

For You are the Resurrection . . .

Ode 4

With us now share our holy watch; let Prophet Habakkuk now stand and for us reveal the first gleaming of the dawn the angel brings with words that pierce our hearts with joy: "This is the day that brings men salvation, for Christ is risen from death as our Almighty Lord."

Christ is risen (3) . . . Jesus, having risen . . .

Ode 5

Come, and let us rise ere comes the dawning, and bring not myrrh but our praises as offering to the Master; then our eyes shall look on Christ, our radiant Sun of Righteousness, rising to lighten the world with light.

Χριστὸς ἀνέστη ... (τρίς). Ἀναστὰς ὁ Ἰησοῦς...

Ὠδὴ ς΄. Ἦχος ὁ αὐτός.

Κατῆλθες ἐν τοῖς κατωτάτοις τῆς γῆς, καὶ συνέτριψας μοχλοὺς αἰωνίους, κατόχους πεπεδημένων Χριστέ, καὶ τριήμερος, ὡς ἐκ κήτους Ἰωνᾶς ἐξανέστης τοῦ τάφου.

Χριστὸς ἀνέστη ... (τρίς.) Ἀναστὰς ὁ Ἰησοῦς...

Ὠδὴ ζ΄. Ἦχος αὐτός.

Ὁ παῖδας ἐκ καμίνου ῥυσάμενος, γενόμενος ἄνθρωπος, πάσχει ὡς θνητός, καὶ διὰ πάθους τὸ θνητόν, ἀφθαρσίας ἐνδύει εὐπρέπειαν, ὁ μόνος εὐλογητὸς τῶν Πατέρων, Θεὸς καὶ ὑπερένδοξος.

Χριστὸς ἀνέστη ... (τρίς.) Ἀναστὰς ὁ Ἰησοῦς...

Ὠδὴ η΄. Ἦχος ὁ αὐτός.

Αὕτη ἡ κλητὴ καὶ ἁγία ἡμέρα, ἡ μία τῶν Σαββάτων, ἡ βασιλὶς καὶ κυρία, ἑορτῶν ἑορτή, καὶ πανήγυρίς ἐστι πανηγύρεων, ἐν ᾗ εὐλογοῦμεν Χριστὸν εἰς τοὺς αἰῶνας.

Χριστὸς ἀνέστη ... (τρίς). Ἀναστὰς ὁ Ἰησοῦς...

Ὠδὴ θ΄. Ἦχος ὁ αὐτός.

Ὁ Ἄγγελος ἐβόα τῇ κεχαριτωμένῃ, ἁγνὴ Παρθένε, χαῖρε, καὶ πάλιν ἐρῶ, χαῖρε· ὁ σὸς Υἱὸς ἀνέστη τριήμερος ἐκ τάφου.

Φωτίζου, φωτίζου, ἡ νέα Ἱερουσαλήμ· ἡ γὰρ δόξα Κυρίου, ἐπὶ σὲ ἀνέτειλε. Χόρευε νῦν καὶ ἀγάλλου Σιών· σὺ δὲ ἁγνὴ τέρπου Θεοτόκε, ἐν τῇ ἐγέρσει τοῦ τόκου σου.

Χριστὸς ἀνέστη ... (τρίς). Ἀναστὰς ὁ Ἰησοῦς...

Christ is risen (3) . . .Jesus, having risen . . .

Ode 6

You went down into the deeps of the abyss to destroy the cruel bars that for ages held men in weary bondage, O Christ, and as Jonah rose from the sea beast in three days, You are risen from Your grave.

Christ is risen (3) . . . Jesus, having risen . . .

Ode 7

The Children from the furnace were saved alive by Him that was born of man, Who as Man knew pain, and by His suffering clothed our flesh with beauty of His immortality; the Lord that alone was blessed by our Fathers, our God exceedingly glorious.

Christ is risen (3) . . . Jesus, having risen . . .

Ode 8

Now has dawned that day most renowned and most holy, the first of the Sabbaths, hailed as queen and sovereign. Fairest Feast of all feasts and most joyous celebration of all celebrations, when we tell how blessed is Christ unto all ages.

Christ is risen (3) . . . Jesus, having risen . . .

Ode 9

The angel, when he saw Mary Full-of-Grace, cried saying: "O holy Maid, I hail you! Yea, once again I hail you, for in the days returning your Son from death has risen; O shine with clear radiance, you new Jerusalem, for now on you is dawning glory from the risen Lord; dance now for joy, and be glad, O Zion; grieve now no more, Maiden Theotokos, but look with joy on your risen Son."

Christ is risen (3) . . . Jesus, having risen . . .

Καὶ εὐθὺς τὸ Αὐτόμελον Ἐξαποστειλάριον.

Ἦχος β΄.

Σαρκὶ ὑπνώσας ὡς θνητός, ὁ Βασιλεὺς καὶ Κύριος, τριήμερος ἐξανέστης, Ἀδὰμ ἐγείρας ἐκ φθορᾶς· καὶ καταργήσας θάνατον. Πάσχα τῆς ἀφθαρσίας, τοῦ κόσμου σωτήριον. (δίς).

Εἶτα ὁ Ἀπόστολος καὶ τὸ Εὐαγγέλιον τῆς ἡμέρας.

Ὁ Χορός· **Δόξα σοι, Κύριε, δόξα σοι.**

Ὁ Διάκονος

Ἐλέησον ἡμᾶς, ὁ Θεός... Ἔτι δεόμεθα...

Τοῦ Κυρίου δεηθῶμεν.

Ἡ Εὐχὴ **Ὁ Θεὸς τῶν Πνευμάτων... Ὅτι σὺ εἶ ἡ ἀνάστασις...** Εἰ δὲ προΐσταται Ἀρχιερεὺς καὶ μία τῶν Συγχωρητικῶν Εὐχῶν **Κύριε ὁ Θεὸς ἡμῶν... Δέσποτα πολυέλεε...** (σελ. 114-115).

Δόξα σοι, ὁ Θεός, ἡ ἐλπὶς ἡμῶν, δόξα σοι. Ὁ ἀναστὰς ἐκ νεκρῶν, Χριστὸς ὁ ἀληθινὸς Θεὸς ἡμῶν, ταῖς πρεσβείαις τῆς παναχράντου αὐτοῦ Μητρός, τῶν ἁγίων ἐνδόξων καὶ πανευφήμων Ἀποστόλων, τῶν ὁσίων καὶ θεοφόρων Πατέρων ἡμῶν, καὶ πάντων τῶν ἁγίων, τὴν ψυχὴν τοῦ ἐξ ἡμῶν μεταστάντος δούλου αὐτοῦ, ἐν σκηναῖς δικαίων τάξαι, ἐν κόλποις Ἀβραὰμ ἀναπαύσαι καὶ μετὰ δικαίων συναριθμήσαι, ἡμᾶς δὲ ἐλεῆσαι, ὡς ἀγαθὸς καὶ φιλάνθρωπος.

Αἰωνία σου ἡ μνήμη...

The Exaposteilarion

Tone 2

On You as Man the sleep of death descended, our King and Lord, but in three days are You risen, and raise Adam from decay and have destroyed the might of Death, Pascha of incorruption, salvation of all the world.

Then the Epistle and the Gospel of the day.

Choir: Glory to You, O Lord; glory to You.

Priest

Have mercy on us . . . Again we pray . . . *(see p. 99)*

Let us pray to the Lord. Lord have mercy.

O God of all spirits . . . *(see page 100)*. For You are the Resurrection . . . *(page 100)*. *If a bishop is present he reads one of the prayers of absolution:* O Lord our God *(page 113) or* Greatly merciful Sovereign Lord *(page 114)*.

Apolysis

Glory to You, O our God and our hope, glory to You. Christ our true God, Who rose from the dead, through the intercessions of His spotless, pure, all-holy Mother; of the holy, glorious and all-praiseworthy Apostles; of the venerable and theophoric Fathers, and of all the Saints, establish the soul of His servant *(Name)*, departed from among us in the tentings of the Just; give him (her) rest in the bosom of Abraham; and number him (her) among the Just; and have mercy on us as our good and loving Lord.

Everlasting be your memory . . .

124

Ἀντὶ δὲ τοῦ   τελευταῖον ἀσπασμόν, ψάλλομεν τὸ ἑξῆς·

Δόξα. Καὶ νῦν. Ἦχος πλ. α΄.

Ἀναστάσεως ἡμέρα καὶ λαμπρυνθῶμεν τῇ πανηγύρει· καὶ ἀλλήλους περιπτυξώμεθα. Εἴπωμεν ἀδελφοί, καὶ τοῖς μισοῦσιν ἡμᾶς· συγχωρήσωμεν πάντα τῇ Ἀναστάσει. Καὶ οὕτω βοήσωμεν·

Χριστὸς ἀνέστη ἐκ νεκρῶν, θανάτῳ θάνατον πατήσας, καὶ τοῖς ἐν τοῖς μνήμασι ζωὴν χαρισάμενος.

Εἶτα ὁ Ἱερεὺς

Χριστὸς ἀνέστη ἐκ νεκρῶν, θανάτῳ θάνατον πατήσας, καὶ τοῖς ἐν τοῖς μνήμασι ζωὴν χαρισάμενος.

Ἐκ τοῦ Ναοῦ μέχρι τοῦ τάφου ψάλλεται τό, **Ἀναστάσεως ἡμέρα...**

◆

Ἐπὶ τοῦ τάφου.

Ὁ Ἱερεὺς ἀναγινώσκει τὸ Νεκρώσιμον Τρισάγιον, ὡς ἐν τῷ οἴκῳ (βλέπε σελ. 98-101). Εἶτα **Ραντιεῖς με ὑσσώπῳ... Τοῦ Κυρίου ἡ γῆ...** Ἀπόλυσις.

Instead of the **Brethren,** come and let us a farewell **kiss,** *we sing the following:*

Glory . . . both now . . .

Resurrection Day is dawning! Let us shine with its light! Pascha, the Lord's own Pascha! For out of death into life, and from earth into His Heaven has Christ our God taken us, in safety singing our triumphal song.

Christ is risen from the dead, by death trampling upon Death, and upon those in the tombs bestowing life.

Priest

Christ is risen from the dead, by death trampling upon Death, and upon those in the tombs bestowing life.

Exiting from the church we say:

Resurrection Day is dawning . . .

At the grave

The priest reads the Trisagion (pages 98-101), then he says: You shall sprinkle me with hyssop . . . and The earth is the Lord's . . . *(page 118), followed by the Apolysis.*

ΑΚΟΛΟΥΘΙΑ ΝΕΚΡΩΣΙΜΟΣ ΕΙΣ ΝΗΠΙΑ

Τὸ Νεκρώσιμον Τρισάγιον.

Ὁ Ἱερεὺς

Εὐλογητὸς ὁ Θεὸς ἡμῶν, πάντοτε· νῦν καὶ ἀεὶ καὶ εἰς τοὺς αἰῶνας τῶν αἰώνων.

Ὁ Διάκονος

Ἀμήν. Ἅγιος ὁ Θεός, Ἅγιος Ἰσχυρὸς, Ἅγιος Ἀθάνατος, ἐλέησον ἡμᾶς (τρίς).

Δόξα Πατρὶ καὶ Υἱῷ καὶ Ἁγίῳ Πνεύματι, καὶ νῦν καὶ ἀεὶ καὶ εἰς τοὺς αἰῶνας τῶν αἰώνων. Ἀμήν.

Παναγία Τριάς, ἐλέησον ἡμᾶς. Κύριε, ἱλάσθητι ταῖς ἁμαρτίαις ἡμῶν. Δέσποτα, συγχώρησον τὰς ἀνομίας ἡμῖν. Ἅγιε, ἐπίσκεψαι καὶ ἴασαι τὰς ἀσθενείας ἡμῶν, ἕνεκεν τοῦ ὀνόματός σου.

Κύριε, ἐλέησον· Κύριε, ἐλέησον· Κύριε, ἐλέησον.

Δόξα Πατρὶ καὶ Υἱῷ καὶ Ἁγίῳ Πνεύματι. Καὶ νῦν καὶ ἀεὶ καὶ εἰς τοὺς αἰῶνας τῶν αἰώνων. Ἀμήν.

FUNERAL SERVICE
FOR INFANTS

The Trisagion for the Dead

Priest

Blessed is our God always, both now and ever, and to the ages of ages.

Reader

Amen. Holy God, Holy Mighty, Holy Immortal, have mercy on us. (3)

Glory to the Father and to the Son and to the Holy Spirit, both now and ever, and to the ages of ages. Amen.

All-Holy Trinity, have mercy on us. Lord, be gracious unto our sins. Master, pardon our transgressions. Holy One, visit and heal our infirmities, for Your Name's sake, and have mercy on us.

Lord have mercy; Lord have mercy; Lord have mercy.

Glory to the Father and to the Son and to the Holy Spirit, both now and ever, and to the ages of ages. Amen.

Πάτερ ἡμῶν, ὁ ἐν τοῖς οὐρανοῖς· ἁγιασθήτω τὸ ὄνομά σου· ἐλθέτω ἡ βασιλεία σου· γενηθήτω τὸ θέλημά σου, ὡς ἐν οὐρανῷ καὶ ἐπὶ τῆς γῆς· τὸν ἄρτον ἡμῶν τὸν ἐπιούσιον δὸς ἡμῖν σήμερον· καὶ ἄφες ἡμῖν τὰ ὀφειλήματα ἡμῶν, ὡς καὶ ἡμεῖς ἀφίεμεν τοῖς ὀφειλέταις ἡμῶν· καὶ μὴ εἰσενέγκῃς ἡμᾶς εἰς πειρασμόν, ἀλλὰ ῥῦσαι ἡμᾶς ἀπὸ τοῦ πονηροῦ.

Ὁ Ἱερεὺς

Ὅτι σοῦ ἐστιν ἡ βασιλεία καὶ ἡ δύναμις καὶ ἡ δόξα τοῦ Πατρὸς καὶ τοῦ Υἱοῦ καὶ τοῦ Ἁγίου Πνεύματος, νῦν καὶ ἀεὶ καὶ εἰς τοὺς αἰῶνας τῶν αἰώνων. Ἀμήν.

Εἶτα τὰ ἑπόμενα Τροπάρια.

Ἦχος δ΄.

Μετὰ πνευμάτων δικαίων τετελειωμένων, τὴν ψυχὴν τοῦ δούλου σου, Σῶτερ, ἀνάπαυσον, φυλάττων αὐτὴν εἰς τὴν μακαρίαν ζωὴν τὴν παρὰ σοί, φιλάνθρωπε.

Εἰς τὴν κατάπαυσίν σου, Κύριε, ὅπου πάντες οἱ Ἅγιοί σου ἀναπαύονται, ἀνάπαυσον καὶ τὴν ψυχὴν τοῦ δούλου σου, ὅτι μόνος ὑπάρχεις ἀθάνατος.

Δόξα.

Σὺ εἶ ὁ Θεὸς ἡμῶν, ὁ καταβὰς εἰς Ἅδην, καὶ τὰς ὀδύνας λύσας τῶν πεπεδημένων· αὐτὸς καὶ τὴν ψυχὴν τοῦ δούλου σου, Σῶτερ, ἀνάπαυσον.

Καὶ νῦν.

Ἡ μόνη ἁγνὴ καὶ ἄχραντος Παρθένος, ἡ Θεὸν ἀφράστως κυήσασα, πρέσβευε ὑπὲρ τοῦ σωθῆναι τὴν ψυχὴν τοῦ δούλου σου.

Ἐπὶ βρεφῶν μὲν δὲν γίνεται μνημόνευσις, μόνον·

Τοῦ Κυρίου δεηθῶμεν.

Our Father, Who is in Heaven,
Hallowed be Your Name; Your Kingdom come.
Your Will be done on earth as it is in Heaven.
Give us this day our daily bread;
And forgive us our trespasses,
As we forgive those who trespass against us.
And lead us not into temptation,
But deliver us from evil.

Priest

For Yours is the Kingdom and the Power and the Glory, of the Father, and of the Son, and of the Holy Spirit, both now and ever, and to the ages of ages. Amen.

Troparia

Tone 4

With the spirits of the righteous made perfect give rest to the soul of Your servant, O Savior; and keep it safe in that life of blessedness that is lived with You, O Friend of Man.

In the place of Your rest, O Lord, where all Your Saints repose, give rest also to the soul of Your servant, for You alone are Immortal.

Glory to the Father . . .

You are our God Who went down to Hades to loose the pains of the dead that were there; give rest also to the soul of Your servant.

Both now . . .

O Virgin, alone pure and immaculate, that in maiden-motherhood brought forth God, intercede for his (her) soul that he (she) may have mercy and salvation.

Let us pray to the Lord. Lord have mercy.

Ὁ φυλάσσων τὰ νήπια, Κύριε... Ὅτι σοῦ μόνου...

Ἐπὶ μεγαλυτέρας δὲ ἡλικίας·

Ὁ Διάκονος

Ἐλέησον ἡμᾶς, ὁ Θεός, κατὰ τὸ μέγα ἔλεός σου, δεόμεθά σου, ἐπάκουσον καὶ ἐλέησον.

Ἔτι δεόμεθα ὑπὲρ ἀναπαύσεως τῆς ψυχῆς τοῦ κεκοιμημένου δούλου τοῦ Θεοῦ (τοῦ δεῖνος) καὶ ὑπὲρ τοῦ συγχωρηθῆναι αὐτῷ πᾶν πλημμέλημα ἑκούσιόν τε καὶ ἀκούσιον.

Ὅπως Κύριος ὁ Θεὸς τάξῃ τὴν ψυχὴν αὐτοῦ, ἔνθα οἱ δίκαιοι ἀναπαύονται· τὰ ἐλέη τοῦ Θεοῦ, τὴν βασιλείαν τῶν οὐρανῶν, καὶ ἄφεσιν τῶν αὐτοῦ πλημμελημάτων παρὰ Χριστῷ τῷ ἀθανάτῳ βασιλεῖ καὶ Θεῷ ἡμῶν, αἰτησώμεθα.

Τοῦ Κυρίου δεηθῶμεν.

Ὁ Ἱερεύς

Ο φυλάσσων τὰ νήπια, Κύριε, ἐν τῷ παρόντι βίῳ, ἐν δὲ τῷ μέλλοντι, διὰ τὸ τῆς γνώμης ἁπλοῦν καὶ ἀνεύθυνον, τοὺς Ἀβραμιαίους κόλπους ἀποπληρῶν καὶ φωτοειδέσι τόποις κατασκηνῶν, ἐν οἷς αὐλίζεται τῶν δικαίων τὰ πνεύματα, πρόσδεξαι ἐν εἰρήνῃ καὶ τοῦ δούλου σου (τοῦ δεῖνος) τὴν ψυχήν· αὐτὸς γὰρ εἶπας, τῶν τοιούτων εἶναι τὴν βασιλείαν τῶν οὐρανῶν.

Ὅτι σοῦ μόνου ἐστὶν ἡ βασιλεία τῶν οὐρανῶν καὶ σοὶ τὴν δόξαν ἀναπέμπομεν, σὺν τῷ ἀνάρχῳ σου Πατρί, καὶ τῷ παναγίῳ καὶ ἀγαθῷ καὶ ζωοποιῷ σου Πνεύματι, νῦν καὶ ἀεὶ καὶ εἰς τοὺς αἰῶνας τῶν αἰώνων. Ἀμήν.

Καὶ ἡ Ἀπόλυσις τῆς Νεκρωσίμου Ἀκολουθίας.

Δόξα σοι, ὁ Θεός, ἡ ἐλπὶς ἡμῶν, δόξα σοι.

Ο καὶ νεκρῶν καὶ ζώντων τὴν ἐξουσίαν ἔχων, ὡς ἀθάνατος Βασιλεύς, καὶ ἀναστὰς ἐκ νεκρῶν, Χρι-

O Lord Who watches over children . . .

For older children

Have mercy on us, O God, according to Your great mercy; we pray You, listen and have mercy.

Again we pray for the repose of the soul of the servant of God (*Name*), departed this life, and for the forgiveness of his (her) every transgression, voluntary and involuntary.

Let the Lord establish his (her) soul where the Just repose; the mercies of God, the Kingdom of the Heavens, and the remission of his (her) sins, let us ask of Christ, our immortal King and our God.

Let us pray to the Lord. Lord have mercy.

Priest

O Lord Who watches over children in the present life and in the world to come because of their simplicity and innocence of mind, abundantly satisfying them with a place in Abraham's bosom, bringing them to live in radiantly shining places where the spirits of the righteous dwell; receive in peace the soul of Your little servant (*Name*), for You Yourself have said: "Let the little children come to Me, for of such is the Kingdom of Heaven."

For only Yours is the Kingdom of Heaven and to You we ascribe glory, together with Your Eternal Father and Your All-Holy, Good, and Life-creating Spirit, both now and ever, and to the ages of ages. Amen.

Glory to You, O God, our hope; glory to You.

May Christ our true God, Who rose from the dead, have mercy on us; He Who as Immortal King has authority

στὸς ὁ ἀληθινὸς Θεὸς ἡμῶν, ταῖς πρεσβείαις τῆς παναχράντου ἁγίας αὐτοῦ Μητρός, τῶν ἁγίων ἐνδόξων καὶ πανευφήμων Ἀποστόλων, τῶν ὁσίων καὶ θεοφόρων Πατέρων ἡμῶν, τῶν ἁγίων καὶ ἐνδόξων προπατόρων, Ἀβραάμ, Ἰσαάκ καὶ Ἰακώβ, τοῦ ἁγίου καὶ δικαίου φίλου αὐτοῦ Λαζάρου, τοῦ τετραημέρου, καὶ πάντων τῶν Ἁγίων, τὴν ψυχὴν τοῦ ἐξ ἡμῶν μεταστάντος δούλου αὐτοῦ (τοῦ δεῖνος) ἐν σκηναῖς δικαίων τάξαι, ἐν κόλποις Ἀβραὰμ ἀναπαύσαι, καὶ μετὰ ἁγίων συναριθμήσαι, ἡμᾶς δὲ ἐλεῆσαι ὡς ἀγαθὸς καὶ φιλάνθρωπος.

Δι᾽ εὐχῶν τῶν ἁγίων Πατέρων ἡμῶν...

Καθ᾽ ὁδὸν μέχρι τοῦ Ναοῦ ψάλλεται ἀργῶς τὸ Ἅγιος ὁ Θεός... (γ΄).

Ἐν τῷ Ναῷ.

Ὁ Ἱερεὺς

Εὐλογητὸς ὁ Θεὸς ἡμῶν...

Καὶ ψάλλεται ὁ Ἄμωμος, ὡς ἐν σελ. 102.

Εἶτα τὰ Εὐλογητάρια, (σελ. 105).

Μετὰ ταῦτα ψάλλεται τὸ Κοντάκιον· **Μετὰ τῶν Ἁγίων**... (σελ. 106).

over both the dead and the living. Through the intercessions of His spotless, pure and holy Mother; of the holy, glorious, and all-praiseworthy Apostles; of our venerable and theophoric Fathers; of the holy and glorious forefathers, Abraham, Isaac, and Jacob; of His holy and righteous friend Lazaros, who lay in the grave four days; and of all the Saints; establish the soul of His servant (*Name*), departed from us, in the tentings of the Just; give him (her) rest in the bosom of Abraham; and number him (her) among the holy, through His goodness and compassion, as our merciful God.

Through the prayers of our holy Fathers . . .

On the way to the church the Holy God *(3) is sung slowly.*

In Church

Priest

Blessed is our God always, now and ever, and to the ages of ages. Amen.

Then the Ah, the blameless in the way . . .*(see page 102); the Eulogetaria,* Blessed are You, O Lord *(page 105); followed by* With the saints give rest *(page 106).*

Προκείμενον. Ἦχος γ΄.

Μακαρία ἡ ὁδός, ᾗ πορεύῃ σήμερον, ὅτι ἡτοιμάσθη σοι τόπος ἀναπαύσεως (γ΄).

Πρὸς σέ, Κύριε, κεκράξομαι, ὁ Θεός μου.

Πρὸς Ῥωμαίους Ἐπιστολῆς Παύλου τὸ Ἀνάγνωσμα.

(Κεφ. Ϛ΄, 9-11)

Ἀδελφοί, Χριστὸς ἐγερθεὶς ἐκ νεκρῶν, οὐκέτι ἀποθνήσκει, θάνατος αὐτοῦ οὐκέτι κυριεύει. Ὃ γὰρ ἀπέθανε τῇ ἁμαρτίᾳ, ἀπέθανεν ἐφ᾽ ἅπαξ, ὃ δὲ ζῇ, ζῇ τῷ Θεῷ. Οὕτω καὶ ὑμεῖς λογίζεσθε ἑαυτοὺς νεκροὺς μὲν εἶναι τῇ ἁμαρτίᾳ, ζῶντας δὲ τῷ Θεῷ ἐν Χριστῷ Ἰησοῦ τῷ Κυρίῳ ἡμῶν.

Ἀλληλούϊα, Ἀλληλούϊα, Ἀλληλούϊα.

Ἐκ τοῦ κατὰ Λουκᾶν.

(Κεφ. ιη΄, 15-17, 26-27)

Τῷ καιρῷ ἐκείνῳ προσέφερον τῷ Ἰησοῦ τὰ βρέφη, ἵνα αὐτῶν ἅπτηται· καὶ ἰδόντες οἱ Μαθηταὶ ἐπετίμησαν αὐτοῖς. Ὁ δὲ Ἰησοῦς προσκαλεσάμενος αὐτὰ εἶπεν· Ἄφετε τὰ παιδία ἔρχεσθαι πρός με, καὶ μὴ κωλύετε αὐτά· τῶν γὰρ τοιούτων ἐστίν ἡ βασιλεία τοῦ Θεοῦ. Ἀμὴν λέγω ὑμῖν, ὃς ἐὰν μὴ δέξηται τὴν βασιλείαν τοῦ Θεοῦ ὡς παιδίον, οὐ μὴ εἰσέλθῃ εἰς αὐτήν. Εἶπον δὲ οἱ ἀκούσαντες· Καὶ τίς δύναται σωθῆναι; Ὁ δὲ εἶπε· Τὰ ἀδύνατα παρὰ ἀνθρώποις, δυνατὰ παρὰ τῷ Θεῷ ἐστι.

Ἐπὶ βρεφῶν μὲν δὲν γίνεται μνημόνευσις, μόνον

Τοῦ Κυρίου δεηθῶμεν.

Ὁ φυλάσσων τὰ νήπια... Ὅτι σοῦ μόνον...

Ἐπὶ μεγαλυτέρας δὲ ἡλικίας·

Prokeimenon, Tone 3

Blessed is the way wherein you walk today, for there is prepared for you a place of rest. (3)

Unto You, O Lord, will I cry.

The reading from the Epistle of the Holy Apostle Paul to the Romans. (Rom. 6:9-11)

Brethren, we know that Christ being raised from the dead will never die again; death no longer has dominion over him. The death he died he died to sin, once for all, but the life he lives he lives to God. So you also must consider yourselves dead to sin and alive to God in Jesus Christ.

Alleluia, Alleluia, Alleluia

Priest

Wisdom! Attend! Let us hear the Holy Gospel. Peace (+) be to all. *Choir:* And with your spirit.

The reading from the Holy Gospel of St. Luke. (Luke 18: 15-17, 26-27) Let us attend.

At that time, they were bringing even infants to him that he might touch them; and when the disciples saw it, they rebuked them. But Jesus called them to him, saying, "Let the children come to me, and do not hinder them; for to such belongs the kingdom of God. Truly I say to you, whoever does not receive the kingdom of God like a child shall not enter it." Those who heard it said, "Then who can be saved?" But he said, "What is impossible with men is possible with God."

Let us pray to the Lord. Lord have mercy.

O Lord Who watches over children . . .For only Yours . . .

Ὁ Διάκονος

Ἐλέησον ἡμᾶς, ὁ Θεός... Ἔτι δεόμεθα ὑπὲρ ἀναπαύσεως... Ὅπως Κύριος ὁ Θεὸς τάξῃ... Τοῦ Κυρίου δεηθῶμεν.

Ὁ Ἱερεὺς

Ὁ φυλάσσων τὰ νήπια, Κύριε, ἐν τῷ παρόντι βίῳ, ἐν δὲ τῷ μέλλοντι διὰ τὸ τῆς γνώμης ἁπλοῦν καὶ ἀνεύθυνον, τοὺς Ἀβραμιαίους κόλπους ἀποπληρῶν, καὶ φωτοειδέσι τόποις κατασκηνῶν, ἐν οἷς αὐλίζεται τῶν δικαίων τὰ πνεύματα, πρόσδεξαι ἐν εἰρήνῃ καὶ τοῦ δούλου σου (τοῦ δεῖνος) τὴν ψυχήν· αὐτὸς γὰρ εἶπας· Τῶν τοιούτων εἶναι τὴν βασιλείαν τῶν οὐρανῶν.

Ὅτι σοῦ μόνου ἐστὶν ἡ βασιλεία τῶν οὐρανῶν καὶ σοὶ τὴν δόξαν ἀναπέμπομεν, σὺν τῷ ἀνάρχῳ σου Πατρί, καὶ τῷ παναγίῳ καὶ ἀγαθῷ καὶ ζωοποιῷ σου Πνεύματι, νῦν καὶ ἀεὶ καὶ εἰς τοὺς αἰῶνας τῶν αἰώνων. Ἀμήν.

Εἶτα ἡ Ἀπόλυσις ὡς ἐν σελ. 128.

Εἰς τὸν ἀσπασμὸν τῶν νηπίων ψάλλονται τὰ ἀκόλουθα προσόμοια ἀντὶ τοῦ Δεῦτε τελευταῖον...

Ἦχος πλ. δ΄. Ὦ τοῦ παραδόξου θαύματος!

Ὦ τίς μὴ θρηνήσῃ τέκνον μου, τὴν ἐκ τοῦ βίου ἡμῶν, πενθηράν σου μετάστασιν; Ὅτι βρέφος ἄωρον, ἐκ μητρικῶν ἀγκαλῶν νῦν, ὥσπερ στρουθίον τάχος ἐπέτασας, καὶ πρὸς τὸν Κτίστην πάντων κατέφυγες; Ὦ τέκνον, τίς ποτε, μὴ θρηνήσῃ βλέπων σου τὸ ἐμφανὲς πρόσωπον εὐμάραντον, τὸ πρὶν ὡς ῥόδον τερπνόν;

For older children

Have mercy on us, O God . . .*(see page 99)* Again we pray for the repose . . . Let the Lord God establish . . .

Let us pray to the Lord. Lord have mercy.

O Lord Who watches over children in the present life and in the world to come because of their simplicity and innocence of mind, abundantly satisfying them with a place in Abraham's bosom, bringing them to live in radiantly shining places where the spirits of the righteous dwell: receive in peace the soul of Your little servant (*Name*), for You Yourself have said, "Let the little children come to Me, for of such is the Kingdom of Heaven."

For only Yours is the Kindom of Heaven and to You we ascribe glory, together with Your Eternal Father and Your All-Holy, Good, and Life-creating Spirit, both now and ever, and to the ages of ages. Amen.

Apolysis. (see page 128)

At the farewell the following are sung:
Tone 8

Who would not lament for you, my child, as your end journey begins from this world to another home? For while still a little child, all too soon from your mother's arms, as might a birdling on speeding wing upborne, are you departed to Him that made all things. O child, who from lament could refrain when he beholds your lovely face, which was like a gladsome rose, now fading fast away?

Ω" τίς μὴ στενάξῃ, τέκνον μου, καὶ μὴ βοήσῃ κλαυθμῷ, τὴν πολλήν σου εὐπρέπειαν, καὶ τὴν ὡραιότητα, τῆς ἁγνῆς πολιτείας σου; Ὥσπερ γὰρ ναῦς τις, ἴχνος οὐκ ἔχουσα, οὕτως ὑπέδυς ἐξ ὀφθαλμῶν μου ταχύ. Δεῦτε οἱ φίλοι μου, συγγενεῖς καὶ γείτονες ἅμα ἐμοί, τοῦτο ἀσπασώμεθα, τάφῳ ἐκπέμποντες.

Ὁ Ἱερεὺς

Δι᾽ εὐχῶν τῶν ἁγίων Πατέρων ἡμῶν, Κύριε Ἰησοῦ Χριστέ ὁ Θεὸς ἡμῶν, ἐλέησον καὶ σῶσον ἡμᾶς. Ἀμήν.

Ἐπὶ τοῦ τάφου.

Ἀναγινώσκεται τὸ Νεκρώσιμον Τρισάγιον, ὡς ἐν τῷ οἴκῳ (σελ. 98-101).

ΑΚΟΛΟΥΘΙΑ ΝΕΚΡΩΣΙΜΟΣ ΕΙΣ ΝΗΠΙΑ ΚΑΤΑ ΤΗΝ ΔΙΑΚΑΙΝΗΣΙΜΟΝ ΕΒΔΟΜΑΔΑ

Αὕτη εἶναι ὁμοία πρὸς τὴν ἐν σελ. 119-125 ἐκτεθεῖσαν, παραλειπομένης τῆς Εὐχῆς. **Ὁ Θεὸς τῶν πνευμάτων...** καὶ ἀντὶ ταύτης λεγομένης τῆς Εὐχῆς **Ὁ φυλάσσων τὰ νήπια, Κύριε..** Ἀπόστολος καὶ Εὐαγγέλιον, καὶ ἐν τῇ περιπτώσει ταύτῃ λέγονται τὰ τῶν Νηπίων.

Who would not with groaning sighs, my child, and floods of clamorous tears mourn the wealth of your comeliness and the beauty shining forth from the innocence of your heart? For like a caravel which leaves no wake behind, so are you vanished, and from my eyes are sped. Come, my beloved friends, kinsfolk, neighbors, now draw nigh to join with me in the kiss of last farewell, and bear him (her) to his (her) grave.

Priest

Through the prayers of our holy Fathers, Lord Jesus Christ our God, have mercy and save us. Amen.

At the grave

The Trisagion is sung. (See pages 98-101)

FUNERAL SERVICE FOR INFANTS
DURING RENEWAL WEEK

Similar to that service on pages 119-125, except that instead of O God *of all spirits we say* O Lord Who watches over children. *The Epistle and Gospel readings are those of the service for infants.*

ΑΚΟΛΟΥΘΙΑ
ΤΩΝ ΕΞΟΜΟΛΟΓΟΥΜΕΝΩΝ

Ὁ Ἱερεὺς

Εὐλογητὸς ὁ Θεὸς ἡμῶν πάντοτε· νῦν καὶ ἀεὶ καὶ εἰς τοὺς αἰῶνας τῶν αἰώνων. Ἀμήν.

Ἐν εἰρήνῃ τοῦ Κυρίου δεηθῶμεν.

Κύριε, ἐλέησον.

Ὑπὲρ τῆς ἄνωθεν εἰρήνης καὶ τῆς σωτηρίας τῶν ψυχῶν ἡμῶν, τοῦ Κυρίου δεηθῶμεν.

Ὑπὲρ τοῦ δούλου τοῦ Θεοῦ (τοῦ δεῖνος) ἀφέσεως τῶν ἁμαρτιῶν καὶ συγχωρήσεως τῶν ἑκουσίων καὶ ἀκουσίων αὐτοῦ πλημμελημάτων, τοῦ Κυρίου δεηθῶμεν.

Ὅπως Κύριος ὁ Θεὸς δωρήσηται αὐτῷ ἄφεσιν ἁμαρτιῶν καὶ καιρὸν μετανοίας, τοῦ Κυρίου δεηθῶμεν.

Ὑπὲρ τοῦ ῥυσθῆναι αὐτόν τε καὶ ἡμᾶς ἀπὸ πάσης θλίψεως, ὀργῆς, κινδύνου καὶ ἀνάγκης, τοῦ Κυρίου δεηθῶμεν.

Ἀντιλαβοῦ, σῶσον, ἐλέησον, καὶ διαφύλαξον...

Τῆς Παναγίας, ἀχράντου, ὑπερευλογημένης...

Ὅτι πρέπει σοι πᾶσα δόξα...

133

THE SACRAMENT OF
HOLY CONFESSION

Priest

Blessed is our God always, both now and ever, and to the ages of ages. Amen.

In peace let us pray to the Lord.

Lord have mercy.

For the peace from above; for the salvation of our souls; let us pray to the Lord.

For the remission of sins of the servant of God (*Name*) and the forgiveness of all his (her) voluntary and involuntary transgressions; let us pray to the Lord.

That the Lord our God may grant him (her) remission of sins and time for repentance; let us pray to the Lord.

That He will deliver him (her) and us from all tribulation, wrath, danger, and necessity; let us pray to the Lord.

Help us; save us; have mercy on us and keep us, O God, by Your Grace.

Calling to remembrance our all-holy, immaculate . . .

For to You are due all glory, honor and . . .

133

Εἶτα λέγει ὁ Ἱερεὺς τὴν παροῦσαν Εὐχήν·

Τοῦ Κυρίου δεηθῶμεν.

Κύριε Ἰησοῦ Χριστέ, Υἱὲ τοῦ Θεοῦ τοῦ ζῶντος, ποιμὴν καὶ ἀμνέ, ὁ αἴρων τὴν ἁμαρτίαν τοῦ κόσμου, ὁ τὸ δάνειον χαρισάμενος τοῖς δυσὶ χρεωφειλέταις καὶ τῇ ἁμαρτωλῷ δοὺς ἄφεσιν ἁμαρτιῶν αὐτῆς· αὐτός, Δέσποτα, ἄνες, ἄφες, συγχώρησον τὰς ἁμαρτίας, τὰς ἀνομίας, τὰ πλημμελήματα, τὰ ἑκούσια καὶ τὰ ἀκούσια, τὰ ἐν γνώσει, τὰ ἐν ἀγνοίᾳ, τὰ ἐν παραβάσει καὶ παρακοῇ γενόμενα παρὰ τῶν δούλων σου τούτων. Καὶ εἴ τι, ὡς ἄνθρωποι σάρκα φοροῦντες καὶ τὸν κόσμον οἰκοῦντες, ἐκ τοῦ Διαβόλου ἐπλανήθησαν, εἴτε ἐν λόγῳ εἴτε ἐν ἔργῳ εἴτε ἐν γνώσει εἴτε ἐν ἀγνοίᾳ εἴτε λόγον Ἱερέως κατεπάτησαν ἢ ὑπὸ κατάραν Ἱερέως ἐγένοντο εἴτε τῷ ἰδίῳ ἀναθέματι ὑπέπεσον ἢ ὅρκῳ ὑπήχθησαν, Αὐτός, ὡς ἀγαθὸς καὶ ἀμνησίκακος Δεσπότης, τούτους τοὺς δούλους σου λόγῳ λυθῆναι εὐδόκησον, συγχωρῶν αὐτοῖς καὶ τὸ ἴδιον ἀνάθεμα καὶ τὸν ὅρκον, κατὰ τὸ μέγα σου ἔλεος. Ναί, Δέσποτα φιλάνθρωπε Κύριε, ἐπάκουσον ἡμῶν δεομένων τῆς σῆς ἀγαθότητος ὑπὲρ τῶν δούλων σου τούτων καὶ πάριδε ὡς πολυέλεος τὰ πταίσματα αὐτῶν ἅπαντα· ἀπάλλαξον αὐτοὺς τῆς αἰωνίου κολάσεως· σὺ γὰρ εἶπας, Δέσποτα· «Ὅσα ἂν δήσητε ἐπὶ τῆς γῆς, ἔσται δεδεμένα ἐν τῷ οὐρανῷ, καὶ ὅσα ἂν λύσητε ἐπὶ τῆς γῆς ἔσται λελυμένα ἐν τῷ οὐρανῷ». Ὅτι σὺ εἶ μόνος ἀναμάρτητος καὶ σοὶ τὴν δόξαν ἀναπέμπομεν, σὺν τῷ ἀνάρχῳ σου Πατρί, καὶ τῷ παναγίῳ καὶ ἀγαθῷ καὶ ζωοποιῷ σου Πνεύματι, νῦν καὶ ἀεὶ καὶ εἰς τοὺς αἰῶνας τῶν αἰώνων Ἀμήν.

Καὶ λέγει τὸ Τρισάγιον· Ἅγιος ὁ Θεός,... (γ΄).
Δόξα. Καὶ νῦν. Παναγία Τριάς, Κύριε, ἐλέησον (γ΄). Δόξα. Καὶ νῦν. Πάτερ ἡμῶν. Ὅτι σοῦ ἐστιν.

Then the Priest says this prayer :

Let us pray to the Lord. Lord have mercy.

O Lord Jesus Christ, Son of the Living God, the Shepherd, the Lamb that takes away the sins of the world, Who gave remittance to the two Γebtors and granted pardon of her sins to the Harlot, do You Yourself, O Master, remit, forgive, and pardon the sins, transgressions, which, in knowledge or in ignorance Your servants have committed. And whatever they have done, as men bearing flesh and living in this world, being beguiled by the Devil; if in word, thought, or deed they have sinned, or despised the word of a Priest; or, under his anathema, or have fallen under their own anathema, or are bound under an oath; do You, as the good Master Who does not requite evil, be pleased that these Your servants be loosed by Your word, forgiving them their own anathema and oath, according to Your great mercy. Yea, O Master, loving Lord, listen to our prayer beseeching Your Grace for these Your servants; and, as our most merciful God, overlook all their offenses and deliver them from everlasting torment, for You, O Master, have said, "Whatsoever you shall bind on earth shall be bound in Heaven, and whatsoever you shall loose on earth shall be loosed in Heaven." For You alone are without sin, and to You do we send up Glory : as to Your Eternal Father and Your All-Holy, Good, and Life-creating Spirit, both now and ever, and to the ages of ages. Amen.

Then he says the Holy God . . . (3). Glory . . . Both now . . . All-Holy Trinity. . . Lord have mercy (3). Glory . . . Our Father . . . For yours . . .

Κύριε, ἐλέησον (ιβ΄). Δεῦτε, προσκυνήσωμεν (γ΄).
Ἐλέησόν με ὁ Θεός... (σελ. 11).

Εἶτα τὰ παρόντα Τροπάρια.

Ἦχος πλ. β΄.

Ἐλέησον ἡμᾶς, Κύριε, ἐλέησον ἡμᾶς...

Δόξα.

Κύριε ἐλέησον ἡμᾶς, ἐπὶ σοὶ γὰρ πεποίθαμεν..

Καὶ νῦν.

Τῆς εὐσπλαγχνίας τὴν πύλην...

Τό, Κύριε, ἐλέησον (μ΄).

Ὁ δὲ ἐξομολογούμενος λέγει καθ᾽ ἑαυτόν.

Ἥμαρτον, Κύριε, συγχώρησόν μοι.

Καὶ τό, Ὁ Θεός, ἱλάσθητί μοι τῷ ἁμαρτωλῷ.

Τοῦ Κυρίου δεηθῶμεν.

Ὁ Θεὸς ὁ Σωτὴρ ἡμῶν, ὁ διὰ τοῦ προφήτου σου
Νάθαν μετανοήσαντι τῷ Δαυῒδ ἐπὶ τοῖς ἰδίοις
πλημμελήμασιν, ἄφεσιν δωρησάμενος, καὶ τοῦ Μα-
νασσῆ τὴν ἐπὶ μετάνοιαν προσευχὴν δεξάμενος· αὐτός, καὶ τὸν δοῦλόν σου (τὸν δεῖνα) μετανοοῦντα, ἐφ᾽
οἷς ἔπραξε πλημμελήμασι, πρόσδεξαι τῇ συνήθει σου
φιλανθρωπίᾳ, παρορῶν πάντα τὰ αὐτῷ πεπραγμένα, ὁ
ἀφιεὶς ἀδικίας, καὶ ὑπερβαίνων ἀνομίας· Σὺ γὰρ εἶπας
Κύριε· «Οὐ θελήσει θέλω τὸν θάνατον τοῦ ἁμαρτωλοῦ
ὡς τὸ ἐπιστρέψαι καὶ ζῆν αὐτόν»· καὶ ὡς ἑβδομη-
κοντάκις ἑπτὰ ἀφιέναι τὰ ἁμαρτήματα. Ἐπεί, ὡς ἡ
μεγαλωσύνη σου ἀνείκαστος, καὶ τὸ ἔλεός σου ἀμέ-
τρητον· ἐὰν γὰρ ἀνομίας παρατηρήσῃς, τίς ὑποστή-
σεται; Ὅτι σὺ εἶ ὁ Θεὸς τῶν μετανοούντων, καὶ σοὶ
τὴν δόξαν ἀναπέμπομεν τῷ Πατρὶ καὶ τῷ Υἱῷ καὶ τῷ
Ἁγίῳ Πνεύματι, νῦν καὶ ἀεὶ καὶ εἰς τοὺς αἰῶνας
τῶν αἰώνων. Ἀμήν.

Lord have mercy (12). Come let us worship . . .(3).
Have mercy on me O God . . .(page 11).

Then the following hymns

Tone 6

Have mercy on us, O Lord . . .
Glory . . .
Lord, have mercy on us . . .
Both now . . .
Open to us the doors of your mercy . . .
Lord have mercy (40).

The penitent says:

I have sinned, O Lord, forgive me. O God, be merciful
to me a sinner.

Let us pray to the Lord. Lord have mercy.

O God our Savior, Who through Your prophet Nathan
granted remission of sins to the penitent David, and accepted the penitent prayer of Manasse, do You Yourself,
O loving Lord, accept this Your servant *(Name)*, who
laments over the transgression which he (she) has committed, overlooking all that he (she) has done. You who
forgive all unrighteousness and pass by all transgressions;
for You, O Lord, have said, "You have no pleasure in the
death of a sinner, but rather he turn from his wickedness
and live"; and that "sins shall be forgiven even unto seventy
times seven." For as Your greatness is incomparable, so
is Your mercy immeasurable. For if You should mark iniquities, who shall stand? For You are the God of the penitent, and to You do we send up Glory: to the Father, and
to the Son, and to the Holy Spirit, both now and ever, and
to the ages of ages. Amen.

Εἶτα ὁ ἐξομολογούμενος, κλίνων τὰ γόνατα καὶ ἄνω τάς χεῖρας ἔχων, λέγει.

Πάτερ, Κύριε τοῦ οὐρανοῦ καὶ τῆς γῆς, ἐξομολογοῦμαί σοι πάντα τὰ κρυπτὰ καὶ φανερὰ τῆς καρδίας καὶ διανοίας μου, ἃ ἔπραξα ἕως τῆς σήμερον. Διὸ ἄφεσιν αἰτῶ παρὰ σοῦ τοῦ δικαίου καὶ εὐσπλάγχνου Κριτοῦ καὶ χάριν τοῦ μηκέτι ἁμαρτάνειν.

Τότε ὁ πνευματικὸς ἱλαρᾷ τῇ φωνῇ λέγει·

Ἀδελφέ· δι᾽ ὃ ἦλθες πρὸς τὸν Θεὸν καὶ πρὸς ἐμέ, μὴ αἰσχυνθῇς· οὐ γὰρ ἐμοὶ ἀναγγέλεις, ἀλλὰ τῷ Θεῷ, ἐν ᾧ ἵστασαι.

Καὶ ἐρωτᾷ αὐτὸν ὁ Πνευματικὸς εἰς πάντα τὰ ἁμαρτήματα καὶ μετὰ τὸ ἐρωτῆσαι καταλεπτῶς, λέγει ταῦτα.

Τέκνον μου πνευματικόν, τὸ τῇ ἐμῇ ταπεινότητι ἐξομολογούμενον, ἐγὼ ὁ ταπεινὸς καὶ ἁμαρτωλὸς οὐκ ἰσχύω ἀφιέναι ἁμάρτημα ἐπὶ τῆς γῆς, εἰ μὴ ὁ Θεός· διὰ δὲ τὴν θεόλεκτον φωνὴν ἐκείνην, τὴν μετὰ τὴν τοῦ Κυρίου ἡμῶν Ἰησοῦ Χριστοῦ Ἀνάστασιν γενομένην πρὸς τοὺς Ἀποστόλους, καὶ λέγουσαν· «Ἄν τινων ἀφῆτε τὰς ἁμαρτίας, ἀφίενται αὐτοῖς· ἄν τινων κρατῆτε, κεκράτηνται», εἰς ἐκείνην καὶ ἡμεῖς θαρροῦντες, λέγομεν· Ὅσα ἐξεῖπες τῇ ἐμῇ ἐλαχίστῃ ταπεινότητι, καὶ ὅσα οὐκ ἔφθασας εἰπεῖν, ἢ κατ᾽ ἄγνοιαν ἢ κατὰ λήθην, οἱαδήποτε, ὁ Θεὸς συγχωρήσοι σοι ἐν τῷ νῦν αἰῶνι, καὶ ἐν τῷ μέλλοντι.

Μετὰ ταῦτα ἐπισυνάπτει καὶ ταύτην τὴν Εὐχήν·

Ο῾ Θεός, ὁ συγχωρήσας Δαυῒδ, διὰ Νάθαν τοῦ προφήτου, τὰ ἴδια ἐξομολογήσαντι ἁμαρτήματα, καὶ Πέτρῳ τὴν ἄρνησιν κλαύσαντι πικρῶς, καὶ πόρνῃ δακρυσάσῃ ἐπὶ τοὺς αὐτοῦ πόδας, καὶ τελώνῃ καὶ ἀσώτῳ· αὐτὸς ὁ Θεὸς συγχωρήσοι σοι δι᾽ ἐμοῦ τοῦ ἁμαρτωλοῦ

The penitent, kneeling and holding up his hands, says :

Father, Lord of heaven and earth, I confess to You all the hidden and open sins of my heart and mind, which I have committed to this day. Therefore, I beg of You, the merciful and righteous Judge, forgiveness and grace to sin no more.

The Priest then says kindly to the penitent :

Brother (sister), inasmuch as you have come to me and to God, be not ashamed; for you speak not to me, but to God, before Whom you stand.

The priest then questions the penitent in detail about his (her) sins, after which he says as follows:

My spiritual child, who has confessed to my humble person, I, humble and a sinner, have no power on earth to forgive sins, but God alone; but through that divinely spoken word which came to the Apostles after the Resurrection of our Lord Jesus Christ, saying, "Whoseoever sins you remit, they are remitted, and whosesoever sins you retain, they are retained," we are emboldened to say: Whatsoever you have said to my humble person, and whatsoever you have failed to say, whether through ignorance or forgetfulness, whatever it may be, may God forgive you in this world, and in the world to come.

The Priest adds this prayer :

May God Who pardoned David through Nathan the Prophet when he confessed his sins, and Peter weeping bitterly for his denial, and the sinful woman weeping at his feet, and the publican and the prodigal son, may that same God forgive you all things, through me a sinner,

πάντα, καὶ ἐν τῷ νῦν αἰῶνι, καὶ ἐν τῷ μέλλοντι· καὶ ἀκατάκριτόν σε παραστήσοι ἐν τῷ φοβερῷ αὐτοῦ βήματι. Περὶ δὲ τῶν ἐξαγορευθέντων ἐγκλημάτων μηδεμίαν φροντίδα ἔχων, πορεύου εἰς εἰρήνην.

Ἀπόλυσις.

Εὐχὴ
ἐπὶ τῶν ἐν ἐπιτιμίοις ὄντων καὶ ἑαυτοὺς ὅρκῳ δεσμούντων.

Δέσποτα, Κύριε, ὁ Θεὸς ἡμῶν, ὁ μονογενὴς Υἱὸς καὶ Λόγος τοῦ Πατρός, ὁ πάντα δεσμὸν ἁμαρτίας ἡμῶν τῷ σῷ πάθει διαρρήξας, καὶ ἐμφυσήσας εἰς τὰ πρόσωπα τῶν σῶν Ἀποστόλων, καὶ εἰπών· «Λάβετε

both in this world and in the world to come, and set you uncondemned before His terrible Judgment Seat. Having no further care for the sins which you have confessed, depart in peace.

Apolysis

Prayer
for those who are under penance.

O Master, Lord our God, the Only-begotten Son and Word of the Father, who through Your Passion have rent asunder every bond of our sins, and breathed into the faces of Your Apostles, saying, " Receive the Holy

Πνεῦμα ἅγιον· ἄν τινων ἀφῆτε τὰς ἁμαρτίας, ἀφίενται αὐτοῖς· ἄν τινων κρατῆτε, κεκράτηνται»· σύ, Δέσποτα, διὰ τῶν ἁγίων σου Ἀποστόλων ἐχαρίσω τοῖς κατὰ καιρὸν ἱερουργοῦσιν ἐν τῇ ἁγίᾳ σου Ἐκκλησίᾳ, ἐπὶ γῆς ἀφιέναι τὰς ἁμαρτίας, καὶ δεσμεῖν καὶ λύειν πάντα σύνδεσμον ἀδικίας. Δεόμεθα οὖν καὶ νῦν ὑπὲρ τοῦ ἀδελφοῦ ἡμῶν (τοῦ δεῖνος) τοῦ παρεστηκότος ἐνώπιόν σου. Ἐπιχορήγησον αὐτῷ τὸ σὸν ἔλεος, διαρρήσσων αὐτοῦ τὸν δεσμὸν τῶν ἁμαρτιῶν, εἴτι ἐν ἀγνοίᾳ ἢ ὀλιγωρίᾳ ἐλάλησεν ἢ ὑπὸ μικροψυχίας ἔπραξεν, εἰδὼς τὴν ἀνθρωπίνην ἀσθένειαν, καί, ὡς φιλάνθρωπος καὶ ἀγαθὸς Δεσπότης, πάντα τὰ ἑκούσια καὶ τὰ ἀκούσια ἁμαρτήματα συγχώρησον αὐτῷ· ὅτι σὺ εἶ ὁ λύων τοὺς πεπεδημένους, ὁ ἀνορθῶν τοὺς κατερραγμένους, ἡ ἐλπὶς τῶν ἀπηλπισμένων, ἡ ἀνάστασις τῶν πεπτωκότων· καὶ τὸν δοῦλόν σου τοῦτον ἐλευθέρωσον ἀπὸ τοῦ δεσμοῦ τῶν ἁμαρτημάτων. Ὅτι δεδόξασταί σου τὸ πανάγιον ὄνομα, σὺν τῷ Πατρὶ καὶ τῷ Ἁγίῳ σου Πνεύματι, νῦν καὶ ἀεὶ καὶ εἰς τοὺς αἰῶνας τῶν αἰώνων. Ἀμήν.

Εὐχὴ
ἐπὶ τῶν ἐξ ἐπιτιμίων λυομένων.

Εὔσπλαγχνε, ἀγαθέ, καὶ φιλάνθρωπε Κύριε, ὁ διὰ τοὺς σοὺς οἰκτιρμοὺς ἐξαποστείλας τὸν μονογενῆ σου Υἱὸν εἰς τὸν κόσμον, ἵνα διαρρήξῃ τὸ καθ᾿ ἡμῶν χειρόγραφον τῶν πλημμελημάτων, καὶ λύσῃ τὰ δεσμὰ τῶν ὑπὸ τῆς ἁμαρτίας πεπεδημένων, καὶ κηρύξῃ αἰχμαλώτοις ἄφεσιν· σύ, Δέσποτα, καὶ τὸν δοῦλόν σου (τὸν δεῖνα) τῇ σῇ ἀγαθότητι ἐλευθέρωσον τοῦ ἐπικειμένου αὐτῷ δεσμοῦ· καὶ δώρησαι αὐτῷ ἀναμαρτήτως ἐν παντὶ καιρῷ καὶ τόπῳ προσιέναι τῇ σῇ μεγα-

Spirit; whosesoever sins you remit, they are remitted unto them, and whosesoever sins you retain, they are retained"; You, O Master, have granted, through Your holy Apostles, to those who minister in Your holy Church the power to forgive sins on earth, and to bind and loose every bond of unrighteousness. We beseech You now for our brother (sister) *(Name)* who stands before You. Pour out Your mercy on him (her), rending asunder the bond of his (her) sins, whether spoke in ignorance or by heedlessness, or has done so through lack of courage, for You know human weakness, and, O good Master, as a lover of mankind, do You forgive him (her) all his (her) sins, voluntary or involuntary; for it is You Who looses those who are cast down, You, the Help of the despairing, the Resurrection of the fallen. O free this Your servant from the bond of sins. For Your All-Holy Name is magnified, of the Father, and of the Son, and of the Holy Spirit, both now and ever, and to the ages of ages. Amen.

Prayer
for those who have fulfilled their penance

O merciful God, Who loves mankind, Who through Your mercies have sent Your Only-begotten Son into the world that he might destroy the handwriting of the transgressions that is against us, and loose the bonds of those who are bound in sin, and preach remission to the captives, do You, O Master, in Your goodness, free Your servant *(Name)* from the bond which is upon him (her), and grant him (her) without sin to draw near to Your Majesty in every time and place, and with boldness and a pure

λειότητι, καὶ μετὰ παῤῥησίας καὶ καθαροῦ συνειδότος αἰτεῖσθαι τὸ παρὰ σοῦ πλούσιον ἔλεος. Ὅτι ἐλεήμων καὶ φιλάνθρωπος Θεὸς ὑπάρχεις, καὶ σοὶ τὴν δόξαν ἀναπέμπομεν, τῷ Πατρὶ καὶ τῷ Υἱῷ καὶ τῷ Ἁγίῳ Πνεύματι, νῦν καὶ ἀεὶ καὶ εἰς τοὺς αἰῶνας τῶν αἰώνων. Ἀμήν.

conscience to ask for Your rich mercy; for You are a merciful God Who loves mankind, and to You we send up Glory, to the Father, and to the Son, and to the Holy Spirit, both now and ever, and to the ages of ages. Amen.

Εὐχ ή
ἐπὶ πᾶσαν ἀσθένειαν.

Τοῦ Κυρίου δεηθῶμεν.

Δέσποτα παντοκράτορ, ἰατρὲ ψυχῶν καὶ σωμάτων, ὁ ταπεινῶν καὶ ἀνυψῶν, παιδεύων καὶ πάλιν ἰώμενος, τὸν ἀδελφὸν ἡμῶν (τὸν δεῖνα) τὸν ἀσθενοῦντα ἐπίσκεψαι ἐν τῷ ἐλέει σου. Ἔκτεινον τὸν βραχίονά σου, τὸν πλήρη ἰάσεως καὶ θεραπείας, καὶ ἴασαι αὐτόν, ἐξανιστῶν ἀπὸ κλίνης καὶ ἀρρωστίας· ἐπιτίμησον τῷ πνεύματι τῆς ἀσθενείας· ἀπόστησον ἀπ᾽ αὐτοῦ πᾶσαν πληγήν, πᾶσαν ἀλγηδόνα, πᾶσαν μάστιγα, πάντα πυρετὸν ἢ ῥῖγος· καὶ εἴ τί ἐστιν ἐν αὐτῷ πλημμέλημα ἢ ἀνόμημα, ἄνες, ἄφες, συγχώρησον διὰ τὴν σὴν φιλανθρωπίαν. Ναί, Κύριε, φεῖσαι τοῦ πλάσματός σου, ἐν Χριστῷ Ἰησοῦ τῷ Κυρίῳ ἡμῶν, μεθ᾽ οὗ εὐλογητὸς εἶ, σὺν τῷ παναγίῳ καὶ ἀγαθῷ καὶ ζωοποιῷ σου Πνεύματι, νῦν καὶ ἀεὶ καὶ εἰς τοὺς αἰῶνας τῶν αἰώνων. Ἀμήν.

Τοῦ Κυρίου δεηθῶμεν.

Κύριε ὁ Θεὸς ἡμῶν, ὁ τὰ χρόνια καὶ δεινὰ πάθη λόγῳ μόνῳ θεραπεύσας, ὁ τὴν πενθερὰν Πέτρου πυρέσσουσαν ἰασάμενος· Αὐτὸς καὶ νῦν, Δέσποτα, ἴασαι τὸν δοῦλόν σοι (τον δεῖνα) ἀπὸ τῆς συνεχούσης αὐτὸν μάστιγος, ὁ παιδεύων συμπαθῶς, καὶ ἰώμενος ἀγαθῶς· ὁ πᾶσαν νόσον καὶ πᾶσαν μαλακίαν ἀφαιρεῖσθαι δυνάμενος· καὶ ἀνάστησον αὐτὸν ἀπὸ κλίνης ὀδυνηρᾶς, καὶ ἀπὸ στρωμνῆς κακώσεως, ἐπιθεὶς ἐπ᾽ αὐτὸν τὸ φάρμακον τοῦ ἐλέους σου· παράσχου δὲ αὐτῷ τελείαν ἴασιν καὶ ὑγείαν. Ὅτι σὺ εἶ ὁ ἰατρὸς τῶν σωμάτων καὶ τῶν ψυχῶν ἡμῶν, καὶ σοὶ τὴν δόξαν ἀναπέμπομεν, σὺν τῷ Πατρὶ καὶ τῷ Ἁγίῳ Πνεύματι, νῦν καὶ ἀεὶ καὶ εἰς τοὺς αἰῶνας τῶν αἰώνων. Ἀμήν.

PRAYERS FOR VARIOUS OCCASIONS

Prayers for the Sick

Let us pray to the Lord. Lord have mercy.

O Lord Almighty, the Healer of our souls and bodies, You Who put down and raise up, Who chastise and heal also; do You now, in Your great mercy, visit our brother (sister) (*Name*), who is sick. Stretch forth Your hand that is full of healing and health, and get him (her) up from his (her) bed, and cure him (her) of his (her) illness. Put away from him (her) the spirit of disease and of every malady, pain and fever to which he (she) is bound; and if he (she) has sins and transgressions, grant to him (her) remission and forgiveness, in that You love mankind; yea, Lord my God, pity Your creation, through the compassions of Your Only-Begotten Son, together with Your All-Holy, Good and Life-creating Spirit, with Whom You are blessed, both now and ever, and to the ages of ages. Amen.

Let us pray to the Lord. Lord have mercy.

O Lord our God, Who by word alone did heal all diseases, Who did cure the kinswoman of Peter, You Who chastise with pity and heal according to Your goodness; Who are able to put aside every malady and infirmity, do You Yourself, the same Lord, grant aid to this Your servant (*Name*) and cure him (her) of every sickness of which he (she) is grieved; lift him (her) up from his (her) bed of pain, and send down upon him (her) Your great mercy, and if it be Your Will, give to him (her) health and a complete recovery; for You are the Physician of our souls and bodies, and to You do we send up Glory: to Father, and to Son, and to Holy Spirit, both now and ever, and to the ages of ages. Amen.

Before an Operation

Let us pray to the Lord. Lord have mercy.

O Lord Jesus Christ our God, Who did patiently endure the scourging and wounding of Your most holy Body, that You might save the souls and bodies of Your people, look graciously, we beseech You, upon the suffering body of this Your servant (*Name*) and give him (her) strength to endure patiently whatsoever You shall see fit to lay upon him (her). Bless the means employed for the working out of his (her) cure, granting that he (she) may so endure his (her) sufferings in the flesh that the wounding of his (her) body may be to avail for the correcting and salvation of his (her) soul, for Yours it is to show mercy and to save, O Christ our God; and to You do we send up Glory, as to Your Eternal Father and Your All-Holy, Good and Life-creating Spirit, both now and ever, and to the ages of ages. Amen.

Thanksgiving for Recovery

Let us pray to the Lord. Lord have mercy.

O Lord God Jesus Christ, the Life and strength of all that put their hope in You, Whose mercies are numberless, and the treasury of goodness that is infinite, we give thanks to You for the blessings which You have bestowed upon Your servant (*Name*); and we humbly beseech You to continue Your goodness toward us; and as You have been well pleased to restore Your servant to his (her) bodily health, so do You imbue his (her) soul with all the heavenly graces, perseverance in good works, and prepare us by Your blessings in this life for the enjoyment of eternal happiness in the Life to come; for to You are due all glory, honor, and worship, as also to Your Eternal Father and Your All-Holy, Good and Life-creating Spirit, both now and ever, and to the ages of ages. Amen.

Communion of the Sick

A small table shall be placed near the bed of the sick one; it shall be covered with a clean white linen cloth, and on it shall be placed an Ikon of the Lord Jesus Christ, a lighted candle, a glass of water, a spoon, and a napkin.

The Priest shall take a particle of the Reserved Holy Mystery, put it into a Cup, and pour therein a little wine (to soften the Particle as much as may be sufficient for the sick one to receive).

Priest

Blessed is our God always, both now and ever, and to the ages of ages. Amen.

Trisagion Prayers (see page 32). All-Holy Trinity ... Our Father ...

Priest

For Yours is the Kingdom ... both now ...

Reader

Amen. Lord have mercy (12). Glory ... both now ...

(+) O come, let us worship and fall down before God our King; (+) O come, let us worship and fall down before Christ our King and our God, (+) O come, let us worship and fall down before Christ Himself, our King and our God.

The Symbol of the Faith

I believe in one God, the Father Almighty, Maker of Heaven and earth, and of all things visible and invisible, and in one Lord Jesus Christ, the Only-Begotten, Begotten of the Father before all worlds; Light of Light, Very God of Very God, Begotten not made, of One Essence with the Father, through Whom all things were made; Who for us and for our salvation came down from Heaven, and was in-

carnate of the Holy Spirit and the Virgin Mary, and was made man. And was crucified also for us under Pontius Pilate, and suffered and was buried. And the third day He rose according to the Scriptures; and ascended into Heaven, and sits on the right hand of the Father; and He shall come again in glory to judge both the quick and the dead; and His Kingdom shall have no end. And I believe in the Holy Spirit, the Lord, the Giver of Life, Who proceeds from the Father, Who with the Father and the Son together is worshiped and glorified; Who spoke through the Prophets. I believe in One, Holy, Catholic and Apostolic Church. I acknowledge one Baptism for the remission of sins. I look for the resurrection of the dead, and the life of the world to come. Amen.

The Priest recites the Communion troparia:

O Son of God, receive me today as a partaker of Your mystic Supper, for I shall not betray Your mysteries to Your enemies, nor will I give You a kiss as did Judas, but with the thief I will confess You, "Remember me, O Lord, when You come into Your Kingdom."

Glory . . .

O Heavenly King, Comforter, Spirit of Truth, Treasury of Blessings and Bountiful Giver of Life, Who are in all places and fill all things, come, take Your abode in us, cleansing us of every sin, and, of Your goodness, O Lord, save our souls.

Both now . . . Amen.

Theotokion

We acknowledged Him God, Who was incarnate of you, O Virgin Theotokos: intercede with Him to save our souls.

Lord have mercy (12).

Let us pray to the Lord. Lord have mercy.

Priest

O Master, Lord Jesus Christ, our Savior, Who alone has the power to forgive sins, and are our Loving God, overlook, we beseech You, the transgressions of Your servant (*Name*), whether of knowledge or ignorance, granting to him (her) to partake without condemnation of Your immaculate Mysteries, not unto judgment, nor to the increase of sins, but to the cleansing of soul and body, and to the inheritance of Your Kingdom; for You are his (her) help and a firm wall and bulwark against the Adversary, and the purification of his (her) iniquities; for You are our merciful and Manbefriending God, and to You do we send up Glory: to the Father, and to the Son, and to the Holy Spirit, both now and ever, and to the ages of ages. Amen.

* * * * *

Lord, I am not worthy that You should enter under my roof, into the house of my soul; for it is all deserted and in ruins, and You have not in me a fitting place to rest Your head; but since You desire to abide with me, I, trusting in Your compassion, have come to You; bid the doors of my unworthy lips to open, that I may be satisfied with You alone; enter into me, and cleanse me from every bodily and spiritual defilement; be You my Helper and Defender, and count me worthy to stand at Your right hand, through the intercessions and supplications of our all-pure Lady, the Theotokos and Ever-Virgin Mary, with all the Saints who in their generation have been well pleasing unto You, for Blessed are You to the ages of ages. Amen.

Prayer of St. John Chrysostom

I believe and confess, O Lord, that You are in truth the Christ, the Son of the Living God, that came into the world to save sinners, of whom I am the chief; and I believe that This is truly Your own immaculate Body, and this is Your own Precious Blood; wherefore, I pray you, have mercy on me, and forgive all my transgressions, both voluntary and involuntary, of thought, word, and deed; of knowledge and ignorance; and account me worthy without condemnation to partake of Your immaculate Mysteries, unto remission of sins and unto everlasting Life. Amen.

When the Confession of the sick one has been heard, Absolution given, the Priest prepares for the Partaking. Spreading the Paten under the chin of the sick one, the Priest gives to him (her) the Holy Mysteries, saying:

The servant of God (*Name*) partakes of the Precious and All-Holy Body and Blood of our Lord God and Savior Jesus Christ unto the remission of sins and everlasting Life.

Lo! This has touched your lips, and your iniquities shall be taken away, and your sin purged.

After the Partaking, the Priest says:

Lord, now let Your servant depart in peace, according to Your word, for my eyes have seen Your salvation, a Light to lighten the Gentiles, the Glory of Your people Israel.

Troparion of the Day

Let us pray to the Lord. Lord have mercy.

Priest

The Lord God most merciful have compassion on you. The Lord Jesus Christ bestow on you every good desire.

The Lord Almighty deliver you from every calamity. The Lord teach you. The Lord give you understanding. The Lord help you; the Lord save you. The Lord protect you; the Lord keep you; the Lord cleanse you. The Lord fill you with spiritual joy. The Lord be Defender of your soul and body. The Lord, as compassionate and loving, give to you forgiveness of sins. The Lord Jesus Christ have mercy on you in the day of judgment and bless you all the days of your life.

Glory . . . both now . . . Amen.

Theotokion of the Day

Priest

Through the prayers of all the Saints, O Lord Jesus Christ, our God, and of the Theotokos, grant us Your peace and have mercy on us, for You alone are compassionate.

Blessing

The blessing (+) of the Lord, through His Divine Grace and manbefriending love, come upon you always, both now and ever, and to the ages of ages. Amen.

Thanksgiving after Communion

Glory to You, our God, glory to You. (3)

I thank You, O Lord my God, Who has granted unto me, though unworthy, to receive Your all-pure and Holy Gifts. May Your Holy Body give profit unto me to everlasting, and Your Precious Blood unto remission of sins; may this Eucharist be unto me for joy, health and gladness, and at Your dread Second Coming, render me, a sinner, worthy to stand at the right hand of Your Majesty, with Your Eternal Father and Your All-Holy, Good and Life-creating Spirit, both now and ever, and to the ages of ages. Amen.

Through the intercessions of Your all-pure Mother, and of all the Saints.

Amen.

Prayer for the Church School

Let us pray to the Lord. Lord have mercy.

O Lord our God, Who has honored us with Your own image, Who has taught Your elect, so that most wise are they who give heed to Your teaching, Who reveals wisdom to babes, Who has imparted wisdom: open the hearts, the minds, and the lips of these Your servants, that they might receive the power of Your Law, and successfully apprehend the useful precepts which shall be taught to them, to the glory of Your Holy Name, to the profit and up-building of Your Holy Church; and that they understand Your good and perfect Will. Deliver them from every hostile oppression: preserve them in Orthodoxy and Your Holy, Catholic Faith, and in all uprightness and purity all the days of their life, that they might advance in wisdom, and in the fulfillment of Your commandments; that being thus prepared they may glorify Your most Holy Name and become heirs of Your Kingdom; for You are the God of Mercy, and gracious in strength; and to You do we send up Glory: to the Father, and to the Son, and to the Holy Spirit, both now and ever, and to the ages of ages. Amen.

Blessing (Sprinkling with Holy Water)

The blessing (+) of the Lord through His divine Grace and manbefriending love come upon you always, both now and ever, and to the ages of ages. Amen.

Service of the Adoption of a Child

Priest

Blessed is our God always, both now and ever, and to the ages of ages. Amen.

Trisagion Prayers. **All-Holy Trinity . . . Our Father . . .** *(see page 32).*

Priest

For Yours is the Kingdom . . . Amen.

Then the Reader recites the Apolytikion (of the day) and the Kontakion (of the Temple).

Let us pray to the Lord. Lord have mercy.

Priest

O Lord our God, Who through Your beloved Child, our Lord Jesus Christ, did call us children of God through adoption, and the Grace of Your All-Holy Spirit, and did say, "I will be to Him a Father, and He shall be to Me a Son." Do You, the same King, Loving God, look down from Your holy dwelling place on high, upon these Your servants and unite their natures which you have begotten separate from one another according to the flesh, through Your Holy Spirit, into parents and son (daughter). Confirm them in Your love; bind them through Your benediction; bless them to Your great glory; strengthen them in Your Faith; preserve them always and renounce them not for that which proceeds from their lips. Be Mediator for their promises, that their love which they have confessed to You be not torn asunder even to the evening of their lives; grant that they may be kept sincerely alive in You, our only Living and True God, and grant unto them to become heirs of Your Kingdom, for unto You is due all Glory: to the Father, and to the Son, and to the Holy

Spirit, both now and ever, and to the ages of ages. Amen.

Peace (+) be to all.

Choir: And to your spirit.

Priest

Let us bow our heads unto the Lord.

Choir: To You, O Lord.

Priest

O Master and Lord, Who are the Maker of all creatures, and by the first Adam did make the bonds of kinship according to the natural flesh, and through Jesus Christ our Lord, Your beloved Son and our God, by Grace did show us also as Your kin, now these Your servants bow their heads before You, Who alone know all things before their happenings, and ask of You a blessing, that in You they may receive that for which they hoped: the bond inscribed in one another, of parents and son (daughter); and that living worthily in You in adoption to sonship (daughtership), they may keep themselves in due constancy, that as in all things, so in this may be glorified in and to Your All-Holy Name of the Father, and of the Son, and of the Holy Spirit, both now and ever, and to the ages of ages. Amen.

Then let the child go up from the Sanctuary, and the parents receive their child from the Sanctuary. And the child shall bow before the parents, who shall place their hands upon the child's head and say:

Today you are our child; this day we have begotten you.

And the parents shall take their child in their arms and kiss one another.

Then the Priest says the Apolysis.

The Prayer for the Blessing of Homes at Theophany

Priest

Blessed is our God always, both now and ever, and to the ages of ages.

Reader

Amen. *Trisagion Prayer. All-Holy Trinity . . . Our Father . . . (see page 32).*

Priest

For Yours is the Kingdom . . . Amen.

Troparion, Tone 1

When You in Jordan for Your baptism were come, O Lord, then was revealed unto us to worship the Trinity, for lo, the Father's voice spoke to bear witness of You, by Name, declaring You His well-beloved Son; and the Spirit in form like a dove appeared to confirm the sure truth of the spoken Word; O Lord made manifest and Light of the world, we give glory to You, O Christ our God.

Priest

Let us pray to the Lord. Lord have mercy.

O God our Savior, the True Light, Who was baptized in the Jordan by the Prophet John, and Who did deign to enter under the roof-tree of Zacchaeus, bringing salvation unto him and unto his house: do You, the same Lord, keep safe also from harm those who dwell herein; grant to them Your blessing, purification and bodily health, and all their petitions that are unto salvation and Life everlasting; for blessed are You, as also Your Father Who is from everlasting, and Your All-Holy, Good and Life-creating Spirit, both now and ever, and to the ages of ages. Amen.

And the Priest shall bless the whole house with Holy Water, saying:

When You in Jordan . . .

Apolysis

May He Who condescended to be baptized in the river Jordan by the Forerunner and Prophet John, for our salvation, through the intercessions of His immaculate Mother, the Theotokos and Ever-Virgin Mary, and of all the Saints, have mercy on us and save us, for He is our good and loving Lord.

The Priest proclaims:

Grant, O Lord, a prosperous and peaceful life, health and salvation, and the furtherance of all good things to all Your servants (*Names*) who dwell herein, and preserve them for many years.

Reader: Many years! (3)

Prayer at the Foundation of a House

Let us pray to the Lord. Lord have mercy.

Priest

O God Almighty, Who made the Heavens with wisdom and has established the earth upon its sure foundations, the Creator and Author of all men, look upon these Your servants (*Names*), to whom it has seemed good to set up a house for their dwelling in the dominion of Your Power, and to rear it by building; establish it upon a stable rock, and found it according to Your divine word in the Gospel,

so that neither wind, nor flood, nor any other thing shall be able to harm it; graciously grant that they may bring it to completion, and deliver all them who shall wish to dwell therein from every attack of the enemy; for Yours is the dominion, and Yours is the Kingdom, and the Power, and the Glory, of the Father, and of the Son, and of the Holy Spirit, both now and ever, and to the ages of ages. Amen.

For the Blessing of Any Object

Let us pray to the Lord. Lord have mercy.

O Creator and Author of the human race; Giver of all spiritual Graces, Bestower of eternal Salvation: do You, the same Lord, send down Your Holy Spirit with a blessing from on high upon this (*name of object being blessed*), that, fortified by the might of Your heavenly protection, it may be potent unto bodily salvation and help and aid unto all who shall make use of it; through Jesus Christ our Lord, Who together with You, the Eternal Father, and Your All Holy, Good and Life-creating Spirit, we send up glory, both now and ever, and to the ages of ages. Amen.

The Blessing and Hallowing of Ikons

Priest

Blessed is our God always, both now and ever, and unto ages of ages:

Chanter

Amen.

The Trisagion Prayers. **O All-holy Trinity . . . Our Father . . .**

Priest

For Yours is the Kingdom . . .

Chanter

Amen.

Kyrie eleison.

O come, let us worship and fall down . . .

O Lord our God, Who created us after Your own Image and Likeness; Who redeems us from our former corruption of the ancient curse through Your manbefriending Christ, Who took upon Himself the form of a servant and became man; Who having taken upon Himself our likeness remade Your Saints of the first dispensation, and through Whom also we are refashioned in the Image of Your pure blessedness;

Your Saints we venerate as being in Your Image and Likeness, and we adore and glorify You as our Creator;

Wherefore we pray You, send forth Your blessing upon this Ikon, and with the sprinkling of hallowed water,

Bless and make holy this Ikon unto Your glory, in honor and remembrance of Your Saint (N);

And grant that this sanctification will be to all who venerate this Ikon of Saint (N), and send up their prayer unto You standing before it;

Through the grace and bounties and love of Your Only-Begotten Son, with Whom You are blessed together with Your All-Holy, Good and Life-creating Spirit; both now and ever, and unto ages of ages.

Amen.

Sprinkling cross-fashion the Ikon with Holy Water, he says:

Hallowed and blessed is this Ikon of St. (N) by the Grace of the Holy Spirit, through the sprinkling of Holy Water: in the Name of the Father (+), and of the Son (+), and of the Holy Spirit: (+). Amen.

Immediately is sung the Troparion and Kontakion of the Saint limned on the Ikon, and we all reverence and kiss the all-pure Ikon. Then follows the little Apolysis including the name of the Saint.

Prayer When One is to Take Up Abode in a New House

Let us pray to the Lord.

Kyrie eleison.

O God our Savior, Who did deign to enter under the roof of Zacchaeus, unto salvation of the same and of all that were in the house;

Do you, the same Lord, keep safe also from harm them who now desire to dwell here,

And who, together with us unworthy ones, do offer unto You prayer and supplication:

Bless this (+) their home and dwelling, and preserve their life free from all adversity;

For unto You are due all glory, honor and worship, as also unto Your Eternal Father, and Your All-Holy, Good and Life-creating Spirit; both now and ever, and unto ages of ages:

Amen.

Prayer at the Blessing of Vehicles of Travel

Let us pray to the Lord:

Kyrie eleison.

O Master, Lord our God, hearken unto the prayer which we now send up to You, and bless this vehicle with Your holy right hand (+);

Send down upon it Thy guardian Angel, that all who desire to journey therein may be safely preserved and shielded from every evil end;

And as the Ethiopian, riding in the chariot and reading of Your holy prophecy, was granted faith and Grace through Your Apostle Philip,

So do You now manifest the path of salvation to Your servants who shall travel in this conveyance, that with Your helping grace they may be clothed upon with good works; and after the completion of this life may be vouchsafed everlasting joy in Your heavenly Kingdom,

For Yours is the might, and the Kingdom, and the power, and unto You do we send up glory; to Father, and to Son, and to Holy Spirit, both now and ever, and unto ages of ages:

Amen.

The priest sprinkles all over the vehicle with Holy Water, saying:

May Christ our true God,
Through the intercessions of His all-pure Mother,
Through the protection of the bodiless powers,
Of the holy, glorious and all-praiseworthy Apostles,
And of St. Nicholas,
And all the Saints,

Have mercy on us and save us, as He is good and loves mankind.

Prayer at the Blessing of a Medal

Let us pray to the Lord:

Kyrie eleison.

O Lord our King, Sovereign of the heavenly and earthly, Father of our Lord God and Savior Jesus Christ,

Who did command Moses Your servant to place the images of the Cherubim in Your holy tabernacle upon either side of the Mercy Seat,

Vouchsafe, we beseech You, O our King to send the grace of Your Holy Spirit and Your Angel upon this medal; and of Your Fatherly goodness to bless (+) and sanctify it, mindful of the mystery which it represents.

And that it may kindle devout affection and increase holiness of life;

Endow it with the aid of Your pretection against all snares of the enemy,

Make it to be a protection of soul and body,

Through the grace and compassion and love of Your Only-Begotten Son, our Lord God and Savior Jesus Christ, and of Your All-Holy, Good and Life-creating Spirit, One God; both now and ever, and unto ages of ages: Amen.

The Priest, blessing the medal with Holy Water, says:

This image is hallowed through the Grace of the Holy Spirit, through the sprinkling of Holy Water: in the Name of the (+) Father, and of the (+) Son, and of the (+) Holy Spirit: Amen.

Then the Dismissal of the Day, including the Saint whose Ikon has been blessed.

Communion Of the Sick in a Hospital

Priest

Blessed is our God always, both now and ever, and to the ages of ages. Amen.

Holy God, Holy Mighty, Holy Immortal: have mercy on us.
Holy God, Holy Mighty, Holy Immortal: have mercy on us.
Holy God, Holy Mighty, Holy Immortal: have mercy on us.

Glory to the Father and to the Son and to the Holy Spirit, both now and ever, and to the ages of ages. Amen.

All-Holy Trinity: have mercy on us; Lord, be gracious unto our sins; Master, pardon our offenses; Holy One, visit and heal our infirmities, for Your Name's sake.

Glory to the Father and to the Son and to the Holy Spirit, both now and ever, and to the ages of ages. Amen.

Lord have mercy; Lord have mercy; Lord have mercy.

Our Father, Who are in Heaven,
Hallowed be Your Name; Your Kingdom come.
Your Will be done on earth as it is in Heaven.
Give us this day our daily bread;
And forgive us our trespasses.
As we forgive those who trespass against us.
And lead us not into temptation,
But deliver us from evil.

Priest

For Yours is the Kingdom and the Power and the Glory, of the Father, and of the Son, and of the Holy Spirit, both now and ever, and to the ages of ages. Amen.

In peace let us pray to the Lord.

For the peace from above; for the salvation of our souls; let us pray to the Lord.

For the remission of sins of the servant of God (Name) and the forgiveness of all his (her) voluntary and involuntary transgressions; let us pray to the Lord.

That He will deliver him (her) and us from all tribulation, wrath, danger, and necessity; let us pray to the Lord.

Help us; save us; have mercy on us and keep us, O God, by Your Grace.

Calling to remembrance our all-holy, pure, exceedingly blessed and glorious Lady Theotokos and Ever-Virgin Mary, with all the Saints; let us commend ourselves and one another and all our life to Christ our God.

For to You are due all glory, honor, and worship: to the Father and to the Son and to the Holy Spirit, both now and ever, and to the ages of ages.

O Master, Lord Jesus Christ, our Savior, Who alone has the power to forgive sins, and are our Loving God, overlook, we beseech You, the transgressions of Your servant (*Name*), whether of knowledge or ignorance, granting to him (her) to partake without condemnation of Your immaculate Mysteries, not unto judgment, nor to the increase of sins, but to the cleansing of soul and body, and to the inheritance of Your Kingdom; for You are his (her) help and a firm wall and bulwark against the Adversary, and the purification of his (her) iniquities; for You are our merciful and Man befriending God, and to You do we send up Glory, to the Father, and to the Son, and to the Holy Spirit, both now and ever, and to the ages of ages. Amen.

The Priest recites the Communion troparia:

O Son of God, receive me today as a partaker of Your mystic Supper, for I shall not betray Your mysteries to Your enemies, nor will I give You a kiss as did Judas, but with the thief I will confess You, "Remember me, O Lord, when You come into Your Kingdom."

When the Confession of the sick one has been heard, Absolution given, the Priest prepares for the Partaking, Spreading the Paten under the chin of the sick one, the Priest gives to him (her) the Holy Mysteries, saying:

The servant of God (*Name*) partakes of the Precious and All-Holy Body and Blood of our Lord God and Savior Jesus Christ unto the remission of sins and everlasting Life.

Prayers of Thanksgiving

Let Your holy Body, O Lord, be unto Life Everlasting for me, and Your precious Blood unto remission of sins. Let this holy Eucharist be a source of joy and gladness for me. At Your second coming make me worthy of standing at Your right hand, through intercessions of your holy Mother, the Theotokos, and all your Saints. Amen.

Dismissal

Through the prayers of our holy Fathers, Lord Jesus Christ, our God, have mercy on us and save us.

Prayers in Times of Trouble

Let us pray to the Lord.

Lord have mercy.

(+) O Lord of Powers, be with us, for in the time of trouble we have no other help but You.

O Lord, God of Powers, have mercy on us.

Priest

O God, our help in time of need, Who are just and merciful, and Who inclines to the supplications of His people;

Look down upon us, miserable sinners, have mercy on us, and deliver us from the trouble that now besets us, for which we acknowledge we are deservedly suffering.

We acknowledge and believe, O Lord, that all the trials of this life are disposed by You for our chastisement, when we drift away from You, and disobey Your commandments;

Deal with us not according to our iniquities, but according to Your manifold mercies, for we are the works of Your hands, and You know our weaknesses:

Grant, we beseech You, Your divine helping Grace, and endow us with patience and strength to endure our tribulations with complete submission to Your Will;

You know our misery and sufferings, and to You, our only hope and refuge, we flee for relief and comfort, trusting in Your infinite love and compassion, that in due time,

When You know best, You will deliver us from this trouble, and turn our distress into comfort,

When we shall rejoice in Your mercy, and exalt and praise Your Holy Name (+) O Father, Son and Holy Spirit; both now and ever, and unto ages of ages. Amen.

Εὐχὴ
ἐπὶ βασκανίαν.

Τοῦ Κυρίου δεηθῶμεν.

Κύριε ὁ Θεὸς ἡμῶν, ὁ Βασιλεὺς τῶν αἰώνων, ὁ παντοκράτωρ καὶ παντοδύναμος, ὁ ποιῶν πάντα καὶ μετασκευάζων μόνῳ τῷ βούλεσθαι· ὁ τὴν ἑπταπλάσιον κάμινον καὶ τὴν φλόγα τὴν ἐν Βαβυλῶνι εἰς δρόσον μεταβαλὼν καὶ τοὺς ἁγίους σου τρεῖς Παῖδας σώους διαφυλάξας· ὁ ἰατρὸς καὶ θεραπευτὴς τῶν ψυχῶν ἡμῶν· ἡ ἀσφάλεια τῶν εἰς σὲ ἐλπιζόντων· σοῦ δεόμεθα καὶ σὲ παρακαλοῦμεν, ἀπόστησον, φυγάδευσον καὶ ἀπέλασον πᾶσαν διαβολικὴν ἐνέργειαν, πᾶσαν σατανικὴν ἔφοδον καὶ πᾶσαν ἐπιβουλήν, περιέργειάν τε πονηρὰν καὶ βλάβην καὶ ὀφθαλμῶν βασκανίαν τῶν κακοποιῶν καὶ πονηρῶν ἀνθρώπων ἀπὸ τοῦ δούλου σου (τοῦδε)· καὶ ἢ ὑπὸ ὡραιότητος ἢ ἀνδρείας ἢ εὐτυχίας ἢ ζήλου καὶ φθόνου ἢ βασκανίας συνέβη, αὐτός, φιλάνθρωπε Δέσποτα, ἔκτεινον τὴν κραταιάν σου χεῖρα καὶ τὸν βραχίονά σου τὸν ἰσχυρὸν καὶ ὕψιστον, καὶ ἐπισκοπῶν ἐπισκόπησον τὸ πλάσμα σου τοῦτο, καὶ κατάπεμψον αὐτῷ Ἄγγελον εἰρηνικόν, κραταιόν, ψυχῆς καὶ σώματος φύλακα, ὃς ἐπιτιμήσει καὶ ἀπελάσει ἀπ᾽ αὐτοῦ πᾶσαν πονηρὰν βουλήν, πᾶσαν φαρμακείαν καὶ βασκανίαν τῶν φθοροποιῶν καὶ φθονερῶν ἀνθρώπων· ἵνα ὑπὸ σοῦ ὁ σὸς ἱκέτης φρουρούμενος, μετ᾽ εὐχαριστίας ψάλλῃ σοι. «Κύριος ἐμοὶ βοηθός, καὶ οὐ φοβηθήσομαι. τί ποιήσει μοι ἄνθρωπος»· καὶ πάλιν· «Οὐ φοβηθήσομαι κακά, ὅτι σὺ μετ᾽ ἐμοῦ εἶ»· ὅτι σὺ εἶ ὁ Θεός, κραταίωμά μου, ἰσχυρὸς ἐξουσια-

PRAYER FOR DELIVERANCE
FROM THE EVIL EYE

Lord, have mercy.

O Lord our God, the King of the ages, Almighty
and Pantocrator: You create and transform all things
by Your will alone. You changed the seven-fold furnace and the flame in Babylon into refreshing dew and
preserved your Three Youths safe. You are the physician and healer of our souls, and the security of all
those who hope in You. We entreat and beseech:
banish, expel and cast away from your servant (*Name*)
every diabolic action, every satanical attack and
assault, every evil influence and harm and the spell of
the evil eye caused by malevolent and evil people. And
if this has occured because of beauty, or hand-
someness, or prosperity, or jealousy, or envy, or the
evil eye, Master, lover of humanity, stretch forth Your
mighty hand and Your powerful and sublime arm and
in Your watchful care look upon this Your servant and
visit him (*her*), and guard him (*her*) with an angel of
peace, a mighty guardian of body and soul, who will
rebuke and expel from him (*her*) every evil design,
every sorcery and the spell of the evil eye of corrupt-
ing and envious people, so that Your servant, defend-
ed by You, may sing with thanksgiving: "the Lord is
my helper and I shall not be frightened. What shall
man do to me," and again: "I shall fear no evil, for
You are with me, for You are God, my strength, a
mighty counsellor, prince of peace, Father of the age

στής, ἄρχων εἰρήνης, πατὴρ τοῦ μέλλοντος αἰῶνος. Ναί, Κύριε ὁ Θεὸς ἡμῶν, φεῖσαι τοῦ πλάσματός σου, καὶ σῶσον τὸν δοῦλόν σου ἀπὸ πάσης βλάβης καὶ ἐπηρείας τῆς ἐκ βασκανίας γινομένης, καὶ ἀνώτερον αὐτὸν παντὸς κακοῦ διαφύλαξον· πρεσβείαις τῆς ὑπερευλογημένης, ἐνδόξου Δεσποίνης ἡμῶν Θεοτόκου καὶ ἀειπαρθένου Μαρίας, τῶν φωτοειδῶν Ἀρχαγγέλων, καὶ πάντων σου τῶν Ἁγίων. Ἀμήν.

****

to come.'' Yes, O Lord, our God, deliver Your creation and save Your servant from all influence and harm caused by the spell of the evil eye and protect him (*her*) from all evil through the intercessions of our most blessed, glorified Lady Theotokos and ever Virgin Mary, the luminous Archangels, and all Your Saints. Amen.